McDougal, Littell

Grammar and Usage

Usage
Complete
Course

McDougal, Littell

Grammar and Usage

Complete
Course

ML

McDougal, Littell & Company

Evanston, Illinois
New York   Dallas   Sacramento   Columbia, SC

Consultants

Dr. Patricia A. Aubin, Director of English/Language Arts, Watertown Public Schools, Watertown, Massachusetts

John Barrett, Language Arts Coordinator, Farmington Public Schools, Farmington, Michigan

Shelley T. Bernstein, Subject Area Coordinator, Mater Dei High School, New Monmouth, New Jersey

John J. Elias, English Supervisor, Wilkes-Barre Area School District, Wilkes-Barre, Pennsylvania

Kay Lunsford, English Teacher and Department Chairman, North Kansas City High School, North Kansas City, Missouri

Jack Pelletier, Chair, English Department, Mira Loma High School, Sacramento, California

William J. Peppiatt, District Director of English and Language Arts, Suffern High School, Suffern, New York

Robert W. Salchert, Language Arts Coordinator, Valley High School, Las Vegas, Nevada

Dr. Jane S. Shoaf, C.E. Jordan High School, Durham, North Carolina

Acknowledgments: Sources of Quoted Materials see page 374.

Cover Photography:	Copyright © Bill Reaves/Viesti Associates, Inc.
Title Page Photography:	Copyright © Willard Clay/TSW—Click/Chicago
Unit Opener Photography:	Pages 2 and 3: David Hughes, Stock Boston

ISBN 0-8123-6727-8 (Softcover)
ISBN 0-8123-6728-6 (Hardbound)

Copyright © 1991 by McDougal, Littell & Company
Box 1667, Evanston, Illinois 60204
All rights reserved. Printed in United States of America.

Grammar, Usage and Mechanics

Grammar and Writing

Special Features

The Arts

Arthurian Legend
Batiking
Bluegrass festival
Commedia dell arte
Comic Strips
Joseph W. Turner
Leonardo da Vinci
Music Composition
Rudyard Kipling
Walt Disney
William Faulkner

History

Horatio Alger
Continental Congress
Cuneiform
Ghost towns
Jane Addams
Haitian liberator, Jean-Jacques
   Dessalines
Jerusalem
Johnstown, Pennsylvania flood
Immigration patterns
Incas
Lincoln's assassination
Religions of India
Peter the Great
Theodore Roosevelt
Rosetta Stone

Science

Aquaculture
Astrology
Thomas Edison
Endangered species
Laser beams
Monsoons
Mushrooms
Alfred Nobel
Rainmaking
Robotics
Tornadoes

Sports

Tyrone Bogues
Wilt Chamberlain
Marathons and marathon runners
Bobby Orr

The Extraordinary-Ordinary

Bookbinding
Chocolate
Hamburger
Honey
Niagara Falls
Pizza
Vanilla

Grammar, Usage, and Mechanics

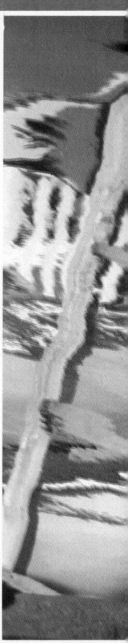

Grammar and Writing

When you opened your first language arts textbook in elementary school, you began a study of English grammar, usage, and mechanics that has continued throughout your school career. From time to time, though, you may have wondered, "Why am I studying this? What good does it do me?"

Teachers and students ask themselves these questions every year. *McDougal, Littell Grammar and Usage* was written to help you find answers to these questions. In the chapters that follow, you will see that the study of language involves more than just rules and exercises. The study of language encompasses writing, thinking, speaking, understanding literature—even humor.

Grammar Does Help

The study of grammar, usage, and mechanics can have many benefits, depending on how you approach it.

Improved Skills in Usage The way you use language can affect many things, from a grade on a paper to the result of a job interview. The details of language—subject-verb agreement, pronoun usage, verb tense—directly affect the clarity of what you say or write. The rules of language, therefore, can make a tremendous difference in the impression you make on others through your school work, in any written correspondence, in interviews, and eventually in your career.

Improved Thinking Skills The study of grammar involves a number of thinking skills, especially the skills of analysis, classification, and application. As you dissect a sentence, classify a word, or apply a concept to a piece of writing, you are stretching your ability to think clearly and effectively.

A Vocabulary for Writing It would be difficult to learn to drive a car if you had to talk about "the round thing in front of the dashboard" instead of a *steering wheel*. Similarly, it would be difficult to discuss ways to improve your writing without the proper vocabulary. For example, you can add variety and interest to your writing through the appropriate use of participial phrases. Conjunctions and clauses can help you combine short, choppy sentences into longer, more graceful ones. Yet without these terms, a teacher or peer editor would have a hard time communicating suggestions to you, and you would have an even harder time trying to implement those suggestions.

More Effective Writing The artist Picasso understood the rules of color, shape, and perspective. Yet, when it suited his purpose, he bent those rules to create a certain effect or make a unique statement. Professional writers do the same thing. How often have you pointed out to a teacher that an author has used sentence fragments in dialogue or unusual capitalization and punctuation in poetry? These writers, however, bend the rules only after understanding how language works. The resulting sentences are still clear and effective. The more you understand the rules, the better you too will be able to use language as a powerful means of expressing ideas.

Appreciation of Literature A sport like football is much more enjoyable if you know something about the strategies that are used to play the game. Similarly, you can appreciate a work of literature much more if you are sensitive to the techniques and strategies that the author is using. For example, you might notice how a writer uses certain modifiers and verbal phrases to create an atmosphere of suspense. In another piece of writing, you might recognize how a writer uses punctuation to introduce rhythm and movement. Through an awareness of language, you can better enjoy and understand each story or poem you read.

Applications in This Book

In *McDougal, Littell Grammar and Usage,* you will find lessons and activities designed to help you achieve all the benefits of language study.

Meaningful Explanations When you learn about a concept, you will be shown how it can affect your writing. You will also be told when everyday language departs from the rules.

Writing Opportunities Throughout the chapters, you will be given opportunities to apply what you have learned in creative writing activities that will stretch your imagination.

Literature-Based Activities Some exercises will give you the opportunity to work with the writing of famous authors, to see how they use the rules—and sometimes why they break them.

On the Lightside Language can be fun. The light essays included in these chapters will show you that words can have a sense of humor, too.

1

The Parts of Speech

*P*ig. Kingdom: Animalia; phylum: Chordata; class: Mammalia; order: Artiodactyla. In order to organize their study of living things, biologists classify animals with similar physical characteristics into groups such as these.

Words, too, are classified into groups called the *parts of speech*. However, unlike biologists, linguists classify each word according to its function in a sentence, which may vary every time the word appears.

In this chapter you will study the parts of speech. Once you become familiar with them, you will have a vocabulary with which to discuss your writing. You will also be able to recognize and correct errors in sentence construction.

Part 1
Nouns

Certain words in English are used as labels to name persons, places, things, and ideas.

A noun is a word that names a person, place, thing, or idea.

Persons Edith Hamilton, author, friend, Caesar
Places Athens, city, mall, Shea Stadium
Things book, cassette, soccer, announcement
Ideas happiness, democracy, sympathy, success

Concrete and Abstract Nouns

A **concrete noun** names something that can be seen, heard, smelled, touched, or tasted: *book, thunder, perfume, soup.*

An **abstract noun** names something that cannot be perceived through the five senses: *belief, joy, strictness, efficiency.*

Concrete Nouns	Abstract Nouns
Golden Gate Bridge	talent
fireworks	bravery
silk	friendship
smoke	peace
sofa	comfort

Common and Proper Nouns

A **common noun** is a general name for a person, place, thing, or idea. It is a name that is common to an entire group: *teacher, city, song.*

A **proper noun** is the name of a particular person, place, thing, or idea: *Ms. Sullivan, Detroit, "This Land Is Your Land."*

As you can see in the following examples, a proper noun always begins with a capital letter and may consist of more than one word.

Common Nouns	Proper Nouns
country	Costa Rica
valley	Star Valley
state	Wyoming
union	United Mine Workers
actor	Emilio Estevez
building	Lincoln Center

Compound Nouns

A **compound noun** contains two or more shorter words. Compound nouns may be written as one word, as separate words, or with hyphens.

One Word	Separate Words	With Hyphens
foodstuff	disc jockey	brother-in-law
grandmother	home run	rock-and-roll

Collective Nouns

A **collective noun** is a singular noun that refers to a group of people or things.

choir   team   family   herd   audience   council

Exercises

A Rewrite each sentence, substituting a proper noun for each italicized common noun and a common noun for each italicized proper noun. You may have to add or delete words.

1. The president of the *company* held a press conference.
2. The class read a passage from the *poem*.
3. Did you hear *Billy Joel* discuss creativity with the emcee?
4. The painting is one of *van Gogh's* most famous works.
5. I read a review of the movie in the *newspaper*.

B Application in Literature Write each italicized noun and identify it by type: *Concrete, Abstract, Compound, Collective*. Some nouns will fit more than one category.

(1) I was . . . disappointed to find the *shades* still drawn and the *family* fast asleep when I unlocked the door and stepped into the *apartment*. (2) I stood in the *doorway* of the kitchen . . . and gazed at the sleeping *figure* of my *brother* on the *daybed* in the *dining room,* and beyond it at the closed door of the one *bedroom* where my *parents* slept. (3) The frayed *carpet* on the floor was the carpet I had crawled over before I could walk. (4) Each *flower* in the badly faded and worn *design* was sharply etched in my *mind.* (5) Each *piece* of furniture in the cramped dim room seemed mildewed with

The Window, Henri Matisse, 1916.

a thousand double-edged *memories.* (6) The *ghosts* of a thousand leaden *meals* hovered over the dining-room table. (7) The dust of countless black-hearted days clung to every *crevice* of the squalid ugly furniture I had known since *childhood.* (8) To walk out of it forever . . . would give *meaning* to the *wonder* of what had happened to me, make *success* tangible, decisive.

From *Act One* by Moss Hart

Part 2
Pronouns

To avoid unnecessary repetition, pronouns are often used to replace nouns. Pronouns can be used in the same ways that nouns are used.

A pronoun is a word used in place of a noun or another pronoun.

The noun for which a pronoun stands and to which it refers is its **antecedent.**

Karen repaired *her* broken bicycle. (*Karen* is the antecedent of the pronoun *her*.)

Sometimes the antecedent appears in a preceding sentence.

Switzerland has many exports. *Its* cheeses and cuckoo clocks are popular around the world. (*Switzerland* is the antecedent of the pronoun *its.*)

There are seven kinds of pronouns: personal pronouns, reflexive pronouns, intensive pronouns, demonstrative pronouns, indefinite pronouns, interrogative pronouns, and relative pronouns. On the pages that follow, you will learn to identify these pronouns. (For problems in pronoun usage, see Chapter 7.)

Personal Pronouns

Personal pronouns are pronouns that change form to express person, number, and gender.

Person Pronouns that identify the person speaking are in the **first person.** Pronouns that identify the person being spoken to are in the **second person.** Pronouns that identify the person or thing being spoken about are in the **third person.**

Number Pronouns that refer to one person, place, thing, or idea are **singular** in number. Pronouns that refer to more than one are **plural** in number.

Singular   The *plant* has lost *its* leaves. (The singular pronoun *its* refers to the singular antecedent *plant.*)

Plural   The *plants* have lost *their* leaves. (The plural pronoun *their* refers to the plural antecedent *plants.*)

The following chart shows the person and number of the personal pronouns.

Personal Pronouns			
	First Person	**Second Person**	**Third Person**
Singular	I, me (my, mine)	you (your, yours)	he, him (his) she, her (her, hers) it (its)
Plural	we, us (our, ours)	you (your, yours)	they, them (their, theirs)

Gender Pronouns that refer to males are in the **masculine gender.** Pronouns that refer to females are in the **feminine gender.** Pronouns that refer to things are in the **neuter gender.**

Although the neuter pronoun *it* refers to things, the female pronouns *she, her,* and *hers* are sometimes used to refer to countries, ships, and airplanes. Animals may be referred to by *it* and *its* or by *he, him, his, she, her,* and *hers.*

Possessive pronouns are special forms of personal pronouns that show ownership or belonging.

> That road map is *his.* (ownership)
> *Our* family likes to travel. (belonging)

In the chart on page 10, the possessive forms of the personal pronouns are in parentheses.

The possessive pronouns *mine, yours, his, hers, its, ours,* and *theirs* are used like other pronouns to replace nouns. The possessive pronouns *my, your, his, her, its, our,* and *their* are used as modifiers. Notice that *his* and *its* appear in both groups.

> This horse is *mine.* (used like other pronouns)
> This is *my* horse. (modifies the noun *horse*)

> The awards are *ours.* (used like other pronouns)
> We claimed *our* awards. (modifies the noun *awards*)

Exercise

On your paper, write the personal pronouns in the following sentences. After each pronoun write its antecedent.

1. Mary Cassatt was a well-known American painter who chose Paris as her permanent residence.
2. The speaker asked the delegates for their attention.
3. When Luis tried to move the trunk, he found it too heavy to lift.
4. Shirley Temple, the child actress, made a million dollars before she was ten years old.
5. Pygmy marmosets must be small indeed, for they can perch on a single blade of grass.
6. When Jim's power mower broke, the Dows let him use theirs.
7. Helen and Nita finished the math section first. They found it easier than the verbal section.
8. "I think these gloves are mine," said Allison.
9. The boys cooked their meals over an open fire.
10. The snake tests its surroundings with its tongue.

Reflexive and Intensive Pronouns

Reflexive and intensive pronouns are formed by adding *-self* or *-selves* to certain personal pronouns.

Singular   myself, yourself, himself, herself, itself
Plural   ourselves, yourselves, themselves

Grammar Note There are no other acceptable reflexive or intensive pronouns. *Hisself* and *theirselves* are never correct.

Reflexive pronouns reflect an action back upon the subject.

Mother treated *herself* to a microwave oven.

The guests helped *themselves* to the cold buffet.

Intensive pronouns add emphasis to a noun or a pronoun in the same sentence, but they are not essential to the meaning of the sentence. If they are removed, the meaning of the sentence does not change.

Have you written to the mayor *himself?*
We drew up the petition *ourselves*.

Usage Note Reflexive and intensive pronouns should never be used without antecedents.

Incorrect   Kip asked Sam and *myself* to go to the movies.
Correct   Kip asked Sam and *me* to go to the movies.

Exercise

Write an appropriate reflexive or intensive pronoun for each of the following sentences. After each pronoun write its antecedent and tell whether the pronoun is intensive or reflexive.

1. They certainly gave _____ the benefit of the doubt.
2. A lizard was sunning _____ on a flat rock.
3. The doctor _____ helped my grandmother into the car.
4. We bought _____ a new cabinet for the VCR.
5. Marianne Moore _____ said poetry should be pleasing to the mind.
6. The horses opened the gates by _____ and headed for the valley.
7. You will have to solve this problem _____ .
8. The President _____ answered our letter about the astronauts.
9. Our basketball players can certainly be proud of _____ .
10. I guess I'll have to finish staining the bookcase _____ .

I NEED HELP ON MY HOMEWORK. WHAT'S A PRONOUN?

A NOUN THAT LOST ITS AMATEUR STATUS.

MAYBE I CAN GET A POINT FOR ORIGINALITY.

Demonstrative Pronouns

The **demonstrative pronouns** *this, that, these,* and *those* point out persons or things. *This* and *these* point out persons or things that are near in space or time. *That* and *those* point out persons or things that are farther away in space or time. Demonstrative pronouns may come before or after their antecedents.

Before   *These* are the *sneakers* I want.

After   Look at the *trophies. Those* were won by my father.

Indefinite Pronouns

Pronouns that do not refer to a definite person or thing are called **indefinite pronouns.** Indefinite pronouns often have no antecedents.

>   *Someone* returned my keys.
>   *Several* have applied, but *few* have been accepted.

The most common indefinite pronouns are listed below.

Indefinite Pronouns	
Singular	another, anybody, anyone, anything, each, everybody, everyone, everything, much, neither, nobody, no one, nothing, one, somebody, someone, something
Plural	both, few, many, several
Singular or Plural	all, any, more, most, none, some

Interrogative Pronouns

The **interrogative pronouns** *who, whom, whose, which,* and *what* are used to introduce questions.

Who is pitching today?   *What* is the schedule?

Relative Pronouns

A **relative pronoun** relates, or connects, a clause to the word or words it modifies. The noun or pronoun that the clause modifies is the antecedent of the relative pronoun. The relative pronouns are *who, whom, whose, which,* and *that.*

> Show me the *camera that* you bought. (The antecedent of the relative pronoun *that* is *camera.*)
> She is the *candidate whom* everyone prefers. (The antecedent of the relative pronoun *whom* is *candidate.*)

Grammar Note   Certain pronouns can also function as adjectives.

Demonstrative Pronouns	*this* hat, *that* car, *these* suitcases, *those* curtains
Indefinite Pronouns	*many* awards, *few* supplies, *each* player
Interrogative Pronouns	*whose* jeans, *what* plans, *which* movie theater

Exercises

A On your paper, write the pronouns in the following sentences. Identify each pronoun according to its kind: *Personal, Reflexive, Intensive, Demonstrative, Indefinite, Interrogative,* or *Relative.*

1. We planned most of the rafting trip ourselves.
2. None of the shop's doors were locked, all of the windows were open, but no one was inside.
3. Is this the watch that you want for your birthday, or is it that one?
4. People hurt themselves when they do not face problems.
5. Did anyone besides you see the comet?
6. Those are handsome vases; they come from China.
7. Everyone who wants to can sign up for our class trip.
8. Whose are those?
9. Who played the part of Jean Valjean in *Les Misérables?*
10. Some of the members were angry, but everybody finally agreed to our plan.

B On your paper, write the pronouns in each of the following sentences. Identify each pronoun according to its kind.

(1) Who would have thought anyone could be fascinated by mushrooms? (2) I wouldn't have, at least not until a friend showed me an article in *Nature World*. (3) What exactly are mushrooms—plants or animals? (4) Technically, they are neither. (5) They are fungi. (6) I decided to find out for myself why people look for mushrooms. (7) I discovered four varieties in a nearby park, and one made a lasting impression. (8) That was the stinkhorn. (9) As I have told anyone who will listen to me, the stinkhorn is appropriately named. (10) Its odor left me breathless! (11) Many of the mushrooms I found were indeed beautiful. (12) Some resemble tiers of organ pipes. (13) Those belonging to the genus *Hercium* resemble icicles.

(14) Since certain mushrooms are poisonous, collecting them for eating is something one should leave to the experts. (15) I plan to admire mushrooms for their appearance only.

c *Write Now* Use the photos below as starting points for a paragraph or two about caves. First, decide on your purpose. Will you describe a cave you've visited, tell a story, or give factual information about caves? Will your tone be serious or humorous? As you write, see how many kinds of pronouns you can use.

Part 3
Verbs

A verb is a word that expresses an action, a condition, or a state of being.

There are two main categories of verbs: **action verbs** and **linking verbs**. Other verbs, called **auxiliary verbs**, are sometimes combined with action verbs and linking verbs.

Action Verbs

An **action verb** is a verb that tells what action someone or something is performing. The action may be physical or mental.

Physical Action We *worked* hard on the fund drive.
Mental Action Everyone *hoped* for success.

Linking Verbs

A **linking verb** does not express action. Instead, it links the subject of the sentence to a word in the predicate.

> Mr. Kachenko *is* our teacher. (The linking verb *is* links the subject *Mr. Kachenko* to the noun *teacher*.)
> That dog *looks* miserable. (The linking verb *looks* links the subject *dog* to the adjective *miserable*.)

Linking verbs may be divided into three groups.

Types of Linking Verbs

Forms of *To Be*
I *am* happy.
My sister *is* a pharmacist.
They *are* my cousins from Ireland.
Our shoes *were* wet.

Verbs That Express Condition
Everyone *looked* hot.
The tomatoes *grew* tall.
Our cat *seems* intelligent.

Sensory Verbs
The baby's skin *feels* smooth.
This yogurt *tastes* different.
The basement *smells* damp.
The music *sounds* loud.

The children *appeared* sleepy.
The audience *became* restless.
The salad *stayed* fresh.

Sometimes the same verb can be a linking verb or an action verb.

Linking Verb	Action Verb
The fish *tastes* delicious.	The cook *tastes* the fish.
Everyone *looked* hungry.	He *looked* for some herbs.

Note If you can substitute *is, are, was,* or *were* for a verb, you know it is a linking verb.

The fish *tastes* delicious.	The fish *is* delicious.
Everyone *looked* hungry.	Everyone *was* hungry.

Exercise

On your paper, write the verbs in the following sentences. Identify each verb according to its kind: *Action Verb* or *Linking Verb*.

1. The deadly funnel cloud appeared without warning.
2. The damage from the tornado appears serious.
3. Denise was the youngest competitor in the tournament.
4. The footprints under the window looked fresh.
5. The criminal investigators looked carefully at the footprints.
6. I am curious about your sudden resignation.
7. I just tasted my first papaya.
8. These apples taste unusually tart.
9. An echo sounded through the valley.
10. Your voice sounds hoarse today.

Auxiliary Verbs

An action verb or a linking verb sometimes has one or more **auxiliary verbs**, also called **helping verbs**. The verb that the auxiliary verb helps is the **main verb**. In the following examples, the auxiliary verbs are in italics. The main verbs are in boldface type.

The skies *should* **clear** by noon.
The wind *has been* **blowing** since midnight.

The most common auxiliary verbs are forms of *be, have,* and *do.*

Be	am, is, are, was, were,	*Have*	have, has, had
	be, been, being	*Do*	do, does, did

Other common auxiliary verbs are listed below.

can	will	shall	may	must
could	would	should	might	

Together the main verb and one or more auxiliary verbs make up a **verb phrase**.

Auxiliary Verb(s) +	Main Verb =	Verb Phrase
had	been	had been
have	had	have had
was	doing	was doing
could have	helped	could have helped
might have been	seen	might have been seen
is being	repaired	is being repaired

In the first three examples above, note that the auxiliary verbs *be*, *have*, and *do* may also be used as main verbs.

Often the auxiliary verb and the main verb are separated by one or more words that are not part of the verb phrase. In the examples that follow, note that the contraction *n't* is not part of the verb phrase.

They certainly *were*n't *being* very helpful.
We *had* just *left* for the airport.
My parents *will* never *forget* your kindness.
Have you really *been* to Saudi Arabia?
*Could*n't rapid action *have helped* you avert this disaster?

Exercises

A On your paper, write the verb phrases in the following sentences. Underline the auxiliary verb once and the main verb twice.

> *Example*   I had never seen the ocean before. had seen

1. According to the forecast, the rain will soon stop .
2. Carmine must feel happy about the elections.
3. Have you ever been to Hawaii?
4. The tanker had apparently run aground in the fog.
5. The benches in the park have been freshly painted .
6. The oxygen supply in a submarine can last for several weeks.
7. No one has ever survived in that desert for more than three days.
8. The new zoning laws aren't being enforced properly.
9. The swimmers were obviously exhausted .
10. Do you have enough blankets for the camping trip?
11. The new gymnasium will surely be ready by September.
12. The driver must have been completely blinded by the rain.
13. The flaws can easily be seen with a magnifying glass.
14. The snow is slowly being cleared from the landing strip.
15. From the highway we could already smell the salty sea air.

B On your paper, write the verbs in the following paragraphs. Remember to include all the words that make up a verb phrase. Identify each verb as an *Action Verb* or a *Linking Verb*.

(1) In my mind's eye I can see the old stone house. (2) It stands about a hundred yards from the edge of the water. (3) The house has not been occupied for years. (4) Its walls are gray. (5) Wooden shutters are nailed over the windows. (6) A steady wind blows in from the sea. (7) Even in the summer the air feels cold. (8) The rains come down with great force; dark clouds bring an early twilight. (9) The house stands quietly amid the overgrown beach grass. (10) It appears indifferent to the forces of nature.

(11) I have never entered the house. (12) Perhaps I will gain admission one day. (13) Will I be frightened inside the gray and lonely house? (14) One can only imagine.

Transitive and Intransitive Verbs

Linking verbs are always intransitive. Action verbs are either transitive or intransitive. An action verb is **transitive** when the action is directed from the subject to the object of the verb. The object comes after the verb and tells *who* or *what* receives the action.

Subject	Transitive Verb	Object
Soula	painted	the fence.
My uncle	owns	a panel truck.
José	won	the trophy.

An action verb is **intransitive** when it does not have an object.

Subject	Intransitive Verb	
The tanker	exploded.	
Maria	sang	beautifully.
Ants	live	in colonies.

In the second example above, the action verb is followed by an adverb, not by an object. In the third example, the action verb is followed by a phrase, not by an object.

Some action verbs may be transitive in one sentence and intransitive in another. Remember that linking verbs are always intransitive.

Transitive Verb	Intransitive Verb
Everyone *applauded* the winner.	Everyone *applauded*.
Are you *selling* your home?	*Are* you *selling*?
Mr. Berra *called* the lawyer.	Mr. Berra *called* yesterday.

Verb or Noun?

Many words may be used either as nouns or as verbs. To distinguish between nouns and verbs, determine whether the word names a person, place, or thing, or expresses an action or state of being.

> We chipped away at the ice with a *pick*. (noun)
> *Pick* a melon that's not too ripe. (verb)

> Our club is in good *shape* financially. (noun)
> Everyone will *shape* up after spring training. (verb)

Exercises

A On your paper, write the verbs and verb phrases in the following sentences. Identify each verb as *Transitive* or *Intransitive*.

1. Deserts can become extremely cold at night.
2. We visited a replica of the *Mayflower*.
3. After seven weeks the sailors had finally sighted land.
4. All oceans contain salt water.
5. The murderer does not appear until the final scene.
6. Our team usually plays well during the first quarter.
7. Everyone seems confident about the outcome of the congressional investigation.
8. My sister Nita willingly accepts responsibility.
9. State troopers are now enforcing the speed laws.
10. The jet disappeared into the distant clouds.

B On your paper, write the verbs in the following sentences. Identify each verb as a *Transitive Verb* or an *Intransitive Verb*. Then write five new sentences using each transitive verb as an intransitive verb and each intransitive verb as a transitive verb.

> *Example*   Hugo played a beautiful melody on the
> French horn. played, Transitive
> Chris played on the tennis team.

1. The tall ships sailed into the harbor.
2. Will your work load lighten after this semester?
3. The Morrisons moved their furniture in a rented van.
4. Who kicked the winning field goal?
5. The explorers crossed the Andes by burro.

c *Write Now* Look at the dogsled driver in the picture below. Imagine that you have the training and endurance to participate in a rigorous activity like this. Who would you be? What would you do? Select an idea from the list below or invent your own. Tell about yourself and your abilities in one paragraph. In a second paragraph, describe one or two events that might occur during your day. Use verbs that will help your reader picture the action.

Olympic athlete	mountain climber
pro football star	white-water canoe guide
jungle explorer	race car driver
slalom ski racer	sunken treasure hunter

Checkpoint *Parts 1, 2, and 3*

A Write the italicized nouns in the following sentences. Identify each as *Concrete, Abstract, Common, Proper, Compound,* or *Collective.* Each noun will fit two or three categories.

> *Example*   My *sister-in-law* wrote a paper about *Babe Didrikson* and her *commitment* to sports.
> sister-in-law, Concrete, Common, Compound
> Babe Didrikson, Concrete, Proper
> commitment, Abstract, Common

1. Few mountains can compare in *splendor* with the *Grand Tetons.*
2. The *store* in the *shopping center* is like a huge *warehouse.*
3. The *pitcher* narrowed his eyes in intense *concentration.*
4. Most medical *breakthroughs* are the *result* of long *years* of blood, sweat, and tears.
5. The plot of that *soap opera* often involves *blackmail.*
6. *Andrew Wyeth* is known for his detailed paintings of rural *scenes.*
7. The *team* had its *picture* taken with the *mayor.*
8. The *screech* of skidding tires was followed by the sound of breaking *glass.*
9. A powerful *tribe* had settled in the *hills* that sloped up from the *riverbank.*
10. To triumph over a *challenge,* one has to overcome fear and *self-doubt.*

B On your paper, write the pronouns in the following sentences. Identify each pronoun according to its kind: *Personal, Reflexive, Intensive, Demonstrative, Indefinite, Interrogative,* or *Relative.*

1. This is the costume I am wearing to our Mardi Gras party.
2. Who is taller, your sister or my brother?
3. Even if Babe Ruth himself were on our team, we could not have beaten them.
4. We built the fire ourselves, so all could enjoy it.
5. We considered ourselves brave, but no one in the group would pet their tame tiger.
6. Is that the project you entered in the Science Fair?
7. She is a person whom one instinctively trusts.
8. Each of the plants is healthy, and several have new leaves.

9. Which of these is yours?
10. Nobody knows how they managed to pull themselves from the water onto the icy ledge.

C On your paper, write the verbs in the following sentences. If the verb is part of a verb phrase, underline the auxiliary verb once and the main verb twice. Identify each verb as an *Action Verb* or a *Linking Verb* and as a *Transitive Verb* or an *Intransitive Verb*.

1. Have you ever seen the classic movie *It's a Wonderful Life* starring James Stewart?
2. A journey in a space shuttle will soon seem as commonplace as a flight in an airplane.
3. By noon Kathy will have collected dozens of shells for her art project.
4. Ahmad's sister worked patiently without a break.
5. Alexander the Great had become a famous conqueror by the age of seventeen.
6. The elderly senator had often dreamed about the office of the Presidency.
7. What will you be doing in the year 2000?
8. Searchers had finally spotted the wreckage of the plane.
9. The exchange students sang a lively French song.
10. The mountains of the West must have seemed insurmountable to the original pioneers.

Part 4
Adjectives

Words that change or limit the meanings of other words are called **modifiers**. One kind of modifier is the **adjective**.

An adjective is a word that modifies a noun or a pronoun.

An adjective answers one of the following questions: *Which one? What kind? How many? How much?*

Which One	this, that, these, those
What Kind	huge, new, green, courageous
How Many	few, several, both, ten, most
How Much	more, less, sufficient, plentiful

Position of Adjectives

Adjectives usually appear before the nouns or pronouns that they modify.

Irate passengers have complained about the *dark* windows on the *new* buses.

Sometimes, for variety, a writer will put adjectives in other positions. Compare the following sentences.

The skier, *swift* and *powerful*, outdistanced his rivals.

Swift and *powerful*, the skier outdistanced his rivals.

Articles

The most common adjectives are the articles *a, an,* and *the*. The word *the* is called a **definite article** because it usually refers to a specific person, place, or thing. The words *a* and *an* are called **indefinite articles** because they refer to no particular person, place, or thing.

Use *a* before a word beginning with a consonant sound: *a check, a history paper.* Use *an* before a word beginning with a vowel sound: *an envelope, an hour.*

Proper Adjectives

A **proper adjective** is formed from a proper noun and is always capitalized.

Proper Noun	Proper Adjective
Spain	Spanish
Canada	Canadian
Shakespeare	Shakespearean
Jackson	Jacksonian

Predicate Adjectives

An adjective that follows a linking verb and modifies the subject of the sentence is called a **predicate adjective.** Unlike most adjectives, predicate adjectives are separated from the words they modify.

Some movies seem *endless.*

The pages of the diary were *yellowed* and *brittle.*

Other Parts of Speech as Adjectives

Nouns, pronouns, and certain verb forms sometimes function as adjectives. To understand the function of a word, decide how it is used in a sentence. If a word tells *what kind, which one, how much,* or *how many* about a noun or pronoun, it is functioning as an adjective. The nouns, pronouns, and verb forms below are functioning as adjectives.

Nouns	The Hawaiian dancers wore *grass* skirts.
	Dorothy walked down a yellow *brick* road.
Pronouns	*This* ticket will admit you to the football game.
	Marty played *her* new tape at least ten times.
Verb Forms	Ellie straightened up her *cluttered* room.
	Rod stirred the soup mix into some *boiling* water.

Exercises

A Write the adjectives in the following sentences. Do not include articles.

1. Honey has been a valuable substance since earliest times.
2. Most foods that early people ate were tough and bland; honey, in contrast, was smooth, sweet, thick, and delicious.
3. Early people began to gather raw honey when they discovered nests of wild bees.
4. The ancient lore about bees included many superstitions.
5. One myth was that loud noises attract bees, but actually bees have very poor hearing.
6. A Hittite law of about 300 B.C. established the value of honey.

7. A tub of honey was as valuable as a tub of butter or one sheep.
8. The ancient Chinese and the medieval Europeans were among those who used honey for medicinal purposes.
9. Honey has been eaten for quick energy since the days of the original Greek Olympic games.
10. There are still many people who eat honey for energy, including marathon runners and Arctic explorers.

B Application in Literature Find at least twenty adjectives in the following excerpt and write them on your paper. Do not include articles. The passage is from a letter written in 1520 by explorer Hernán Cortez to his king, Charles V of Spain. In it Cortez describes the Aztec capital Tenochtitlán (now Mexico City).

Detail, *The Great City of Tenochtitlán,* Diego Rivera, 1945.

(1) Most powerful Lord, an account to Your Royal Excellency of the magnificence, the strange and marvelous things of this great city . . . will, I well know, be so remarkable as not to be believed. (2) This great city is built on the salt lake. (3) There are four artificial causeways leading to it, and each is as wide as two cavalry lances. (4) The city itself is as big as Seville or Córdoba . . . . (5) This city has many squares where trading is done and markets are held continuously. (6) There is also one square . . . where more than 60,000 people come each day to buy and sell, and where every kind of merchandise produced in these lands is found.

c *Write Now* Test your ability to use adjectives effectively by writing a description of what you are wearing right now. Try to go beyond ordinary words such as *old, new, red,* or *blue*. Search for adjectives that can show why a pair of jeans or a sweater is unique. Are the jeans stiff, worn, faded, or patched? Is the sweater fuzzy, ragged, or stretched?

Part 5
Adverbs

Another kind of modifier is the **adverb**.

An adverb is a word that modifies a verb, an adjective, or another adverb.

Modifying a Verb	The ship sailed *slowly* out of the harbor.
Modifying an Adjective	We all had a *rather* hectic day of sightseeing in San Francisco.
Modifying an Adverb	The traffic moved *very* quickly.

Adverbs answer the questions *Where? When? How?* and *To what extent?*

Where	We moved the table *outside*.
When	The picnic begins *later*.
How	The storm came *unexpectedly*.
To What Extent	Everyone got *very* wet.

Grammar Note Adverbs that modify adjectives or other adverbs by adding emphasis are called **intensifiers**. These include *too, very, extremely, truly,* and *really*. Avoid overuse of intensifiers. Too many *very*'s and *really*'s can weaken your writing.

Forms of Adverbs

Many adverbs are formed by adding *-ly* to an adjective: *correct, correctly; prompt, promptly; easy, easily*. Some modifiers that end in *-ly*, however, are adjectives: *friendly* dog, *lonely* soldier, *ugly* bruise.

Some common adverbs do not end in *-ly*. These include the negatives *no, not,* and *never*, and time words such as *soon, later,* and *often*.

Position of Adverbs

An adverb usually follows the verb it modifies.

Their bus arrives *there tomorrow*.

Sometimes, however, an adverb comes before the verb.

Frequently, the bus leaves on time.

The bus *frequently* leaves on time.

Intensifiers or other adverbs that modify adjectives or other adverbs usually come right before the word they modify.

Ours is a *very* common name.

We worked *extremely* hard on his campaign.

Nouns as Adverbs

Several words that are generally thought of as nouns can also function as adverbs. These adverbs tell *where* and *when*. Look at the following examples.

Noun	Adverb
My *home* is in Tulsa.	She went *home* early. (where)
Tomorrow will be sunny.	I'll study *tomorrow*. (when)

Adjective or Adverb?

Words like *fast* and *early* have the same form when used as adjectives or as adverbs. To tell whether a word is an adjective or an adverb, determine which word it modifies. If the word modifies a noun or a pronoun, it is an adjective. If it modifies a verb, an adjective, or another adverb, it is an adverb.

Adjective   My grandmother has always been an *early* riser. (The adjective *early* modifies the noun *riser* and tells *what kind*.)

Adverb   My grandmother rises *early*. (The adverb *early* modifies the verb *rises* and tells *when*.)

Grammar Note Many adverbs are combined with verbs to make idioms. An **idiom** is a group of words whose meaning is different from the literal meanings of the individual words. Some idiomatic verb phrases are *break down, bottle up, check out, fill in, grow up, set up,* and *strike out*.

Exercises

A Each sentence below contains an adverb in italics. Write the word or words each adverb modifies. Tell which question the adverb answers: *Where? How? When? To what extent?*

1. Kelly tied the square knot *skillfully*.
2. It began to rain, and we all ran *indoors*.
3. Last summer was *extremely* hot.
4. The President will address the nation *tonight*.
5. After the long cold winter, the settlers' food supply was *completely* exhausted.

B Application in Literature Find at least fifteen adverbs in the following passage and write them on your paper. As you read the passage, notice how the adverbs add specific details that make the writing more vivid.

(1) "Nicholas, Nicholas!" she screamed, "you are to come out of this at once. (2) It's no use trying to hide there; I can see you all the time."

(3) Presently the angry repetitions of Nicholas's name gave way to a shriek, and a cry for somebody to come quickly. (4) Nicholas shut the book, restored it carefully to its place in a corner, and shook some dust from a neighboring pile of newspapers over it. (5) Then he crept from the room, locked the door, and replaced the key exactly where he had found it. (6) His aunt was still calling his name when he sauntered into the front garden.

(7) "Who's calling?" he asked.

(8) "Me," came the answer from the other side of the wall. (9) "Didn't you hear me? (10) I've been looking for you in the gooseberry garden, and I've slipped into the rain-water tank. (11) Luckily there's no water in it, but the sides are slippery and I can't get out. (12) Fetch the little ladder from under the cherry tree–"

(13) "I was told I wasn't to go into the gooseberry garden," said Nicholas promptly.

(14) "I told you not to, and now I tell you that you may," came the voice from the rain-water tank rather impatiently.

(15) "Your voice doesn't sound like aunt's," objected Nicholas. (16) "You may be the Evil One tempting me to be

disobedient. (17) Aunt often tells me that the Evil One tempts me and that I always yield. (18) This time I'm not going to yield."

From *The Lumber Room* by H. H. Munro (Saki)

c *Write Now* Visualize yourself traveling down the road pictured in the photo above. Write a description of your journey. Tell where you have been and where you are going. Use at least five of the words below in your writing. When you are done, underline these words and tell whether you have used them as adverbs or adjectives.

low	slow	right	late	straight
high	fast	north	early	far

Checkpoint *Parts 4 and 5*

A Write the modifiers in the following sentences and identify each as an adjective or adverb. Then write the word each adjective or adverb modifies. Do not include articles.

1. We were tense as our plane approached the thunderclouds.
2. Which of the runners had the fastest time?
3. A large calico cat crept silently across my yard.

4. A tiny tugboat slowly towed the enormous oil tanker out of the narrow harbor.
5. The game lasted much longer than most because of an extremely long half-time program.
6. Some rock stars are incredibly wealthy.
7. The audience laughed loudest at the antics of the sad clown with the baggy pants.
8. Yesterday we discovered a dinosaur fossil near the base of the mountain trail.
9. France is smaller than Texas.
10. The fishermen hauled the empty nets onto the deck of the boat and headed for home.
11. The trunk in the attic appeared rather old.
12. A very unpleasant odor gradually filled the chemistry lab and the hallway.
13. After the sudden storm, the crickets remained unusually quiet for several hours.
14. Maria operates the finest art gallery in town.
15. Usually, elephants move rather slowly.

B Application in Literature Find at least five adverbs and ten adjectives in the following paragraphs and write them on your paper. Identify each modifier as an adverb or adjective and tell what word each modifies. Notice how a careful choice of modifiers can create a strong, clear description. Remember that many words can function as more than one part of speech.

(1) In many ways he looked like something that was awkwardly put together. (2) Both his nose and his lips seemed a trifle too large for his face. (3) To say he was ugly would be unjust and to say he was handsome would be gross exaggeration. (4) Truthfully, I could never make up my mind about him. (5) Sometimes he looked like something out of a book of ancient history . . . looked as if he was left over from that magnificent era before the machine age came and marred the earth's natural beauty.

(6) His great variety of talent often startled the teachers. (7) This caused his classmates to look upon him with a mixed feeling of awe and envy.

From "The Boy Who Painted Christ Black" by John Henrik Clarke

What Is and Ain't Grammatical

In the excerpt below, humorist Dave Barry reflects upon the importance of English grammar and speculates about its "origins."

I cannot overemphasize the importance of good grammar.

Actually, I could easily overemphasize the importance of good grammar. For example, I could say: "Bad grammar is the leading cause of a slow, painful death in North America," or "Without good grammar, the United States would have lost World War II."

The truth is that grammar is not the most important thing in the world. The Super Bowl is the most important thing in the world. But grammar is still important. For example, suppose you are being interviewed for a job as an airplane pilot, and your prospective employer asks you if you have any experience, and you answer: "Well, I ain't never actually flied no actual airplanes or nothing, but I got several pilot-style hats and several friends who I like to talk about airplanes with."

If you answer this way, the prospective employer will immediately realize that you have ended your sentence with a preposition. (What you should have said, of course, is "several friends with who I like to talk about airplanes.") So you will not get the job, because airline pilots have to use good grammar when they get on the intercom and explain to the passengers that, because of high winds, the plane is going to take off several hours late and land in Pierre, South Dakota, instead of Los Angeles.

We did not always have grammar. In medieval England, people said whatever they wanted, without regard to rules, and as a result they sounded like morons. Take the poet Geoffrey Chaucer, who couldn't even spell his first name right. He wrote a large poem called *Canterbury Tales,* in which people from various professions—knight, monk, miller, reever, riveter, eeler, diver, stevedore, spinnaker, etc.—drone on and on like this:

> *In a somer sesun whon softe was the sunne*
> *I kylled a younge birde ande I ate it on a bunne.*

When Chaucer's poem was published, everybody read it and said: "Good grief, we need some grammar around here." So they formed a Grammar Commission, which developed the parts of speech, the main ones being nouns, verbs, predicants, conjectures, particles, proverbs, adjoiners, coordinates, and rebuttals. Then the commission made up hundreds and hundreds of grammar rules, all of which were strictly enforced. ***Dave Barry***

Part 6
Prepositions

A preposition is a word used to show the relationship between a noun or a pronoun and another word in the sentence.

> Several *of* America's best poets have come *from* New England. (The preposition *of* relates the pronoun *Several* to the noun *poets;* the preposition *from* relates the verb *have come* to the noun *New England.*)

Prepositions often express relationships of location (*by, near*), direction (*to, down*), and association (*of, with*). Look for prepositions like these as you study the following list.

Commonly Used Prepositions

about	before	down	of	throughout
above	behind	during	off	to
across	below	except	on	toward
after	beneath	for	onto	under
against	beside	from	out	underneath
along	between	in	outside	until
among	beyond	inside	over	up
around	but	into	past	upon
as	by	like	since	with
at	despite	near	through	within

Usage Note The words *but* and *as* are usually conjunctions. However, *but* is used as a preposition when it means "except." *As* functions as a preposition when it means "in the capacity of."

A **compound preposition** is formed by combining words.

Commonly Used Compound Prepositions

according to	by means of	in place of	on account of
aside from	in addition to	in spite of	out of
because of	in front of	instead of	prior to

Objects of Prepositions

A preposition never appears alone. It is followed by a word or a group of words called the **object of the preposition.**

> The box fell behind the *refrigerator*. (The word *refrigerator* is the object of the preposition *behind*.)
>
> Before *baking a cake,* you should read the recipe. (The group of words *baking a cake* is the object of the preposition *before*.)

A preposition and its object, plus any modifiers, form a **prepositional phrase.**

> into the house   because of the icy roads
>
> among her papers   on the northeast corner
>
> near the train tracks   to the moon

In most prepositional phrases, the object follows the preposition. Occasionally, however, the object comes first. This usually occurs in sentences that have interrogative or relative pronouns.

> *Whom* did you write the letter *to?* (The interrogative pronoun *whom* is the object of the preposition *to*.)
>
> Is this the town *that* you came *from?* (The relative pronoun *that* is the object of the preposition *from*.)

Adverb or Preposition?

A number of words may be used either as prepositions or as adverbs. One simple test may help you to tell the difference. A preposition is never used alone. It is always followed by a noun or a pronoun as part of a phrase. If the word is in a phrase, it is probably a preposition. If the word has no object, it is probably an adverb.

> Sue put on her coat and went *out*. (*Out* is an adverb. It has no object.)
> Sue put on her coat and went *out* the door. (*Out* is a preposition. It has an object, *door*.)

> The sundial had been knocked *down*. (adverb)
> The cart rolled *down* the hill. (preposition)

> Will you all please stand *up?* (adverb)
> The mountaineers struggled *up* Pike's Peak. (preposition)

For more information on prepositional phrases, see Chapter 3, page 71.

Exercises

A On your paper, write the prepositions in the following sentences. After each preposition, write its object.

1. During the intermission, the crowd rushed toward the snack bar.
2. A man jumped onto the train and shouted at the passengers.
3. Everyone but me saw the car crash into the fence.
4. We all felt better after our talk with the coach.
5. Aside from the cost, we have no objection to your proposal.
6. Whom did you address the package to?
7. Is there a law against fireworks outside the city?
8. Because of the storm, most schools were closed on Friday.
9. Every night the dog sniffs around the kitchen for its dinner.
10. To the east sharp peaks rose above the floor of the valley.

B Write the prepositions. After each preposition, write its object.

1. Prior to 1689 Russia was an agricultural society controlled by nobles and farmed by peasants.
2. There was little contact with Western Europe.
3. A major problem was the lack of seaports.
4. During this time, Sweden blocked passage to the Atlantic Ocean in the west, while the Ottoman Empire (Turkey) controlled the waterways in the south.
5. When Peter the Great came to power in 1689, he immediately began plans for the introduction of Western culture throughout Russia, the capture of neighboring ports, and the creation of a navy.
6. Peter made extensive trips to Europe, where he observed, studied, and even worked as a carpenter for a shipbuilder.

Left: Peter the Great.
Right: Petrodvorets, the Grand Cascade, Leningrad, Russia (formerly St. Petersburg).

7. When he returned to Russia, he brought a number of European scientists and craftsmen with him. He also brought European ideas of dress, politics, education, and military training, which he forced upon his subjects.
8. Many of Peter's Western ideas were not popular among the nobility, but this did not stop him.
9. In 1721, four years before his death, Peter captured some Baltic seaports from Sweden and established the Russian navy.
10. Peter also built a new capital called St. Petersburg near the Baltic. He called the town his "window to the world."

Part 7
Conjunctions

Prepositions show relationships between words. Conjunctions connect words or groups of words.

A conjunction is a word that connects words or groups of words.

There are three kinds of conjunctions: coordinating conjunctions, correlative conjunctions, and subordinating conjunctions.

Coordinating Conjunctions

A **coordinating conjunction** is used to connect words or groups of words that have the same function in a sentence.

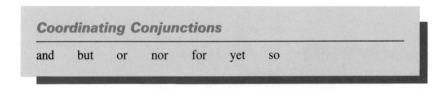

Coordinating Conjunctions

and	but	or	nor	for	yet	so

Coordinating conjunctions can connect the following:

Nouns	**Rain** *and* **fog** made travel impossible.
Pronouns	This package is for **you** *and* **me**.
Verbs	We **bathed** *and* **groomed** the dog.
Adjectives	Our principal is **strict** *yet* **fair**.
Adverbs	They worked **slowly** *but* **efficiently**.
Prepositions	Are you **with** *or* **against** us?

A coordinating conjunction can also connect phrases or independent clauses. Clauses are groups of words containing both a subject and a verb. For a discussion of clauses, see Chapter 3.

Phrases   The fog crept <u>over the water</u> *and* <u>toward the city</u>.
Clauses   <u>They acted human</u>, *yet* <u>their feet were definitely webbed</u>.

The conjunctions *for* and *so* always connect clauses.

> <u>We know spring is coming</u>, *for* <u>the river is beginning to thaw</u>.
> <u>We needed extra chairs</u>, *so* <u>we borrowed some from our neighbor</u>.

Nor is used as a coordinating conjunction only when it is preceded by such negative words as *no, not,* or *neither*.

> The team has *no* coach, *nor* does it have a catcher.

Correlative Conjunctions

Correlative conjunctions are similar to coordinating conjunctions. However, correlative conjunctions are always used in pairs.

Correlative Conjunctions

both . . . and	neither . . . nor	whether . . . or
either . . . or	not only . . . but (also)	

> *Both* my grandfather *and* my aunt are physicians.
> The peaches are *neither* in the refrigerator *nor* on the table.
> *Either* that cat is grinning at us, *or* I am imagining things.
> The lettuce is *not only* wilted *but also* moldy.
> I wondered *whether* you would come by train *or* by bus.

Subordinating Conjunctions

A **subordinating conjunction** introduces certain subordinate clauses—clauses that cannot stand by themselves as complete sentences. A subordinating conjunction joins a subordinate clause to an independent clause—a clause that can stand by itself as a complete sentence.

> ┌independent┐┌————— subordinate ————┐
> A crowd gathers *whenever* there is an accident. (The subordinating conjunction *whenever* connects the subordinate clause to the independent clause.)

Subordinating conjunctions show various kinds of relationships including those of time, manner, place, reason, comparison, condition, or purpose.

Subordinating Conjunctions	
Time	after, as, as long as, as soon as, before, since, until, when, whenever, while
Manner	as, as if
Place	where, wherever
Cause or Reason	because, since
Comparison	as, as much as, than
Condition	although, as long as, even if, even though, if, provided that, though, unless, while
Purpose	in order that, so that, that

Conjunctive Adverbs

A **conjunctive adverb** is an adverb that is used to connect clauses that can stand by themselves as sentences.

> We were not certain that this was the correct address; *nevertheless,* we rang the doorbell.
> Michelangelo is best known for his painting in the Sistine Chapel; *however,* he thought of himself primarily as a sculptor.

The words most often used as conjunctive adverbs are listed in the chart below.

Conjunctive Adverbs		
accordingly	furthermore	nevertheless
also	hence	otherwise
besides	however	still
consequently	indeed	then
finally	moreover	therefore

Punctuation Note A conjunctive adverb is preceded by a semicolon and followed by a comma.

Exercises

A On your paper, write the conjunctions in the following sentences. Identify each conjunction according to its kind: *Coordinating Conjunction, Correlative Conjunction, Subordinating Conjunction,* or *Conjunctive Adverb.*

1. The search party worked quickly and carefully.
2. We must either sell more subscriptions or give up the early morning paper route.
3. Is Juan or Kate responsible for buying the tickets?
4. We were not at home when the mail carrier knocked; nevertheless, the package arrived safely.
5. The car stalled, so we hiked to the nearest service station.
6. She seemed confident before she gave her speech.
7. Neither the awards nor the speeches were very surprising.
8. The dictionary is a valuable tool; however, not all dictionaries agree on spelling and pronunciation.
9. We'll bicycle through the park Saturday unless it rains.
10. Because the sub was lying silently three hundred feet down, the planes could not detect it.
11. Although the army was starving, Washington led them forward.
12. The eggs were overcooked; otherwise, the breakfast was good.
13. The Japanese and the Italian delegates opposed the plan.
14. The traffic moves slowly whenever it rains.
15. The ride on the *Metroliner* was fast and comfortable.

B Write each pair of sentences as one sentence by joining the italicized words with the kind of conjunction indicated in parentheses. Delete words as necessary.

1. The rocket shot *off the pad*. It shot *into the air*. (coordinating)
2. *Mother sprained her ankle. She is not going to work tomorrow.* (conjunctive adverb)
3. Germanium is a *rare metal*. It is *useful*. (coordinating)
4. You may take *biology*. You may take *earth science*. (correlative)
5. The test was *fair*. The test was *difficult*. (coordinating)
6. *The museum was closed. We went to the zoo.* (subordinating)
7. *Dad tossed the salad. He made the dressing.* (correlative)
8. *I enjoyed the book. I wanted to see the movie.* (conjunctive adverb)
9. A stray dog crept *through the broken front gate*. It crept *into the yard*. (coordinating)
10. *Everyone rose. The judge entered.* (subordinating)

Interjections

An interjection is a word or a group of words that expresses feeling or emotion.

An interjection may precede a sentence or appear within a sentence.

> *Good grief!* Are those your new sneakers?
> His new sneakers, *alas,* were ruined.
> *Well,* what are we going to do now?

Punctuation Note An interjection that precedes a sentence is followed by an exclamation point or a comma. An interjection within a sentence is set off by commas or a comma.

Exercise

On your paper, write the following sentences, replacing each blank with an appropriate interjection. Do not use an interjection more than once. Remember to use the correct punctuation and capitalization.

1. _____ it can't be six o'clock already.
2. _____ You just won first prize.
3. _____ Everyone is taking a nap.
4. _____ That skunk really smells.
5. _____ it's time to go.

Checkpoint *Parts 1–8*

A On your paper, write the adverbs and prepositions in the following sentences. After each adverb, write the word it modifies. After each preposition, write its object.

1. The lights of the distant airplanes were almost invisible among the stars.
2. In the Gettysburg Address, Lincoln firmly stated that ours was a government of the people, by the people, and for the people.
3. Jacques Cousteau "eavesdrops" on marine life by means of extremely sensitive sonar equipment.
4. Diane awoke early in the morning and went down to the beach looking for seashells.
5. The first kindergarten in the United States was begun by Margaretha M. Schurz in 1856.
6. The Yukon River flows down through Alaska and empties into the Bering Sea.
7. Many children in Zaire must row back and forth to school across dangerous swamps.
8. Tiles from Spain have been carefully installed on the ceiling of the Holland Tunnel in place of the original tiles.
9. The blue whale was nearly hunted to extinction in the late 1800's for its oil and meat.
10. Muscles will eventually become covered with fat if they are not exercised.

B On your paper, write the conjunctions in the following sentences. Identify each conjunction according to its kind: *Coordinating Conjunction, Correlative Conjunction, Subordinating Conjunction,* or *Conjunctive Adverb.*

1. Shakespeare did not attend college, but he did master several languages and both ancient and modern history.
2. A chemical waste dump was found near the reservoir; consequently, the water supply was shut off.
3. Elise told the guidance counselor that she wants to be either a concert violinist or a composer.
4. Firecrackers and similar explosives are illegal in this state; however, they are not illegal in the adjoining one.
5. Zeus was the foremost Greek god, yet even he was subject to fate.

6. Let's plan to spend a weekend camping in Wisconsin when the weather is warmer.
7. A cut usually requires stitches if the edges are jagged and uneven.
8. The motion of the boat made me seasick; nevertheless , I would not have missed the tour of the Gulf.
9. Neither rain nor sleet nor snow keeps my little sister from her daily newspaper route.
10. It was once believed that not only water but also canals existed on the surface of Mars.

C Identify the part of speech of each italicized word in the sentences below. Then, write a new sentence using the word as indicated in parentheses.

1. The gravitational *pull* of the sun and moon on the earth creates tides. (verb)
2. Of all the things we've discussed, *which* is the problem that bothers you the most? (adjective)
3. The wind blew *hard* all night long and by morning the lawn was littered with debris. (adjective)
4. At the North Pole, the sea is very *deep*. (adverb)
5. The crowds were so enormous that our tour guide was left *behind*. (preposition)
6. There will be no *afternoon* games next year unless the school board reconsiders its decision. (noun)
7. His last movie did not *further* his career. (adverb)
8. My grandparents have a very *fast* boat but they rarely use it anymore. (adverb)
9. By early afternoon, the yellow 1955 Chevrolet had taken the *lead* in the race. (verb)
10. A great crowd gathered *around* the movie star and began to ask for autographs. (adverb)
11. Do you know at *what* time the shuttle liftoff will occur this morning? (pronoun)
12. Because poor quality mortar had been used, the *brick* wall was already crumbling. (noun)
13. There's a part that's perfect for you, so *promise* me that you will come to auditions. (noun)
14. When we were in Africa last year, we visited a wildlife preserve *in* Kenya. (adverb)
15. A local ice-cream manufacturer is planning to *branch* out into other parts of the country. (noun)

Linking Grammar & Writing

Think of a time when you were very frightened. Perhaps you were home alone in a storm or walking through a forest on a moonless night. Write a paragraph that describes your experience.

Prewriting and Drafting Try to remember the time and place of your experience along with as many sights, sounds, and other sensations as possible. To brainstorm for descriptive language, make columns for *Nouns, Adjectives, Verbs,* and *Adverbs.* Begin by listing a noun, and then list related words as shown below.

Nouns	Adjectives	Verbs	Adverbs
branches	shadowy	threatened	menacingly
wind	gusting	blew	eerily

Revising and Proofreading When revising, consider the following questions:

1. Have you used vivid, dramatic details?
2. Have you shown your reader *why* you were afraid?
3. Is the organization of your description easy to follow?

Additional Writing Topic Pretend that you are witnessing the final moments of an important sporting event such as the one in the picture below. Write two paragraphs. In the first, describe the crowd, the setting, and the general atmosphere. In the second, describe the action during the last moments of the event.

Chapter 1
Application and Review

A Understanding How Words Are Used Determine how the italicized words are used in each sentence. Tell whether each is a *Noun, Pronoun, Verb, Adjective, Adverb, Preposition, Conjunction,* or *Interjection.*

1. *Several* of the people *on* the beach played volleyball.
2. The campers *soon* learned that the *plant* with *three* leaves was poison ivy.
3. Although she *seemed* calm, Char was *nervous and* tense about appearing in the play.
4. *Wow! That* really sailed out of the stadium.
5. The lighthouse *keeper sounded* the foghorn.
6. Scientists *are finding* many *uses* for the *laser* beam.
7. Belinda *guided* the chestnut-brown horse *along* a wooded trail.
8. Carlos celebrated his *birthday* by going *to* the carnival.
9. For supper we *ate some* of the vegetables that grew in our garden.
10. *Who* actually discovered *America*?
11. *Ashley* used both *palms* and ferns *in* her terrarium.
12. The cafeteria serves hamburgers *or* hot dogs *nearly* every day.
13. *Frequently,* Lisa *uses* a jump rope to exercise.
14. The game stopped while Derek hunted *for* his contact *lens.*
15. *Aha!* You're the *one* making that noise!

B Recognizing Parts of Speech Determine the part of speech of each italicized word in the following paragraph.

(1) A *monsoon* is a seasonal wind often accompanied *by heavy* rainfall. (2) In Japan, monsoons are extremely important because they bring the moisture *that* nourishes *the* country's rice fields. (3) *Since* the Japanese depend *heavily* on this crop for food—the word "gohan" is used in Japan for both "food" and "rice"—failure of the monsoon to appear has *often* resulted in famine. (4) In other words, the monsoon is both a giver *and* taker of life. (5) In early fall, *it* often brings *typhoons,* Pacific Ocean counterparts to Atlantic hurricanes. (6) These roaring winds *sometimes* churn up *monstrous* tidal waves that wreak havoc *along* the shorelines of the *island* kingdom. (7) Monsoons also bring tremendous amounts of rain *to* the lands that *they* move across. (8) In fact, one *Asian* city receives an average of 240 inches of rain *annually.*

C Using Words as Different Parts of Speech Identify the part of speech of the italicized word in each of the following sentences. Then, write a new sentence using the same word as the part of speech indicated in parentheses.

1. "*Tomorrow* is the day we've all been waiting for," said Heather excitedly. (adverb)
2. The operator of the Ferris wheel assured me that no one had ever fallen *out*. (preposition)
3. Not only was *that* western novel a best seller, but it also won a Pulitzer Prize several years ago. (pronoun)
4. "*Wonderful!*" he said. "I thought you would win first place at the science fair." (adjective)
5. *Help* arrived in the form of a country doctor driving a battered 1963 Chevy. (verb)
6. When the tomato was first introduced to Europe, many people thought that the *plant* was poisonous. (verb)
7. When you're driving to work, *what* radio station do you listen to most often? (pronoun)
8. The pitch was *high* and outside, but the umpire called it a strike anyway. (adverb)
9. The swallows would *dart* back and forth between the feeder and the birdbath. (noun)
10. Spider monkeys *hold* onto tree branches with their tails to keep from falling. (noun)

D Identifying Parts of Speech Identify the part of speech of each of the italicized words in the following sentence pairs.

1. a. The home team's quarterback almost fumbled the ball but made a *fast* recovery.
   b. The line for tickets to the new movie was long, but it moved *fast* once it got started.
2. a. Will someone *time* Maria's speech for her?
   b. What *time* does the debate begin?
3. a. I always bring my bicycle *inside* when the weather forecaster predicts rain.
   b. The mailboxes are *inside* the lobby.
4. a. Have you already mailed *those* letters?
   b. *Those* are the letters she wrote.
5. a. Weighing up to 1,800 pounds, the North American moose is the largest member of the *deer* family.
   b. The smallest *deer* is the Chilean pudu.

2

The Sentence and Its Parts

*T*ake the mainspring out of a watch, and the rest of the clock-works ceases to work. Take the verb out of a sentence, and the remaining group of words no longer functions as a sentence. Neither sentence nor watch is complete without these essential parts. Furthermore, for the watch to tell time accurately and the sentence to clearly convey the message its author intended, these parts must be arranged in proper working order.

In this chapter you will learn how the parts of speech work together so that you can arrange them to express your thoughts clearly.

Part 1

The Sentence

Sentences make statements, ask questions, give commands, and show feelings. Each sentence expresses a complete idea. As you learn more about sentences, you will expand on the following definition.

A sentence is a group of words that expresses <u>a complete thought</u>.

When part of an idea is missing from a sentence, the group of words is a **sentence fragment.**

Sentence Fragment	The owner of the car. (What about the owner?)
Sentence	The owner of the car filed an accident report.
Sentence Fragment	Seemed dull. (Who or what seemed dull?)
Sentence	The movie seemed dull.

You will work more with sentence fragments in Chapter 4.

Exercises

A On your paper, write *S* for each group of words below that is a sentence. Write *F* for each group of words that is a fragment.

1. A bearded man with a Seeing Eye dog.
2. The registered letter has already come.
3. Washed in on the tide.
4. Several highlights of his illustrious career.
5. Waited impatiently for the announcement.
6. Shelters for the disadvantaged and homeless.
7. Fortunately nobody in the life raft panicked.
8. An entirely new approach.
9. Will be constructed on the same spot.
10. A water main has broken.

B Some of the following groups of words are sentence fragments. Rewrite the fragments so that they are complete sentences.

1. Actually, were not at all surprised.
2. No clear-cut plan for creating school spirit.
3. Never spoke to us or even noticed us, though we were standing right next to him.

4. They scraped and painted the walls.
5. Disappearing in the fog and howling mournfully.
6. Always asking questions, but never getting a valid response.
7. Still trying to discourage the plan of the Indian Council.
8. Was too much emphasis placed on winning?
9. The change in demographics throughout the country.
10. Coming to a screeching stop in the middle of the intersection.

Part 2
Kinds of Sentences

A sentence may be classified according to the purpose it serves. Four principal purposes are listed below.

A **declarative sentence** expresses a statement of fact, wish, intent, or feeling. It ends with a period.

> Hulda Crooks climbed Mt. Fuji at the age of 91.
> Everyone wished the balloonist a successful flight.

An **interrogative sentence** asks a question. It always ends with a question mark.

> Why do some people wear sunglasses indoors?
> Will the Olympic pool be finished on time?

An **imperative sentence** gives a command, request, or direction. It usually ends with a period. If the command or request is strong, an imperative sentence may end with an exclamation point.

> You return that book as soon as possible.
> Follow that car.   *or*   Follow that car!

An **exclamatory sentence** expresses strong feeling. It always ends with an exclamation point.

> What a great time we had!
> I won first prize!

Punctuation Note When an exclamatory sentence is preceded by a separate exclamation, either a period or an exclamation mark can be used at the end of the sentence.

> Oh, no! I left the tickets at home! (*or.*)

Exercises

A Identify each sentence below according to its kind: *Declarative, Interrogative, Imperative,* or *Exclamatory.* Then indicate the end punctuation. Some sentences may be punctuated in more than one way.

1. Keep your seat belts securely fastened until the plane has come to a complete stop
2. Which design will be easiest to produce
3. Soprano Marjorie Lawrence sings from a wheelchair
4. What a wild landing that was
5. Don't wear those dirty sneakers and ragged jeans to school
6. My parents are taking a vacation from alarm clocks
7. B-r-r-r That lake water is like ice
8. A small creek wandered between tree-shaded banks near my friend's cottage
9. Who is our most reliable pitcher
10. Tyrone and I carefully maneuvered the canoe through the marshy channels

B Application in Literature The following passage contains all four kinds of sentences. The author uses them to vary the dialogue and help convey the feeling of the speaker. Note that the end marks for the sentences are missing. Number your paper from 1 to 15. Identify each sentence according to its kind. Then write the appropriate end mark for each sentence. Be sure to find at least one sentence that can end with an exclamation point.

(1) Cockerill ushered [Nellie] to the door (2) "You go home now and wait, Miss Bly (3) Leave your address at the desk downstairs as you go out"

(4) She turned to go (5) Again Joseph Pulitzer did an unprecedented thing (6) "Have you any money (7) Can you wait those few days or perhaps a week"

(8) "Oh . . . I forgot" (9) She told them the story of her lost purse (10) "I can't even pay my rent"

(11) Pulitzer fumbled in his pocket and . . . gave up (12) "Give her a voucher, John (13) Give her twenty-five dollars" (14) Then to Nellie: "This money, this is not a loan; it is an advance on your salary"

(15) She didn't walk downstairs; she floated

From *Nellie Bly: First Woman Reporter* by Iris Noble

c *Proofreading* On your paper, rewrite the following paragraph, correcting all errors in punctuation, capitalization, and spelling. Before you change any end punctuation, decide whether the sentence is declarative, interrogative, imperative, or exclamatory.

> Have you seen this article. It tells about Rudyard Kipling, the English author who wrote novels, peoms, stories, and tails for children. Did you know that Kipling was borne in 1865 in india, the setting for much of his writeing! What an interesting life he must have lead. He traveled throughout the british Empire and spent several years in the United States. Read "Gunga Din" "The Rode to Mandalay," *The Jungle Book,* and *Just So Storys* to sample this Nobel prize winner's work?

Left: Rudyard Kipling's room in Allahabad, India, 1888–1889.
Right: Rudyard Kipling.

Part 3
Complete Subjects and Predicates

A sentence has two parts: a complete subject and a complete predicate. The **complete subject** includes all the words that identify the person, place, thing, or idea that the sentence is about. The **complete predicate** includes all the words that tell what the subject did or what happened to the subject.

Complete Subject	Complete Predicate
Children	play.
The children on our block	always play in a nearby park.

Exercise

Write the following sentences on your paper. Underline the complete subject once and the complete predicate twice.

1. The trees along the nature trail are labeled.
2. A cocoon was attached to the underside of the leaf.
3. Our landlord has promised us a new refrigerator.
4. Several pages in this paperback are stuck together.
5. My parents became United States citizens recently.
6. Everything in the Edgar Allan Poe Cottage in the Bronx has been carefully restored by the County Historical Society.
7. Mt. McKinley attracts hundreds of climbers every summer.
8. The most popular sculpture in the museum is a forgery.
9. Most islands in the South Pacific are surrounded by coral.
10. The plants in an aquarium provide oxygen for the fish.

Checkpoint *Parts 1, 2, and 3*

A In all but two of the following groups of words, either the complete subject or the complete predicate is missing. Identify each sentence fragment and rewrite it as a complete sentence by providing the missing part. Then underline each complete subject once and each complete predicate twice. Write *Sentence* for those groups of words that are already complete sentences.

> *Example*   This year's country music special.
> This year's country music special was not as good as last year's.

1. Is working in the supermarket this summer.
2. The villain's face, partially hidden by a long, black moustache.
3. Parking spaces in our neighborhood are very scarce.
4. Gathered around the subway entrance.
5. Are making stuffed animals for all of the infants at Children's Memorial Hospital.
6. A bicycle with a quick-release front wheel.
7. The captain's desk was covered with charts and maps.
8. Usually directs traffic at that corner.
9. A thick Irish stew with lamb and potatoes.
10. Scrambled for a first down.

B On your paper, identify each of the following sentences according to its kind: *Declarative, Interrogative, Imperative,* or *Exclamatory*. Indicate the correct end punctuation by writing *Period, Question Mark,* or *Exclamation Point*. Then rewrite each sentence so that it is the kind indicated in parentheses. Use appropriate end punctuation.

> *Example*   Buy a ticket for the matinee. (Interrogative)
> Imperative, Period
> Did you buy a ticket for the matinee?

1. What a gorgeous day it is (Declarative)
2. It is illegal to hunt crocodiles in Florida (Interrogative)
3. Did Shakespeare write comedies and tragedies (Declarative)
4. You are lucky (Exclamatory)
5. Stop at the store on your way home (Declarative)
6. The gym is large enough for the flea market (Interrogative)
7. Does their school have a rugby team (Declarative)
8. He has written his grandparents a postcard (Interrogative)
9. Return your library books on time (Declarative)
10. Has that book become a best seller (Declarative)

Part 4
Simple Subjects and Predicates

The simple subject is the key word or words in the complete subject.

To find the subject, ask *who* or *what* before the verb.

> Holly called yesterday.   **Verb**   called
> **Who called?**   Holly
> **Subject**   Holly

The simple subject does not include modifiers. In the examples below, the simple subjects are in boldface type.

> Every **atom** in the universe has an effect on every other atom.
> The late **Roman Jakobson** could read in twenty-five languages.

Do not confuse the simple subject with other words that appear between the subject and the predicate. In the first example above, the subject is *atom*, not *universe*.

A simple subject made of two or more key words is a **compound subject.** The parts of a compound subject are joined by a conjunction such as *and* or *or.*

The **Nile,** the **Amazon,** *and* the **Mississippi** are three of the world's longest rivers.

The simple predicate, also called the *verb,* is the key word or words in the complete predicate.

The verb may be a phrase consisting of more than one word: *had seen, should have seen, was singing, had been singing.* The words making up the verb phrase may be interrupted by a modifier. Such a modifier is not part of the verb. The verbs below are in boldface type.

Hair **grows** more quickly in warm climates.
Two bears **had ransacked** the garbage during the night.
We **will** not **be going** to the lake this summer.

A **compound verb** is made up of two or more verbs or verb phrases joined by a conjunction.

The park ranger **found** *and* **destroyed** the traps.
The flowers **were swaying** *and* **dancing** in the breeze.

In this text, *subject* will be used to refer to the simple subject; *verb* will be used to refer to the simple predicate.

Sentence Diagraming For information on diagraming subjects, verbs, and their modifiers, see pages 350–351.

Exercises

A On your paper, write the subject and verb of each of the following sentences. Underline the subject once and the verb twice.

1. A flock of migrating ducks landed on the pond.
2. A long freight train was rumbling by.
3. The Secret Service protects the President of the United States.
4. The bear rose slowly, stretched, and shook itself.
5. Several of the club members are helping with the decorations.
6. Soup, whole-grain bread, and fruit make a nutritious lunch.
7. Several tenants cleaned the vacant lot and planted a garden.
8. Either the drummer or the violinist will perform a solo.
9. Most of Greenland is covered by a great icecap.
10. Aristotle was a tutor to young Alexander the Great.

B Application in Literature On your paper, write the subject and verb of each sentence in the following literature passage. Underline each subject once and each verb twice. Remember that sentence parts can be compound.

(1) Jade Snow's parents had conceded defeat. . . . (2) [Now] Jade Snow came and went without any questions. (3) In spite of her parents' dark predictions, her new freedom in the choice of companions did not result in a rush of un-desirables. (4) As a matter of fact, the boys were more concerned with copying her lecture notes than with anything else.

(5) As for Joe, on the evening of Jade Snow's seventeenth birthday, he gave her as a remembrance a sparkling grown-up bracelet. (6) There under the stars he gently tilted her face and gave her her first kiss.

(7) Awkward in her full-skirted red cotton dress, Jade Snow was caught by surprise and without words. (8) She had been kissed at seventeen . . . a cause for rejoicing.

From *Fifth Chinese Daughter* by Jade Snow Wong

c *Write Now* Following are notes for a brief report about the life of Jade Snow Wong. As you can see, the notes are not written as complete sentences. Incorporate the notes into one or two paragraphs. Be sure to write complete sentences. Try to make some of the subjects and verbs compound.

born in 1922
parents from China
emigrated to San Francisco
only Chinese spoken in her
home
worked in tailoring shop in San
Francisco
unusual middle name
born during rare California
snowfall
first college graduate in her
family
chose chemistry as major

primarily interested in pottery
and ceramics
autobiography, *Fifth Chinese
Daughter*, published in 1950
admits her experiences may not
be typical
wrote about struggle between
Chinese ways and American
customs
written in third person because
of Chinese habit
second book, *No Chinese
Stranger*, published in 1975

Part 5

Subjects in Unusual Positions

In most sentences the subject appears before the verb. In some types of sentences, however, this order is not followed.

Subjects in Inverted Sentences

Inverted sentences are those in which a verb or part of a verb phrase is positioned before the subject. Following are the three most common types of inverted sentences.

Questions In most questions, the subject appears between the words that make up the verb phrase. In the examples below, the subject is underlined once and the verb twice.

> Have you called yet?
> Are your neighbors moving to Detroit?
> Where should we put these boxes?

In most questions beginning with the interrogative words *where, when, why, how,* or *how much,* the subject falls between the parts of the verb. In questions beginning with an interrogative adjective or pronoun, the verb may follow the subject in normal order.

> Which picture fell off the wall?
> Who shouted?
> What happened?

Notice that *who* and *what* sometimes function as subjects.

© 1981 United Feature Syndicate, Inc.

Sentences Beginning with *There* and *Here* When a sentence begins with *there* or *here,* the subject usually follows the verb. Remember that *there* and *here* are never the subjects of a sentence.

> There <u>are</u> my red <u>sneakers</u>.
> Here <u>is</u> your <u>passport</u>.

In the examples above, *there* and *here* are adverbs. They modify the verb and tell *where.* To find the subject, reword the sentence.

> My red <u>sneakers</u> <u>are</u> there. (*Sneakers* is the subject.)
> Your <u>passport</u> <u>is</u> here. (*Passport* is the subject.)

Sometimes, however, *there* is used as an **expletive,** a word that merely helps to get a sentence started. If you can rearrange the sentence and drop the word *there,* you can assume it is an expletive.

> There is Ms. Dobkin's office.
> Ms. Dobkin's <u>office</u> <u>is</u> there. (*There* is an adverb.)

> There were several people in line.
> Several <u>people</u> <u>were</u> in line. (*There* is an expletive.)

Occasionally, a sentence beginning with the adverb *there* or *here* will follow regular subject-verb order.

> Here <u>she</u> <u>comes</u>.
> There <u>he</u> <u>is</u>.

Sentences Inverted for Emphasis For emphasis or variety a speaker or writer may intentionally place the verb before the subject. This technique focuses extra attention on the subject. When used sparingly, this type of sentence adds drama. When it is overused, the result can sound artificial.

Normal Order   A <u>wall</u> of flood water <u>burst</u> through the door.
Inverted Order   Through the door <u>burst</u> a <u>wall</u> of flood water.

Normal Order   An abandoned <u>cottage</u> <u>was</u> at the end of the path.
Inverted Order   At the end of the path <u>was</u> an abandoned <u>cottage</u>.

Finding Subjects in Inverted Sentences One way to find the subject in an inverted sentence is to find the verb first. Then ask *who* or *what* before the verb.

> From the distance came the howl of a timber wolf. (The verb is *came.*
> What came? Howl came. The subject is *howl.*)

Another way to find the subject is to reorder the sentence. Putting the words in a different order often makes the subject easier to identify.

> After the rain came the wind.
> The wind came after the rain.

Subjects in Imperative Sentences

The subject of an imperative sentence is always *you*. When the subject is not directly stated, as is usually the case, *you* is "understood" to be the subject.

> You look at these pictures.
> (You) Speak to the landlord tomorrow.

Sentence Diagraming For information on diagraming imperative sentences, see page 351.

Exercises

A On your paper, write the subject and verb of each of the following sentences. Underline the subject once and the verb twice. If the subject is understood, write *you* in parentheses and underline it.

> *Example*   Put this in your locker.
> (You) put

1. There in the mud lay my brand new scarf.
2. Don't forget to mow the lawn today, Mike.
3. How much money can we raise at the bake sale?
4. Could you see anything from the back row?
5. Ask Harrison for his five-alarm chili recipe.
6. Inside the elegant white florist's box was one perfect long-stemmed yellow rose.
7. There are very few pandas living in the wild.
8. The gentle call of the emperor's nightingale floated away on the evening breeze.
9. Should I have tried to see the doctor sooner?
10. Through the swirling mists appeared the outline of a long-deserted castle.
11. Please get me a ticket, too.
12. Here are the registration forms.
13. From the stands came a roar of approval.
14. How can I get from here to the auditorium?
15. There are six typing errors in your paper.

B On your paper, write the subject and verb of each of the sentences in the paragraph below. Underline the subject once and the verb twice.

(1) In the future, we will find robots as much a part of our daily lives as automobiles or television sets. (2) Where will robots be utilized? (3) You will find robots in homes, schools, and businesses. (4) What will these mechanical servants do for us? (5) They will perform many of our more tedious tasks. (6) Here are the only requirements for a basic robot. (7) It needs a computer, of course, and a mechanical arm with claws. (8) Along the arm run cables. (9) Instructions from the computer to the claws are transmitted through these cables. (10) Robots can only follow instructions programmed into their computer "brains." (11) Where can you learn more about robots? (12) Ask your librarian or science teacher.

c *Write Now* You are a musical composer in the 1800's working side by side with the great masters Beethoven and Brahms. Your first symphony, *Rock-and-Roll Rhythms in G Minor,* has just been performed, but it is not a success. The critics are outraged and the audience is confused. Write a brief essay that defends and explains your music. Make your writing as interesting as your music by including some inverted and imperative sentences.

Part 6
Complements

Some sentences, such as *Joan sings,* contain only a subject and a verb. Most sentences, however, require additional words placed after the verb to complete the meaning of the sentence. These additional words are called **complements.**

A complement is a word or a group of words that completes the meaning of the verb.

Friction produces *heat.* (Produces what? Produces heat. *Heat* completes the meaning of *produces.*)

The guide showed the *visitors* from Japan some unusual *minerals.* (Showed what to whom? Showed minerals to visitors. *Visitors* and *minerals* complete the meaning of *showed.*)

Old Faithful is a well-known *geyser.* (Is what? Is geyser. *Geyser* completes the meaning of *is.*)

Many volcanoes are *dormant.* (Are what? Are dormant. *Dormant* completes the meaning of *are.*)

Now you will study four kinds of complements: direct objects, indirect objects, objective complements, and subject complements.

Direct Objects

A **direct object** is a word or group of words that receives the action of an action verb. It answers the question *What?* or *Whom?* about the verb. Verbs that take direct objects are called **transitive verbs.** See page 19 for more information about transitive verbs.

Everyone knows your *secret.* (Knows what?)
The fans cheered *Paul Molitar.* (Cheered whom?)

Do not confuse a direct object with an adverb that follows an action verb. A direct object tells *what* or *whom.* An adverb tells *where, when, how,* or *to what extent.*

Direct Object   We followed the *trail.* (Followed what?)
Adverb   We followed *closely.* (Followed how?)

The direct object may be compound.

I misplaced my *pad* and *pencil.* (Misplaced what?)
The officer helped my *sister* and *me.* (Helped whom?)

Indirect Objects

An **indirect object** is a word or group of words that tells *to whom* or *for whom* the action of the verb is being performed. A verb has an indirect object only if it also has a direct object. The indirect object always comes before the direct object.

> The book club sent *us* a refund. (Sent a refund to whom?)
> My aunt made *Lisa* a sweater. (Made a sweater for whom?)

The indirect object may be compound.

> Our grandmother taught my *cousin* and *me* Greek.

The words *to* and *for* never appear before the indirect object. *To* and *for* are prepositions when they are followed by a noun or pronoun. The noun or pronoun is the object of the preposition.

Indirect Object   The team sent the *coach* a telegram.
Object of a Preposition   The team sent a telegram to the *coach*.

For more information on prepositions, see pages 33–35.

Exercises

A Make three columns labeled *Verb, Indirect Object,* and *Direct Object.* For each sentence, write the verb and the object or objects in the proper columns. If there is no indirect object, write *None*.

1. The reporter wrote the mayor a letter of apology.
2. Have you ever given an elephant a bath?
3. We found a magazine and several letters under the doormat.
4. The new vacuum has attachments that clean furniture and drapes.
5. We handed Rico and Paula the money for our tickets.
6. My aunt made Dad and me a huge pot of beef and barley soup.
7. Ernest lent Alice his trumpet for the band auditions.
8. Has the ticket agent guaranteed you good seats for the concert?
9. The rain brought little relief to the drought-stricken plains.
10. Those plants need fresh air and direct sunlight.

B Write the following sentences. Underline each subject once and each verb twice. Write *DO* over each direct object and *IO* over each indirect object.

1. One of the ushers found me a seat in the front row.
2. The judges awarded Melissa first prize in the piano competition.
3. The doctor has prescribed vitamins for the whole family.

4. Has Juan read you his letter to the editor?
5. My mother finally found my brother an affordable secondhand car in good condition.
6. The supervisor offered my cousin the job of assistant manager.
7. At the holidays we send our relatives a family photograph.
8. During the Soviet blockade, Western powers airlifted the people of West Berlin badly needed supplies.
9. The superintendent awarded five students scholarships.
10. A helicopter lowered a ladder to the survivors.

Objective Complements

An **objective complement** is a word or group of words that follows a direct object and renames or describes that object. Objective complements follow certain verbs and their synonyms: *appoint, call, choose, consider, elect, find, make, keep, name, think.*

An objective complement may be a noun or an adjective.

Noun   Tennis experts consider Steffi Graf a unique *player*. (*Player* renames or describes the object *Steffi Graf*.)

Adjective   Many even call her *unbeatable*. (*Unbeatable* describes the object *her*.)

Exercise

Identify each complement in the following sentences according to its kind: *Direct Object, Indirect Object,* or *Objective Complement.*

> *Example*   Our class elected Tricia Fox president.
> Tricia Fox, Direct Object
> president, Objective Complement

1. The new baseball coach considers Laura a reliable but mediocre pitcher.
2. Has the manufacturer sent Michael a new jacket?
3. We found the film long and dull, but my parents enjoyed it.
4. The superintendent handed Ursula the keys to the store room.
5. The senator appointed Dad her legal assistant.
6. Violence on television makes many people uncomfortable.
7. Chicago's voters elected him mayor for an unprecedented fourth consecutive term.
8. The jury must have thought the witness unreliable.
9. *Treasure Island* made Robert Louis Stevenson famous.
10. Automated assembly lines made Ford cars affordable.

Subject Complements

A **subject complement** is a complement that follows a linking verb and renames or describes the subject. Subject complements often come after a form of the verb *be*. For a discussion of linking verbs, see page 17. There are two kinds of subject complements: **predicate nominatives** and **predicate adjectives.**

Predicate Nominatives A **predicate nominative** is a word or a group of words that follows a linking verb and names or identifies the subject of the sentence. Predicate nominatives can be either **predicate nouns** or **predicate pronouns.**

Predicate Noun   My favorite sport is *football*.
Predicate Pronoun   The winner should have been *she*.

The predicate nominative may be compound.

Benjamin Franklin was a *statesman* and an *inventor*.

Predicate Adjectives A **predicate adjective** is an adjective that follows a linking verb and modifies the subject of the sentence.

Everyone on the team felt *confident* of victory.

The predicate adjective may be compound.

Medieval castles were usually *cold, damp,* and *gloomy*.

Sentence Diagraming For information on diagraming subject complements, see page 352.

Exercises

A Write each subject complement in the following sentences and identify it according to its kind: *Predicate Nominative* or *Predicate Adjective*. Remember that a subject complement may be compound.

1. "Does your chewing gum lose its flavor on the bedpost overnight?" was the first line of a song popular in the 1960's.
2. Gum-chewing has been popular in many cultures for over 2,000 years.
3. Spruce gums were the first ones available in the United States.
4. Some spruce gums used by early American settlers were waxy and tough.
5. The later chicle-based gums were sweeter and tastier.
6. Chicle is an ingredient in most modern gums.

7. Some people have become avid collectors of the baseball cards given away with certain gums.
8. Children have been fond of bubble gum since it was first put on the market in 1933.
9. Kurt Bevacqua was the winner of a 1975 bubble-blowing contest.
10. The size of his winning bubble was eighteen inches.

B Complete each group of words by adding a subject complement. Then tell whether the complement is a predicate nominative or a predicate adjective. Use at least three compound complements.

1. Two well-known singers are
2. Outer space is
3. The abandoned factory looked
4. Your excuse for missing class seems
5. The water in the pond appears

6. This salad tastes
7. My best friend is
8. A current fad is
9. The team remained
10. That tape sounds

Checkpoint Parts 4, 5, and 6

On your paper, write the following sentences. Underline each subject once and each verb twice. Identify each complement by writing *DO* (direct object), *IO* (indirect object), *OC* (objective complement), *PN* (predicate nominative), or *PA* (predicate adjective) over the appropriate word. Not every sentence has a complement.

1. The opening ceremony of the Olympics is usually very impressive.
2. Why do some people consider thirteen an unlucky number?

3. Along the shore the tourists found some unusual shells.
4. The coach appointed them co-captains of the B team.
5. Our neighbor gives his dogs and cats the run of the house.
6. The baseball manager considers the rookie outfielder a valuable addition to the team.
7. Dust and carbon monoxide can form a thick smog.
8. There are sandwiches and cold drinks in the refrigerator.
9. The first prize will be five hundred dollars and a trip to New York City.
10. Thunder crashed overhead and rattled the windowpanes.
11. The new owners of the cottage have planted geraniums and marigolds along the front walk.
12. They named their hamsters Napoleon and Josephine.
13. Vidkun Quisling was the Norwegian leader who betrayed his country to the Germans during World War II.
14. Did England award Florence Nightingale the Order of Merit?
15. Our new dog is both pugnacious and quarrelsome.

Part 7
The Sentence Redefined

Here and at the end of Chapter 3, you will add to the basic definition of the sentence given on page 47. You now know a sentence is a group of words that (1) expresses a complete thought, (2) contains at least one subject and verb, and (3) may contain a complement.

Exercise

Proofreading Combine the fragments in the following paragraph into complete sentences. Also correct any errors in punctuation, capitalization, or spelling.

Citadelle Henry is one of the largest forts. In the world. It sits atop a jungle peek. On the Caribbean island of haiti. The fort was begun in the early nineteenth Century. By Haitian liberator Jean-Jacques Dessalines. Under his leadership, the slaves of Haiti. Rebelled and defeated they're French masters. The next ruler, King henry Christophe, oversaw most of the Citadelles' construction. King Christophe hoped the forte would proteckt his subjects. From any future European invasions. He wiseley decided that fighting from the Hills. Was the best plan of defence for the island.

Linking
Grammar *&* Writing

Did you know that 92,000 Americans have reservations with Pan American Airlines for a trip to the moon? Imagine that you were on such a trip. What would the experience be like? Write one or more paragraphs in which you describe your voyage.

To make your description more interesting, use all four kinds of sentences (declarative, imperative, interrogative, and exclamatory).

Prewriting and Drafting Look at the photos below as you think about what you might see on your space voyage. Limit your description to the one part of the voyage that you think would be the most exciting—the take-off, the landing, or the flight itself. Imagine what you would see and hear and feel. Try freewriting or brainstorming to develop colorful details for your description.

Revising and Proofreading When revising your description, consider these questions:

1. Does your description include vivid, sensory details?
2. Does your description follow a logical order?
3. Have you used all four kinds of sentences?

Additional Writing Topic A local millionaire has decided to sponsor a writing contest at your school. He will award a prize of ten thousand dollars to the person who can write the most entertaining description of himself or herself. In one paragraph, describe who you are. Use several predicate nouns and predicate adjectives.

Chapter 2
Application and Review

A Writing Complete Sentences All but two of the following groups of words do not express complete thoughts. Identify these groups and change them into sentences. Write *Sentence* for those groups of words that are already complete sentences.

1. The scientist in the laboratory.
2. Swayed and trembled in the violent wind.
3. The girl with the short, curly hair.
4. Stopping abruptly, he turned and stalked away.
5. Offered Joyce one scoop of rocky road ice cream.
6. The scariest movie I have ever seen.
7. Rushed toward the goal post while the fans roared.
8. Is flying in tonight from Philadelphia on a DC-10.
9. Tried unsuccessfully to hold back his tears.
10. Working in the emergency ward is exhausting for the hospital staff.

B Finding Subjects and Verbs Find the verb and its simple subject in each of the following sentences.

1. There were thirty-two new players at the first football practice of the season.
2. Along the horizon twinkled the lights of the city.
3. Between the band and the next float rode sixteen clowns on multicolored motorbikes.
4. Rudolf Nureyev and Mikhail Baryshnikov were both born in Russia.
5. Maurice Sendak writes and illustrates many wonderful and popular children's books.
6. How are you getting to work during the bus strike?
7. Into the harbor sailed the double-masted schooner.
8. Here are the videotapes of the game.
9. From the cave entrance flew a cloud of bats.
10. On this island grow many carnivorous plants.
11. Are you in intermediate ballet or the advanced class?
12. St. Paul's Cathedral is located in London.
13. West Virginia became a state during the administration of President Abraham Lincoln.
14. Some lizards change color when frightened.
15. Who will wear the green jerseys?

C Identifying the Parts of a Sentence Label six columns *Subject, Verb, Direct Object, Indirect Object, Objective Complement,* and *Subject Complement*. Place those parts of the following sentences in the proper columns. Some of the sentence parts may be compound.

1. Our drama class wrote and produced a serious musical about substance abuse.
2. My aunt in Mexico sent me some hand-crafted silver jewelry.
3. A *B* on that paper would make me ecstatic!
4. During the trial, the defendant admitted her guilt.
5. I found your report confusing and misleading.
6. The magician showed Arleta several illusions.
7. The Latin class wore togas for their Roman banquet.
8. The baby sitter gave the children crackers and cheese.
9. My helicopter ride was rough and noisy.
10. Pigs and cattle were loaded onto railroad cars.
11. This cave looks treacherous.
12. A gust of wind scattered Jason's homework around the parking lot.
13. Three airplanes performed stunts for the crowd.
14. The gymnastics coach spotted Kendra during her back flip.
15. The politicians consider Ms. Weiss a prime candidate for nomination.
16. Billie Holiday was a famous blues singer.
17. Cindy asked the veterinarian questions about pet care.
18. Dad taught us a new dive.
19. Cassie seemed curious about the algebra assignment.
20. Whom did their class elect for president?

D Using Sentence Parts Complete the following sentences by adding the material indicated in parentheses.

1. The rescue volunteers distributed _____ to the flood victims. (compound direct object)
2. I made _____ peanut butter and banana sandwiches. (compound indirect object)
3. The President _____ at the photographers and the White House journalists. (compound verb)
4. Marnie _____ to make the decision on her own. (verb)
5. The game show contestants were _____ . (compound predicate adjective)
6. Christopher named his pet snakes _____ . (compound objective complement)
7. The nominees were _____ . (compound predicate nominative)
8. _____ are great qualities in a friend. (compound subject)

Cumulative Review

Chapters 1 and 2

A Identifying Parts of Speech Write the function of each italicized word, telling whether it is a *Noun, Pronoun, Verb, Adjective, Adverb, Preposition, Conjunction,* or *Interjection*.

1. It appeared that the battle was almost *certainly* lost.
2. *Whenever* she imagined the possibility of winning the scholarship, she worked even harder.
3. Only the crackling sound of footsteps on the snow interrupted the *still* beauty of the wintry night.
4. The final responsibility for all decisions belongs to *her*.
5. With each swish of the basket, the crowd's enthusiasm *mounted*.
6. If you only could have been *there*, you would have been amazed to see everyone working so hard.
7. *Which* of the desserts are you going to choose?
8. That woman's secretive manner and mysterious appearance remind me of a spy *that* I once read about.
9. Once you know him better, you will discover that *underneath* that tough, selfish exterior lies a tough, selfish interior.
10. After the storm, the captain went *below* to check the damage.
11. The Thomas Hardy poem "During Wind and Rain" repeats the phrase, "*Ah*, no; the years, the years" in each stanza.
12. Of all of those who had entered, only *fifteen* remained.
13. Either Sherry *or* Nathan will be able to tell you the answer to that question.
14. She seemed *confident* of her ability, though she had never played.
15. The human body can survive without food longer than it can survive *without* water.

B Recognizing Parts of a Sentence Study each italicized word or group of words in the sentences below. Write whether it is a *Subject, Verb, Direct Object, Indirect Object, Objective Complement, Subject Complement,* or *Object of a Preposition*.

1. Maria made herself a tostada with the fresh *tortilla*.
2. From the distance came the lively *sounds* of the street musicians.
3. Frederick Douglass *published* a famous abolitionist newspaper.
4. Many high-school students have read the *fiction* of John Steinbeck.

5. The French impressionists often painted outside in order to capture the immediacy of their *sensations*.
6. Augustus appointed himself first *emperor* of Rome.
7. Churchill's wartime speeches sounded *fearless* and *resolute* to the people of Great Britain.
8. While telling his imaginary story of a haunted house, he gave *himself* a good scare.
9. Margaret Atwood *wrote* a powerful poem about the accidental drowning of her young son.
10. Author Virginia Woolf and her friends once disguised *themselves,* impersonated foreign dignitaries, and fooled the British Navy.
11. Cable television reaches nearly 50 percent of the *households* in the United States.
12. The audience gave the long-winded *speaker* a lukewarm reception, even though they had paid an extravagant sum of money to see him.
13. The parents of the football player Jim Plunkett were both legally *blind*.
14. Who answered the front *door* when the mysterious, late-night visitors rang the bell?
15. She appeared *poised* and knowledgeable as she answered the questions from the senators.

C Using Parts of Speech and Parts of Sentences Complete the following sentences by adding the material indicated in parentheses.

1. After the party, the room looked _____ . (compound predicate adjective)
2. The war between Iran and Iraq had been intensifying; _____ athletes from the two countries competed in a volleyball match. (conjunctive adverb)
3. In his new role as team captain, he _____ dedicated and disciplined. (linking verb)
4. Her performanced showed _____ the astounding range of her voice. (indirect object)
5. The ruthless dictator named himself _____ . (objective complement)
6. _____ had already left the dance floor. (indefinite pronoun)
7. Her favorite spectator sports were _____ . (compound predicate nominative)
8. The father looked _____ at his playful child. (adverb)
9. Gandhi gave _____ to rich and poor alike. (direct object)
10. The old man saw in _____ a glimpse of his own past. (object of a preposition)

3

Using Phrases and Clauses

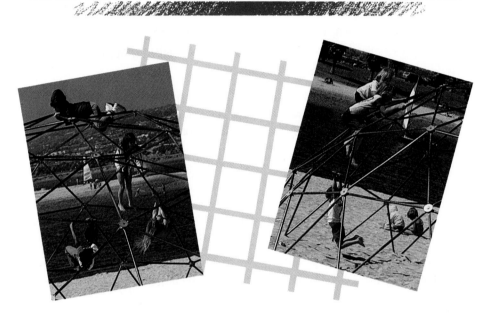

*L*ike kids hanging on a jungle gym, phrases and clauses can be attached anywhere in a sentence—at the beginning, at the end, or somewhere in between—to add information and interest to the basic message.

In this chapter you will learn to recognize the types of phrases and clauses and how they function in sentences. You will also discover how to use these flexible components to make your own writing and speaking come alive.

Part 1
Prepositional Phrases

A **phrase** is a group of related words that does not have a subject and a predicate and that functions in a sentence as a single part of speech. One kind of phrase is a **prepositional phrase.**

A prepositional phrase is a phrase that consists of a preposition, its object, and any modifiers of the object.

> The mockingbird imitates the calls *of other birds*. (*Birds* is the object of the preposition *of*.)

As you have learned, the object of a preposition is always a noun, pronoun, or a group of words used as a noun. A prepositional phrase may have two or more objects joined by a conjunction.

> Deliver the letter *to whoever answers the door*. (The group of words *whoever answers the door* is the object of the preposition *to*.)

> A majority of members *of both the House and the Senate* strongly supported the bill. (*House* and *Senate* are the compound objects of the preposition *of*.)

A prepositional phrase is a modifier and functions in a sentence as an adjective or an adverb.

Adjective Phrases

A prepositional phrase that modifies a noun or pronoun is called an **adjective phrase.** An adjective phrase can modify a subject, direct object, indirect object, or predicate nominative. The phrase usually tells *which one* or *what kind* about the word it modifies.

Modifying a Subject	The clock *in the church steeple* struck ten. (*Which* clock?)
Modifying a Direct Object	Kim repaired the shutter *on my camera*. (*Which* shutter?)
Modifying an Indirect Object	Mom gave the family *next door* a plum pudding. (*Which* family?)
Modifying a Predicate Nominative	A marmoset is a monkey *from South America*. (*What kind* of monkey?)

An adjective phrase sometimes modifies the object in another prepositional phrase.

Several scenes in the documentary *about grizzlies* were frightening. (*Which* documentary?)

Adverb Phrases

A prepositional phrase that functions as an adverb is called an **adverb phrase.** An adverb phrase modifies a verb, an adjective, or another adverb. Like an adverb, an adverb phrase tells *how, when, where,* or *to what extent* about the word it modifies.

Modifying a Verb	The milk spilled *on the floor*. (Spilled *where*?)
Modifying an Adjective	Charles Dickens was very skillful *at characterization*. (Skillful *how*?)
Modifying an Adverb	Autumn color begins soon *after the first frost*. (*How* soon?)

More than one adverb phrase may modify the same word.

Who knocked *on our door at dawn?* (Both phrases modify *knocked*. *On our door* tells where. *At dawn* tells when.)

Punctuation Note There are three times when a prepositional phrase at the beginning of a sentence is followed by a comma.

1. If the phrase is followed by a natural pause when read: According to the fire marshall, smoke detectors save lives.
2. After a series of prepositional phrases: After three weeks of heavy rain in April, the fields were wet and muddy.
3. To avoid confusion: Next to the school, houses were being built.

Placement of Prepositional Phrases

A prepositional phrase may come before or after the word it modifies. However, to avoid confusion, place a prepositional phrase close to the word it modifies.

Confusing	Edward explained how to raise earthworms in his report.
Clear	*In his report,* Edward explained how to raise earthworms.

Sentence Diagraming For information on diagraming prepositional phrases, see page 355.

A Cat in Underwear?

As anyone knows who has ever written so much as a letter home to mother, the English language is full of traps and pitfalls. It is harder to write a clear sentence than to keep a clear conscience.

Some time ago, while trying to explain why I thought my neighborhood had that exclusive quality known as ambience[1], I wrote this sentence. . . .

"A man chasing a cat with a broom in his underwear is ambience by any definition."

Oddly enough, several people evidently misunderstood that simple sentence. . . .

"It was with considerable interest," wrote Bob Byrne, "knowing that you also have long suffered with a back problem, that I read that you keep a broom in your underwear. Is this good?"

The problem seems to be that the reader's understanding is colored or distorted by his own experience. . . ."A gray tomcat with a broom in his underwear is ambience," wrote Mrs. Cecil T. Brown, "in anyone's language. Please call us collect the next time. We will take pictures."

"I do agree," wrote yet another, . . . "Mt. Washington must have ambience—a cat in underwear, indeed! And even more ambient—a cat with a *broom* in his underwear?"

"I have known cats for many years," wrote N. S. Elliott of Hollywood, "but have never seen one wearing underwear. Or outerwear, either, for that matter. Or was it you with the broom in your underwear? If so, why?"

What I would like to do now is to explain exactly what happened that night. . . .

We have a new tomcat in the neighborhood, and he had begun to exasperate me beyond the limits of my patience, if not my sanity. He would wait until I had gone to bed, or was about to, then skulk into our yard and crouch in the ivy under my windows to caterwaul his loathsome lovesong.

Among all my virtues, I like to think that tolerance for my fellow creatures is first. But the screech of a . . . tomcat strings me out. So that night, when he did it again, I snapped. I won't go into the ludicrous details.

But if you had been here, you would have seen a man chasing a cat with a broom in his underwear.

As you see, the difficulty of saying exactly what you mean, so that your reader can't fail to understand, is not a common skill, which is why most writing is not so much read as puzzled out.

Jack Smith

---

[1] **ambience:** a special atmosphere

Exercises

A On your paper, write the prepositional phrases in the following sentences. After each phrase write the word or words the phrase modifies and tell whether the phrase is used as an *Adjective* or *Adverb*. Each sentence has more than one prepositional phrase.

> *Example*   At the end of autumn, the lake is covered with ice.
> At the end, is covered, Adverb
> of autumn, end, Adjective
> with ice, is covered, Adverb

1. Lines of ginkgo trees have been planted along the parkway.
2. The birds of the evergreen forests have a varied diet of seeds, berries, and insects.
3. Georgia O'Keeffe is famous for her dramatic paintings of the American Southwest.
4. By the side of the road, a motorist was changing one of the tires of her car.
5. The identity of the man in the iron mask remained a mystery until the death of Louis XIV.
6. Before long, a spontaneous burst of applause rose from the bystanders.
7. For eight hours, the survivors clung to the small iron buoy.
8. A cloud of thick smoke appeared on the horizon.
9. An otter slithered down the riverbank into the water.
10. Before a holiday, a feeling of excitement pervades the school.

B Application in Literature List the prepositional phrases in the following passage. Tell whether the phrase is an adjective or adverb phrase. Notice how the writer uses prepositional phrases to add clarity and interest to the nouns and verbs in the passage.

> (1) The inhabitants of the wall were a mixed lot, and they were divided into day and night workers, the hunters and the hunted. (2) At night the hunters were the toads that lived among the brambles, and the geckos, pale, translucent, with bulging eyes, that lived in the cracks higher up the wall. (3) Their prey was the population of stupid, absent-minded crane-flies that zoomed and barged their way among the leaves; moths of all sizes and shapes . . . fluttered in soft clouds. . . .
>
> From "The World in a Wall" by Gerald Durrell

c *Write Now* Scientists believe that one answer to the world's hunger problems may lie in farming the sea. Imagine that you are a staff member of the first oceanic farm. Use a variety of prepositional phrases to write a paragraph describing your first harvest.

Part 2
Appositives and Appositive Phrases

An appositive is a noun or a pronoun that usually follows another noun or pronoun and identifies or explains it.

The adventurous balloonist *Julian Nott* is planning an around-the-world flight. (The appositive *Julian Nott* identifies *balloonist*.)

An appositive phrase consists of an appositive and its modifiers.

Nott's balloon, *a revolutionary new model with a pressurized gondola,* can ascend seven miles into the jet stream. (The appositive *model* explains the subject *balloon*. The adjectives *revolutionary* and *new* and the adjective phrase *with a pressurized gondola* modify the appositive *model*.)

"Dang it, Monica! I can't live this charade any longer! I'm not a telephone repairman who stumbled into your life— I'm a Komodo dragon, largest member of the lizard family and a filthy liar."

Appositives and Appositive Phrases 75

Sometimes the appositive phrase comes before the word it identifies or explains.

> *A noted pilot of her era,* Anne Morrow Lindbergh was also a writer of exceptional ability. (The appositive *pilot* explains the subject *Anne Morrow Lindbergh*.)

An appositive may be compound.

> Antoine de Saint-Exupéry, a *writer* and an *artist,* began his career in aviation as a mail pilot.

An appositive may be essential or nonessential. An **essential appositive** is one that is needed to make the intended meaning of a sentence complete.

> The aviator *Beryl Markam* wrote about her historic flight across the Atlantic. (Without the appositive, the intended meaning would not be complete.)

A **nonessential appositive** is one that adds extra meaning to a sentence in which the meaning is already clear and complete.

> Nevil Norway, *a British pilot,* wrote novels under the name of Nevil Shute.

Sometimes special circumstances affect whether an appositive is essential or nonessential. Consider the example below.

> My nephew Alex just graduated from college.

If the writer has several nephews, and only Alex graduated, then the appositive is essential. Usually, however, an appositive such as the one above would be considered nonessential.

Punctuation Note As shown above, nonessential appositives are set off with commas. Commas are not used with essential appositives.

Sentence Diagraming For information on diagraming appositives and appositive phrases, see page 357.

Exercises

A Write the appositive or the appositive phrase in each of the following sentences. A sentence may have more than one appositive.

1. Kim can do her math problems faster with an abacus, an ancient form of calculator, than I can with a modern calculator.

2. Robinson Crusoe and Friday are the principal characters in Defoe's classic novel *Robinson Crusoe*.
3. The metal tungsten is added to steel to make it hard.
4. Captain Kidd, a well-known pirate, may have buried treasure in New York.
5. The unforgettable actor Lionel Barrymore was also an accomplished musician.
6. The songstress Jenny Lind toured the United States under the management of P. T. Barnum, the world-famous showman.
7. Does the name Johnny Appleseed mean anything to you?
8. Herbert Pocket was a friend of Pip, the hero of *Great Expectations*.
9. A delicate, lacy-winged insect, the mayfly lives only a few days.
10. Yellowstone, the world's first national park, was established in 1872.

B On your paper, combine the following pairs of sentences into a single sentence by using an appositive phrase. Eliminate words as needed and use appropriate punctuation.

> *Example*   They entered their dog in the dog show. Their dog's name is Pockets.
> They entered their dog Pockets in the dog show.

1. The highlight of our vacation was the logrolling contest in Itasca. Itasca is the source of the Mississippi River.
2. The *Nightingale* is named for Florence Nightingale. It is a U.S. Air Force hospital plane with a red cross on its tail.
3. Attila overran a large part of Eurasia in the fifth century. Attila was king of the Huns.
4. The Iditarod covers 1,100 miles from Anchorage to Nome and lasts twelve days. It is the most grueling dogsled race in the world.
5. Red Grange was the first football player to have his jersey retired. He was known as the Galloping Ghost of the University of Illinois.
6. Beyond the tundra, ice and snow remain year round. The tundra is a region of land in the Arctic.
7. Why would you visit a chiropodist? A chiropodist is a doctor who treats ailments of the feet.
8. Prince Otto von Bismark created the nation of Germany. Prince Otto was the Iron Chancellor.
9. Uranium is a radioactive element. Radioactive elements give off alpha, beta, and gamma rays.
10. Chess gets its name from a Persian word meaning "king." The Persian word for "king" is *shah*.

Part 3
Verbals and Verbal Phrases

A **verbal** is a verb form that functions as a noun, an adjective, or an adverb. A **verbal phrase** consists of a verbal, its modifiers, and its complements. There are three kinds of verbals: **infinitives, participles,** and **gerunds.**

Infinitives and Infinitive Phrases

An infinitive is a verb form that usually begins with *to* and functions as a noun, an adjective, or an adverb.

Noun	*To leave* was a difficult decision. (subject)
	King Edward did not choose *to rule*. (direct object)
	His choice was *to abdicate*. (predicate nominative)
Adjective	That is the game *to see*. (modifies the noun *game*)
Adverb	Everyone stood *to stretch*. (modifies the verb *stood*)
	Kiwis are unable *to fly*. (modifies the adjective *unable*)

Grammar Note Do not confuse an infinitive (*to* plus a verb form) with a prepositional phrase (*to* plus a noun or pronoun).

An infinitive is often used with one or more auxiliary verbs.

Selma was proud *to have been elected*.

To, which is called "the sign of the infinitive," is sometimes left out of the sentence.

Someone will help you *pack*. (Someone will help you [*to*] *pack*.)

Infinitives used with the following verbs do not usually include *to: dare, help, make, see, hear, let, please, watch*.

An infinitive phrase consists of an infinitive, its modifiers, and its complements.

Infinitives may be modified by adverbs and by adverb phrases.

Firefighters have *to practice daily*. (*Daily* is an adverb modifying *to practice*.)

We packed sandwiches *to eat on the bus*. (*On the bus* is an adverb prepositional phrase modifying *to eat*.)

Since an infinitive is a verb form, it can have complements.

> Rita offered *to make everyone pizza.* (*Everyone* is the indirect object of the infinitive *to make; pizza* is the direct object.)

When the infinitive is formed from a linking verb, its complement is a predicate adjective or predicate nominative.

> We tried *to look serious.* (*Serious* is a predicate adjective after the infinitive *to look.*)

Like infinitives, infinitive phrases can function as nouns, adjectives, or adverbs.

Noun	*To chase after the dog* would be futile. (subject)
Adjective	Ms. Lawry is the candidate *to watch in this election.*
Adverb	We meet every Friday night *to play Scrabble*™ *or Trivial Pursuit.*™

Usage Note Careful writers avoid placing a modifier between *to* and the rest of the infinitive. A modifier in that position is said to "split the infinitive." A split infinitive usually sounds awkward and should be reworded.

Awkward	The principal hopes to substantially increase our reading scores.
Improved	The principal hopes to increase our reading scores substantially.

Exercises

A Write the infinitives and infinitive phrases in the following sentences. Do not confuse infinitives with prepositional phrases.

1. Some poetry is difficult to interpret.
2. Our neighbors helped us carry the tree stump to the dumpster.
3. The President seems to recognize the problem.
4. To get the frightened cat down from the tree, the firefighter used an extension ladder.
5. Vi watched the weaver bird skillfully construct the nest.
6. To escape the heavy rain, the cyclists rode into a deserted barn.
7. The proposal to table the motion failed.
8. The people downstairs want to sublet their apartment to us.
9. Most elected officials like to hear from their constituents.
10. Many actors also want to write and direct.

B On your paper, write the infinitives and infinitive phrases in the following sentences. Then tell how each infinitive or infinitive phrase is used in the sentence: as a *Noun*, an *Adjective*, or an *Adverb*.

1. In the eighteenth century, an Arab worker helped discover one of the most famous stones in history, the Rosetta Stone.
2. Thinking the oddly shaped black basalt stone was magical, the worker's first impulse was to destroy it.
3. Fortunately, the engineer in charge of the crew became interested in the stone and decided to clean it.
4. On its polished surface were three broad bands of etched writing that proved very difficult to read.
5. To decipher the writing on its surface, scholars examined it carefully.
6. Once they realized that the three messages were the same and that one was written in Greek, scholars were able to read the hieroglyphics.
7. However, it took more than twenty years to unlock the entire Egyptian script.
8. In time, the Rosetta Stone was so important it became booty, to be fought over by nations warring in Egypt.
9. Meanwhile, many people worked to piece together the puzzling facts and unlock the stone's message.
10. Finally, Jean François Champollion was to get credit for deciphering the hieroglyphics.

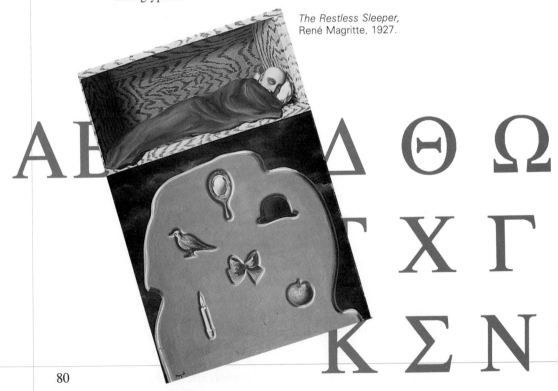

The Restless Sleeper,
René Magritte, 1927.

Participles and Participial Phrases

A participle is a verb form that functions as an adjective.

Like adjectives, participles modify nouns and pronouns.

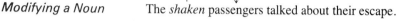

Modifying a Noun   The *shaken* passengers talked about their escape. (*Shaken* modifies the noun *passengers*.)

Modifying a Pronoun   *Bored,* everyone soon became restless. (*Bored* modifies the pronoun *everyone*.)

There are two kinds of participles: **present participles** and **past participles.** For all verbs, the present participle ends in *-ing.* The past participle has several different forms but usually ends with *-d, -ed, -t,* or *-n.* See Chapter 5, pages 132–171, for lists of irregular verbs and their past participles.

When a present participle or past participle is used with an auxiliary verb to form a verb phrase, it functions as a verb. When it is used as an adjective, it is a verbal.

Verb Phrase   The child on the monkey bars *was laughing.*

Verbal   *Laughing,* the child swung from the monkey bars.

A participle used as an adjective is sometimes used with one or more auxiliary verbs.

Having finished, we turned in our test papers and left.

A participial phrase consists of a participle and its modifiers and complements. Participial phrases function as adjectives.

Participles may be modified by adverbs and by adverb phrases.

Already soaked by the rain, I struggled with my umbrella. (In the participial phrase, the participle *soaked* is modified by the adverb *already* and the adverb phrase *by the rain.*)

Since a participle is a verb form, it can have complements.

Handing the sailor the navigational charts, the captain went below. (*Sailor* is the indirect object of the participle *handing; charts* is the direct object.)

Punctuation Note Introductory participles and participial phrases are followed by a comma.

Participial phrases may be essential or nonessential. An **essential participial phrase** is one that is needed to make the meaning of a sentence complete. A **nonessential participial phrase** is one that adds extra meaning to the sentence.

Essential	The puppy *curled up in the corner* is ours. (The participial phrase points out a particular puppy.)
Nonessential	The puppy, *curled up in the corner*, slept through all the excitement. (The participial phrase adds to the description of the puppy.) Note the use of commas.

Misplaced Participles For clarity, a participle or participial phrase should be placed as close as possible to the word that it modifies.

Confusing	Holsteins are the most popular cows among dairy farmers *producing the most milk.* (The participial phrase appears to modify *farmers.*)
Clear	*Producing the most milk,* Holsteins are the most popular cows among dairy farmers. (The participial phrase clearly modifies *Holsteins.*)

Dangling Participles A participle or a participial phrase that does not clearly modify anything in a sentence is called a **dangling participle.** A dangling participle causes confusion because it appears to modify a word that it cannot sensibly modify. Correct a dangling participle by providing a word for the participle to modify.

Confusing	*Calculating the danger,* the victims were rescued. (The participial phrase has no word to modify.)
Clear	Calculating the danger, the paramedics rescued the victims.

Sentence Diagraming For information on diagraming participles and participial phrases, see page 356.

Absolute Phrases An **absolute phrase** is made up of a participle and the noun or pronoun it modifies. An absolute phrase has no grammatical connection with a particular word in the rest of the sentence, but it does modify the independent clause by indicating time, reason, or circumstance.

Example	Our discussion finished, we all shook hands.

Exercises

A On your paper, write the participles and participial phrases in the following sentences. After each participle or participial phrase, write the word it modifies.

1. Can a broken promise ever be mended?
2. We visited a castle built in the twelfth century.
3. The witness carrying the umbrella will testify for the defense.
4. Best known for her novels, Willa Cather also wrote short stories.
5. The sunken treasure, encrusted with barnacles, certainly didn't look very valuable.
6. The school soccer team has a losing record.
7. Having heard the election results, Thomas Dewey retired for the night, thinking he was President.
8. Frothing beakers and smoking test tubes gave the laboratory an eerie atmosphere.
9. Walking in pairs, the elephants lumbered into the ring.
10. Movies intended for a general audience are rated *G*.
11. Wilting in the hot sun, both teams played listlessly.
12. The approaching band has won the state championship.
13. Crowded with colorful characters, *Shogun* depicts the life of samurai swordsmen.
14. Candidates running for public office must become experts at time management.
15. The cast appeared discouraged after the dress rehearsal.

B Each of the following sentences contains a misplaced participle or a dangling participle. On your paper, revise each sentence to make the meaning clear.

1. Walking across the front lawn, the geraniums and marigolds looked colorful.
2. Broken down and dented, Paul paid very little for the car.
3. The posters seemed beautiful to Laura hanging on the wall.
4. Pickled and chilled, the family enjoyed the kiwi fruit.
5. Swimming in the aquarium, the cat peered at the guppies.
6. Rowing steadily, the boat was maneuvered safely to shore.
7. The chimpanzees were observed by scientists swinging from the branches.
8. Having accidentally bumped the table, the lamp crashed to the floor.
9. Lying under the kitchen table, I found the note Dad had left.
10. Performing maneuvers in the air, we watched the Blue Angels.

c *Write Now* By using verbal phrases you can add energy and movement to your writing. For example, compare the following descriptions of an accident.

> The truck swerved wildly. It went around a corner. Then it jumped
> the curb and crashed through a storefront.
> Swerving wildly around a corner, the truck jumped the curb and
> crashed through a storefront.

Imagine that you are a reporter. You have just covered one of the following events (or one of your choice). Write a brief article that captures the action and contains at least four participial phrases.

> an earthquake in downtown Los Angeles
> a firefighter's rescue of a small girl
> a movie crew filming a chase scene through city streets
> a bear—having escaped from the zoo—rummages through the local
> produce market

Gerunds and Gerund Phrases

A gerund is a verb form that ends in *-ing* and functions as a noun.

A gerund can be used in a sentence in almost every way that a noun can be used.

Subject	*Jogging* is not recommended for everyone.
Direct Object	Never cease *dreaming*.

Object of a Preposition	If you swim too soon after *eating*, you may get a muscle cramp.
Predicate Nominative	My favorite Olympic event is *kayaking*.
Appositive	Her hobby, *skydiving*, sounds risky.

A gerund phrase consists of a gerund and its modifiers and complements.

Like verbs, gerunds are modified by adverbs and adverb phrases.

Running away from a problem won't solve it. (The adverb *away* and the adverb phrase *from a problem* modify the gerund *running*.)

Unlike a verb, however, a gerund may also be modified by an adjective.

Proper lighting on stage is a necessity. (The adjective *proper* and the adverb phrase *on stage* modify *lighting*.)

Since it is a verb form, a gerund may have complements.

Telling <u>me</u> that <u>story</u> has certainly changed my outlook. (*Me* is the indirect object of the gerund *telling*; *story* is the direct object.)
Being a <u>dancer</u> requires great discipline. (*Dancer* is the predicate nominative after the gerund *being*.)

Like gerunds, gerund phrases function as nouns.

Subject	*Playing tennis on a tour* is not always fun.
Direct Object	The photographer tried *adjusting the shutter*.
Predicate Nominative	Their biggest mistake was *giving my brother a trombone*.
Object of a Preposition	Read everything carefully before *signing a contract*.
Appositive	On vacation we had one unforgettable experience, *fishing for tarpon*.

Sentence Diagraming For information on diagraming gerunds and gerund phrases, see pages 355–356.

Exercises

A Write the gerunds and gerund phrases in the sentences below.

1. We added to the resale value of the bike by painting it.

2. Counterfeiting is illegal.
3. For surfing, Hawaiian beaches are best.
4. Sleeping late in the morning is a great luxury.
5. Douse the fire thoroughly before leaving the campsite.
6. Watching the clock is a poor work habit.
7. Silas Marner was known for hoarding his money.
8. Concentration is important in playing chess.
9. Rattling the presents is half the fun of Christmas Eve.
10. At the dairy, some of us tried milking a cow by hand.
11. Our neighbor's hobby is raising tropical fish.
12. Her ambition, performing in a ballet, was never realized.
13. Glazing makes pottery waterproof.
14. Steel gets its strength from the process of tempering.
15. A method for turning metals into gold was sought by alchemists.

B Write the gerunds and gerund phrases in the following sentences. Tell whether each is a *Subject*, *Direct Object*, *Predicate Nominative*, *Object of a Preposition*, or *Appositive*. If there is no gerund or gerund phrase, write *None*.

(1) Batik, using wax to dye fabric in intricate patterns, is a process that originated in Java. (2) Planning the design is very important since some areas of the fabric will be colored, and some areas will remain plain. (3) Liquid wax, paraffin, or rice paste forms a coating that is painted onto the areas that are not to be dyed. (4) When the fabric is dipped into the dye, the covered areas resist the pigment. (5) After the

cloth is dry, the wax can be removed by boiling. (6) With no coating, the design stands out against the colored background.

(7) Two difficult tasks are achieving multiple shades of the same color and introducing a second color. (8) Two shades of one color can be made by protecting the parts that are not to be dyed darker. (9) The fabric is then dipped into the dye again. (10) Repeating the same process with a different dye, allows a new color to be added.

Checkpoint *Parts 1, 2, and 3*

A On your paper, write the phrases in the following sentences. Tell whether each phrase is a *Prepositional Phrase,* an *Appositive Phrase,* an *Infinitive Phrase,* a *Participial Phrase,* or a *Gerund Phrase.* Keep in mind that a prepositional phrase may be part of a verbal phrase.

1. Sitting on the roof, we watched the fireworks over Shea Stadium.
2. Crippled and already beaten, the Spanish Armada sailed north to its final battle.
3. The skillful gemcutter looked for a place to make the first cut in the diamond.
4. We hoped to see many of our former neighbors at the reunion.
5. Helen Hunt Jackson, a schoolmate and lifelong friend, was Emily Dickinson's literary champion.
6. Finding new sources of water is essential for our cities.
7. Marcia's hobby is carving chess pieces from blocks of wood.
8. To give their children a good education is the dream of parents around the world.
9. Some people enjoy going for a brisk hike before breakfast.
10. Sturdy and maneuverable vessels, Columbus's ships marked a major advance in the seafaring technology of the time.

B Write the verbals in the following sentences. Identify each as a *Gerund,* an *Infinitive,* or a *Participle.* Tell whether each gerund is acting as a *Subject, Direct Object,* or *Object of a Preposition.* Tell whether each infinitive is acting as a *Noun, Adjective,* or *Adverb.* Also tell which word each participle is modifying.

1. Cultivated for centuries, the aromatic vanilla plant has a long and fascinating history.
2. To the ancient Aztecs vanilla was a highly cherished gift from the gods.

3. Considered very precious, vanilla was once reserved for European royalty.
4. Classified as part of the orchid family, the vanilla plant must be pollinated by hand.
5. A plant needs four years to mature before producing beans.
6. Then the skilled workers pollinating the plants don't dare waste any time.
7. Having matured, the plants flower only one day a year.
8. Fertilizing the plants needs to occur between nine and ten in the morning when the blossoms are completely open; only then will the fertilized flower develop.
9. Treated like customers in an expensive spa, the beans then get a sunning treatment by day and a sweating session at night.
10. Once it undergoes the processes of drying and sorting, the valuable product goes to market branded with the owner's special mark to protect it from vanilla rustlers.
11. Buyers must also beware of counterfeiters who sprinkle white powder on inferior beans to make them resemble the frosted crystals on the outside of superior beans.
12. Could you dare call vanilla plain again?

C Application in Literature Write the phrases in the following passage. Tell if each phrase is *Prepositional*, *Participial*, *Gerund*, or *Infinitive*. Notice how the writer uses a variety of phrase constructions to create an interesting and vivid passage.

(1) Why he couldn't possibly recognize her. . . . (2) John would be looking for a young woman with a peaked Spanish comb in her hair and the painted fan. (3) Digging post holes changed a woman. (4) Riding country roads in the winter . . . was another thing: sitting up nights with sick horses and sick children . . . [but] it was time to go in and light the lamps. . . . (5) Lighting the lamps had been beautiful. (6) The children huddled up to her and breathed like little calves waiting at the bar in the twilight. (7) Their eyes followed the match and watched the flame rise and settle in a blue curve, then they moved away from her. (8) The lamp was lit. (9) They didn't have to be scared . . . any more. Never, never, never more.

From *The Jilting of Granny Weatherall*
by Katherine Anne Porter

Part 4
Clauses

A clause is a group of words that contains a subject and a verb.

There are two kinds of clauses: **independent** and **subordinate**.

Independent Clauses

A clause that can stand alone as a sentence is an independent, or main, clause.

The sentence below contains two independent clauses.

> <u>Beethoven</u> gradually <u>became</u> deaf; nevertheless, <u>he</u> <u>continued</u> to write great music.

In the example above, the subject of each independent clause has been underlined once, and the verb has been underlined twice. Each clause can stand alone as a sentence.

> Beethoven gradually became deaf. He continued to write great music.

Subordinate Clauses

A clause that cannot stand alone as a sentence is a subordinate, or dependent, clause.

Both of the clauses that are shown below have a subject and a verb. However, they are not sentences because they do not express complete thoughts.

> If <u>you</u> <u>like</u> houses with a history. (Then what happens?)
> Where <u>George</u> <u>Washington</u> <u>stayed</u> after the surrender at Yorktown.
> (What about where he stayed?)

To form a sentence, you must combine the subordinate clause with an independent clause.

> ┌── subordinate clause ──┐   ┌──────────── independent
> If you like houses with a history, you will enjoy a trip through the
> clause ──┐
> Hudson Valley.

> ┌ independent clause ┐   ┌──────────────── subordinate
> We visited the house where George Washington stayed after the
>   clause ──────┐
> surrender at Yorktown.

Do not confuse a subordinate clause with a verbal phrase. A verbal phrase does not have a subject and a verb.

Subordinate Clause	Unknowingly, ancient Egyptians used treatments *that contained penicillin.* (The subject is *that* and the verb is *contained.*)
Verbal Phrases	Unknowingly, ancient Egyptians used treatments *containing penicillin.* (The participial phrase does not have a subject and a verb.)
	The treatments were used *to cure skin ailments.* (The infinitive phrase does not have a subject and a verb.)

The subject of a subordinate clause may be a relative pronoun such as *who, whom, whose, that,* or *which.* In the first example above, *that* is a relative pronoun.

Exercises

A On your paper, write the italicized group of words in each of the following sentences. Identify each group as a *Phrase* or a *Clause.* When you identify a clause, tell whether it is an *Independent Clause* or a *Subordinate Clause.*

1. Washoe, the ape, uses sign language *to ask for things.*
2. To photograph the ocean bottom, *the divers descended in a metal sphere.*

3. Scientists are now more hopeful of *finding a cure for muscular dystrophy*.
4. *When it clawed at the door*, the dog finally attracted its owner's attention.
5. *It is hard to believe* that they are moving to Alaska.
6. Tires must be inflated properly, or *they will not wear well*.
7. That player is a rookie *whose future looks very bright*.
8. The whale swam around the wrecked boat, *churning the water in its vengeful wake*.
9. Remember to turn off your stereo *before you fall asleep*.
10. Whenever there is a heavy snowfall in the city, *ground transportation comes to a halt*.
11. Set up the easel *wherever the light is best*.
12. Why is caviar, *which is just fish eggs*, so expensive?
13. *Found throughout Australia*, dingos are wild dogs.
14. *Interpret his comment* however you like.
15. Designed as a universal language, *Esperanto is spoken by few people*.

B Write the following sentences on your paper. Underline each independent clause once and each subordinate clause twice. Note that a sentence may contain two independent clauses or an independent clause and a subordinate clause.

1. Jane Addams was a social reformer who had led an aimless existence for several years.
2. Until she visited a settlement house in London, she did not find her vocation.
3. A settlement house is an institution that provides needed community services.
4. Miss Addams came to Chicago where she helped establish Hull House.
5. The story of Hull House, which is a long one, illustrates Ms. Addams's perseverance.
6. She was active in labor and social reform, but she remained the chief fund-raiser for Hull House.
7. Jane Addams soon became a public figure, and her early interest in woman's suffrage was revived.
8. When Theodore Roosevelt asked for help, she campaigned vigorously for the Progressive Party.
9. After Hull House moved its headquarters in 1963, most of the settlement buildings were demolished.
10. The house itself still stands, and it serves as a memorial to Jane Addams.

Part 5
Kinds of Subordinate Clauses

There are three kinds of subordinate clauses: **adjective clauses, adverb clauses,** and **noun clauses.**

Adjective Clauses

The single-word adjective, the adjective phrase, and the adjective clause are used in the same way. They modify a noun or a pronoun.

An adjective clause is a subordinate clause that is used as an adjective to modify a noun or a pronoun.

Like adjectives, adjective clauses tell *what kind* or *which one.* An adjective clause is usually placed immediately after the word the clause modifies.

The stamps *that commemorate American locomotives* feature four different models. (*what kind* of stamps?)

That is the wealthy collector *who bought the rare stamp.* (*which* collector?)

Words Used to Introduce Adjective Clauses Most adjective clauses begin with a relative pronoun: *who, whom, whose, that, which.* A **relative pronoun** relates the clause to the word it modifies. The modified word is the antecedent of the relative pronoun.

Isaac Newton, the English scientist, was born the same year *that Galileo, the famous Italian astronomer and physicist, died.* (*Year* is the antecedent of the relative pronoun *that* and is modified by the entire adjective clause.)

Sometimes the relative pronoun functions in the adjective clause as a subject, a direct object, an object of a preposition, or a modifier.

Subject	Westwater Canyon cuts through rock *that* is almost two billion years old. (The relative pronoun *that* is the subject of the verb *is* in the adjective clause.)
Direct Object	The artist *whom* I admire most is Mary Cassatt. (The relative pronoun *whom* is the direct object of the verb *admire* in the adjective clause.)

Object of a Preposition	The tourists to *whom* we spoke are from Germany. (The relative pronoun *whom* is the object of the preposition *to* in the adjective clause.)
Modifier	He is the friend *whose* father is an engineer. (The relative pronoun *whose* modifies *father*, the subject of the adjective clause.)

An adjective clause introduced by a relative pronoun is sometimes called a **relative clause.**

Usage Note As you use adjective clauses in description and other writing, be aware that the case of the pronoun, *who* or *whom,* is determined by the use of the pronoun in the adjective clause. *Who* can be used as a subject or predicate nominative within a clause. *Whom* can function as a direct object, indirect object, or object of a preposition.

The **relative adverbs** *after, before, since, when, where,* and *why* may also introduce adjective clauses. Like relative pronouns, relative adverbs relate the clause to the word it modifies. Unlike a relative pronoun, however, a relative adverb modifies the verb in the adjective clause.

> In Minnesota we visited a workshop *where birch bark canoes are made by hand.* (The adjective clause modifies the noun *workshop.* The relative adverb *where* modifies the verb *are made* in the adjective clause.)

Sometimes the introductory word in an adjective clause is omitted.

> The trail *the guide indicated* led to a mill. (The relative pronoun *that* is omitted: *that* the guide indicated.)

Essential and Nonessential Adjective Clauses An adjective clause may be essential or nonessential. An **essential adjective clause** is one that is needed to make the intended meaning of a sentence complete.

> We asked for a houseplant *that is not overly fond of direct sunlight.* (The clause is needed to complete the meaning of the sentence.)

A **nonessential adjective clause** is one that adds additional information to a sentence in which the meaning is already complete.

> The wax begonia, *which can be red, white, or pink,* blooms all year long. (The clause adds an idea to the sentence.)

That is always used to introduce essential clauses. In formal writing, *which* introduces nonessential clauses. *Who* may be used to introduce essential or nonessential clauses when the antecedent is a person. *Which* is never used to refer to people.

Punctuation Note As shown in the examples on the previous page, commas are used to set off a nonessential clause from the rest of the sentence. Commas are not used with essential clauses.

Sentence Diagraming For information about diagraming adjective clauses, see page 358.

Exercises

A On your paper, write the adjective clauses in the following sentences and the word each modifies. Then underline the relative pronoun or the relative adverb that introduces the clause. In two sentences the introductory word has been omitted.

1. The North and South poles belong to no time zone; therefore technically, there are places where time stands still.
2. Senator Bradley is the official to whom we wrote.
3. Early summer is the time of year when tornadoes most often strike.
4. The energy we are using came originally from the sun.
5. What is the most embarrassing thing that ever happened to you?
6. Easter Island, which is located off the coast of Chile, is noted for its colossal pre-Columbian statues.
7. Windsurfing requires participants who are agile.
8. Where are the peppers you sautéed for the pizza?
9. Julius Caesar was a Roman general whose success in the Gallic Wars earned him a loyal following.
10. The letter to which you refer must have been misfiled.

B Combine each of the following sentence pairs into a sentence with an adjective clause. Remember to punctuate the clauses correctly.

> *Example*   I read an article about Mount Olympus. Zeus was believed to have held court there.
> I read an article about Mount Olympus, where Zeus was believed to have held court.

1. The National Weather Service is part of the Department of Commerce. The service was established by Congress in 1871.
2. The representative was helpful. We spoke to her on the phone.

3. Elinor Wylie was known for the visual imagery of her poetry. Her published works include *Nets to Catch the Wind*.
4. Scientists have invented a light. It does not produce heat.
5. The man hosts a popular game show. We saw him in a restaurant.
6. Springs are fed by rain. The rain seeps through the soil.
7. E.H. Shepard is an artist. He did the illustrations for the Winnie the Pooh books.
8. I have seen the house. Betsy Ross lived in the house.
9. The mynah bird sings in two languages. My aunt bought the bird.
10. Verona is a town in northern Italy. It is the setting for Shakespeare's *Romeo and Juliet*.

c *Proofreading* Revise the following paragraph by using adjective clauses to combine some thoughts. Be alert for errors in existing adjective clauses as well as other errors in usage or mechanics.

The Incas were a South American indian people. These people ruled one of the largest and richest empires in the americas. Because the Incas did not develop a writing system before the Spanish conquest of thier civilization, archaeological remains provide the major source of information about them.

Historians know a number of interesting facts about the incas. The Incas had special officials to who was given the duty of record keeping. The officials used a *quipe*. The *quipe* was a cord. The cord was tyed with knotted strings of various lengths and colors. There were also surgeons. These surgeons performed an operation which involved cutting away part of the skull. They held the belief that this would relieve pressure on the brain and let out evil spirits.

Adverb Clauses

An adverb clause is a subordinate clause that is used as an adverb to modify a verb, an adjective, or an adverb.

Modifying a Verb	The sheriff posted the notice *where everyone could see it.*
Modifying an Adjective	In cooking class we learned that dough is proofed *when it has risen.*
Modifying an Adverb	The cave was darker *than you can imagine.*

Like adverbs, adverb clauses tell *where, when, why, how,* or *to what extent* about words they modify. Adverb clauses can also explain *under what circumstances* and *why.*

If demand exceeds supply, prices will go up. (Go up *under what circumstances?*)

He lost the debate *because he was not prepared.* (Lost *why?*)

Like verbs, verbals also may be modified by an adverb clause.

Modifying an Infinitive	Erin wants to visit Ireland *so that she can kiss the Blarney Stone.* (Why?)
Modifying a Participle	Waiting *until the nurse slept,* Juliet drank the potion. (Under what circumstances?)
Modifying a Gerund	Guessing *if you don't know the answer* may help. (Under what circumstances?)

Words Used to Introduce Adverb Clauses   Most adverb clauses begin with subordinating conjunctions. A **subordinating conjunction** relates the clause to the word it modifies. Subordinating conjunctions can be used to show a variety of relationships between ideas.

Time	after, as, as soon as, before, since, until, when, whenever, while
Cause	because, since
Comparison	as, as much as, than
Condition	although, as long as, even though, provided that, unless
Purpose	in order that, so that
Manner	as, as if, as though
Place	where, wherever

Elliptical Clauses *Elliptical* comes from *ellipsis,* which means "omission of a word or words." An **elliptical clause** is an adverb clause from which a word or words have been omitted.

> *When applying for a job,* you should dress appropriately. (The words *you are* have been omitted: when *you are* applying.)
> You seem happier with the results *than I.* (The word *do* has been omitted: than I *do.*)

Punctuation Note An adverb clause at the beginning of a sentence is followed by a comma.

Sentence Diagraming For information on diagraming adverb clauses, see page 358.

Exercises

A On your paper, write the adverb clauses in the following sentences. Underline the subordinating conjunction. After each clause write the word or words that it modifies.

> *Example*   Whenever drought is a problem, people hope for rain.
>   <u>Whenever</u> drought is a problem, hope

1. Even though it seems difficult, if not impossible, humans have long tried to make rain.
2. When an ancient rainmaker cast a spell, people could not always count on rain.
3. More recent "pluviologists" have proved no better at the task than the ancient rainmakers were.
4. One rainmaker was almost lynched because he "caused" a twenty-inch rain and washed out a dam.
5. Until Vincent Schaefer had a happy accident, rainmaking remained a hoax.
6. Seeding clouds so that drops of water would form had been tried by many different scientists.
7. Would seeding work if the temperature of the clouds was below freezing?
8. After Schaefer tried out this idea in a series of almost comical experiments with his home freezer, he succeeded.
9. One day, as he was putting a block of dry ice into the freezer, Schaefer exhaled.
10. Soon his improvised laboratory looked as if a miniature snowstorm were in progress.

B Compose sentences that use the following adverb clauses. Underline the word or words each clause modifies.

1. Because nonpoisonous snakes destroy rodents
2. Because the judge entered the court
3. Until there was no sound or movement
4. When the Liberty Bell cracked
5. Since it is difficult to recognize harmful wild mushrooms
6. Provided that your registration fee is paid
7. If you have the sales receipt
8. Although the car needed repair
9. Unless more funds are raised
10. Where the soil is sandy
11. So that we can finish the experiment
12. While I am running errands

C *Write Now* Good horror films always seem to have dramatic special effects. For example, think of Dr. Frankenstein's lab. Whenever lightning strikes, electric arcs bounce around his mysterious machines. Describe a scene from one of your favorite horror films or devise a scene of your own. Use a variety of adverb clauses to add drama to your description.

Noun Clauses

A noun clause is a subordinate clause that is used in a sentence as a noun.

A noun clause may be used in any way that a noun is used. Consequently, noun clauses most frequently function as subjects, direct objects, indirect objects, predicate nominatives, objects of prepositions, and appositives.

Subject	*Where the hostages are* remains a mystery to the police.
Direct Object	Hoyle believed *that his theory would revolutionize the study of the universe.*
Indirect Object	Give *whoever comes in last* a consolation prize.
Predicate Nominative	My question is *how do I load this computer program.*
Object of a Preposition	We have to limit expenses to *whatever funds are available.*
Appositive	My parents vetoed the idea *that we buy a sports car instead of a wagon.*

A noun clause may function as the direct object of a verbal.

> Alice tried to decide *if she had been dreaming*. (The noun clause is the direct object of the infinitive *to decide*.)
> Henry VIII had no trouble deciding *whether he should remarry*. (The noun clause is the direct object of the gerund *deciding*.)

Words Used to Introduce Noun Clauses Noun clauses are introduced by pronouns and by subordinating conjunctions.

Pronouns   who, whom, which, what, that, whoever, whomever, whatever

A pronoun that introduces a noun clause may also function as a subject or an object within the clause.

> The American Red Cross provides shelter and emergency relief aid for *whoever needs it*. (*Whoever* is the subject of the verb *needs* in the noun clause.)

Subordinating Conjunctions   how, that, when, where, whether, why (For a complete list of subordinating conjunctions, see page 38.)

Notice that some of the same words that introduce noun clauses can also introduce adjective and adverb clauses. To determine if a clause is functioning as a noun, decide if the clause is doing the job of a noun in the sentence. In the first example below, the clause is a noun clause because it is functioning as a direct object. The clauses in the second and third examples are modifying other words; therefore, they are not functioning as noun clauses.

> The orchestra conductor announced *when the concert would begin*. (Announced *what*? The noun clause is the direct object of the verb *announced*.)
> This is the time of year *when the Canada geese fly over*. (*Which* time? The adjective clause modifies the noun *time*.)
> The engine knocks *when you use low octane gas*. (Knocks *when*? The adverb clause modifies the verb *knocks*.)

Sometimes the introductory word is omitted from a noun clause.

> The report said *unemployment was at an all-time low*. (The report said *that* unemployment was at an all-time low.)

Sentence Diagraming For information on diagraming noun clauses, see pages 358–359.

Exercises

A Identify each noun clause. Tell whether it is used as a *Subject, Object of a Verb, Object of a Preposition, Predicate Nominative,* or *Appositive.*

1. The suspect would not tell us where she had been.
2. What the reporter really wanted remained a mystery to us.
3. Fred was apologetic about what he had said.
4. The doctor said that Marion could get up tomorrow.
5. Do you know who invented the microscope?
6. We had no idea of what might happen.
7. The police know who wrote the threatening letters.
8. Who will win the playoffs is anyone's guess.
9. Everyone wondered when the fog would lift.
10. The date of the surprise birthday party was what they did not write on the invitation.
11. What happened to the missing paintings was never discovered by the police or the FBI.
12. The neighborhood council will be grateful for whatever you do.
13. Who had the brilliant idea that we should clean out the attic during spring vacation?
14. We did not know Harold had such amazing powers of concentration.
15. Is your new job what you expected?

B On your paper, write the noun clauses in the following quotations. Tell how each clause functions in the sentence by writing *Subject, Object of a Verb, Object of a Preposition, Predicate Nominative,* or *Appositive.*

1. Genius does what it must, and talent does what it can. Owen Meredith
2. I regret that I have but one life to give for my country. Nathan Hale
3. Don't invent with your mouth what you don't see with a smile.
   Mother Teresa
4. Whoever gossips to you will gossip about you. Spanish proverb
5. The best way to be thankful is to make use of what the gods have given you. Anthony Trollope
6. What is wanted is not more law, but a better public opinion.
   James G. Blaine
7. A Bill of Rights is what the people are entitled to. Thomas Jefferson
8. Paradise is where I am. Voltaire
9. Remember that time is money. Benjamin Franklin
10. Whoever does not rise early will never do any good. Samuel Johnson

C Write sentences using the following noun clauses as indicated in parentheses.

1. what the excited witness was saying (direct object)
2. who the murderer was (subject)
3. when the treasure is buried (predicate noun)
4. whichever skater wins (object of preposition)
5. that all men are created equal (appositive)

D *Write Now* A good mystery or adventure novel can keep a reader intrigued for hours. Recount the plot of your favorite mystery or adventure story, using a variety of noun clauses.

Checkpoint Parts 4 and 5

A On your paper, write the italicized groups of words in the following sentences. Tell whether each group of words is a *Phrase* or a *Clause*. When you identify a clause, tell whether it is an *Independent Clause* or a *Subordinate Clause*.

1. *When I was last in New Orleans,* it was during Mardi Gras.
2. *After winning the Olympic gold medal,* the U.S. hockey team received congratulations from the President.
3. Poison ivy is a dangerous plant, but *it can be easily identified.*
4. *While Gina worked diligently on the crossword puzzle,* Renetta read the sports section.

5. *Charging out of the woods,* a six-pronged deer appeared on the path ahead of us.
6. Islam, *the official religion of many Arabic countries,* was founded in the seventh century A.D.
7. If the litmus paper turns blue, *the substance is basic.*
8. The professor, *who teaches at Rutgers University,* spoke to us about careers in the media.
9. *Caught in the monstrous traffic jam,* some drivers got out of their cars and began to chat.
10. Some caterpillars live in tentlike webs *that they spin among tree branches.*

B On your paper, write the subordinate clauses in the following sentences. Tell whether each is an *Adjective, Adverb,* or *Noun Clause.* For each adjective or adverb clause, tell the word it modifies. Tell whether each noun clause is used as a *Subject, Object of a Verb, Object of a Preposition, Predicate Nominative,* or *Appositive.*

1. Chief Inspector Holmes looked thoughtful as he inspected the contents of the safe.
2. Warm Springs, Georgia, is where President Franklin Roosevelt spent the last days of his life.
3. Many visitors go each year to Stratford, the town where William Shakespeare was born.
4. Paul Zindel's novel *Pigman* is as serious as it is funny.
5. Chaing did better on the history exam than she had expected.
6. Henry Ford, who was a pioneer in the automobile industry, called his first car the "quadricycle."
7. The stray cat that wandered into our yard has adopted us.
8. After *Brighton Beach Memoirs* became a hit on Broadway, it was made into a motion picture.
9. If the coach agrees, we will wear our jerseys for the homecoming game.
10. Queen Victoria ruled in an age when England was the head of a great colonial empire.
11. Although his native tongue was Polish, Joseph Conrad became a famous English novelist.
12. The shop teacher showed the class how an adz is used.
13. Most reputable scientists scorn the belief that earth has been visited by UFO's.
14. That Duke Ellington was a great musician is unquestionable.
15. Dr. Robert Goddard, whose inventions launched the Space Age, built the first liquid-fueled rocket in 1926.

Part 6
The Structure of the Sentence

You have learned that sentences may be classified according to their purpose: declarative, interrogative, imperative, and exclamatory. Sentences may also be classified according to their structure—the number and kinds of clauses they contain. The four kinds of structural classifications are (1) simple sentences, (2) compound sentences, (3) complex sentences, and (4) compound-complex sentences.

Simple Sentences

A simple sentence is a sentence that contains one independent clause and no subordinate clauses.

> The candidate is confident.

A simple sentence may have any number of phrases.

> The candidate, Mrs. Schulman from Queens, is confident about the outcome of the mayoral race.

The parts of a simple sentence may be compound.

Compound Subject	Both the *Montagues* and the *Capulets* contributed to the feud.
Compound Verb	Someone *had split* the logs and *stacked* the wood in the shed.
Compound Complement	Mark Twain was both a *writer* and an *inventor*.

More than one part of a simple sentence may be compound.

> The firefighters and several police officers rushed into the building and warned the tenants of the bomb threat. (simple sentence with a compound subject and a compound verb)

Compound Sentences

A compound sentence is a sentence that has two or more independent clauses that are joined together.

The clauses in a compound sentence may be joined with a comma and a coordinating conjunction: *and, but, nor, or, for, yet.*

> Everyone stopped work, **and** the factory became silent.

The independent clauses may be joined with a semicolon.

There is no joy in Mudville; Mighty Casey has struck out.

In some compound sentences the clauses may be joined by a semi-colon and a conjunctive adverb. (For a list of conjunctive adverbs see page 38.)

Our library may be small; **however,** it has an extensive collection of reference books.

Punctuation Note As shown above, a conjunctive adverb is usu-ally preceded by a semicolon and followed by a comma.

Sentence Diagraming For information on diagraming simple and compound sentences, see pages 350–359.

Exercises

A On your paper, write the following sentences. Underline the subject of each independent clause once and the verb twice. Label each sen-tence *Simple* or *Compound*. Keep in mind that a simple sentence may have one or more compound parts.

1. The governor will address the committee and endorse the bill.
2. The house itself is small, but the grounds are spacious.
3. In Norway, people drive or ski from one village to another.
4. Both strawberries and asparagus are in season.
5. The fans were ecstatic; their team had made it to the semifinals.
6. Hamilton and Washington wrote Washington's Farewell Address.
7. Plastics are nonconductors; therefore, they make ideal electrical parts.
8. The climbers reached the summit and spent the afternoon there.
9. Beavers help conserve soil; thus, they should be protected.
10. Gnats and mosquitoes are most numerous in early June and July.

B On your paper, rewrite the following sentences changing them to the structure indicated in parentheses.

> *Example*　　Isaac Stern played at the benefit. Loretta
> 　　　　　　　Lynn played there too. (simple sentence
> 　　　　　　　with compound subject)
> 　　　　　　Isaac Stern and Loretta Lynn played at
> 　　　　　　　the benefit.

1. Two deer bolted across the road. They disappeared into a grove of birch trees. (simple sentence with compound predicate)

2. Birds are born blind. They can recognize their mothers by using their other senses. (compound sentence with conjunctive adverb)
3. For years the Great Lakes were very polluted. The situation is improving. (compound sentence with coordinating conjunction)
4. Da Vinci painted only a few pictures. They are all masterpieces. (compound sentence with coordinating conjunction)
5. The drought forced the price of citrus up. The early frost also forced the price of citrus up. (simple sentence with compound subject)

Complex Sentences

The complex sentence consists of one main clause and one or more subordinate clauses.

In a complex sentence, the subordinate clause is used as a noun or as a modifier. If it is used as a modifier, the subordinate clause usually modifies a word in the main clause.

> *When you leave,* shut the door. (Clause modifies *shut.*)
> *If he quits that job,* he will regret it later on. (Clause modifies *will regret.*)

In each preceding example, the main clause can stand as a sentence by itself: *Shut the door. He will regret it later on.*

The subordinate clauses, however, cannot stand alone because their meaning is incomplete.

> When you leave . . . (What then?)
> If he quits that job . . . (What will happen?)

The complex structure of the Georges Pompidou Center, Paris, France.

105

Complex sentences containing noun clauses are somewhat different from those with adjective or adverb clauses. The noun clause is used as a noun within the main clause. The noun clause, in other words, is part of the main clause.

> *What we saw* is impossible! (Noun clause is subject of *is*.)
> Kira is sorry about *what she said*. (Noun clause is object of preposition *about*.)

Usually, as in the examples above, neither the main clause nor the noun clause can stand by itself. Nonetheless, a sentence containing one main clause and noun clause is regarded as a complex sentence.

Sentence Diagraming For information on diagraming complex sentences, see page 359.

Exercises

A On your paper, write the following complex sentences. Underline each independent clause once and each subordinate clause twice.

1. Simmer the pudding until it thickens.
2. Is that the house Frank Lloyd Wright built for himself?
3. Our school, which has only 227 students, ordered more than 2,000 paperbacks last year.
4. Over two centuries have passed since the Constitution was signed.
5. In 1494 Spain and Portugal signed the Treaty of Tordesillas, which divided the New World between them.
6. Some scholars believe that writing began as a form of word magic.
7. If you finish your paper by Thursday, we can go to the movies.
8. I can't decide whether Charlie Chaplin or Groucho Marx is my favorite movie comedian.
9. What is science fiction today, may become real-life science tomorrow.
10. The city that had the first zoo in America was Philadelphia.

B On your paper, write the following sentences. Label each sentence *Simple, Compound,* or *Complex.* Underline the subordinate clauses in the complex sentences.

1. Anyone who has come under the spell of a great piece of music may have wondered what inspired the composer.
2. Many contemporary composers deny working from inspiration.
3. According to one, he composes because he can't help it!
4. As a rule, creative artists do not sit around waiting for inspiration.

5. They turn to their creative tasks, and they do their best.
6. Many composers, however, seem to write music as though they had the gift of automatic writing.
7. Mozart and Schubert, two of the most spontaneous composers, seemed to write music with little or no conscious effort.
8. Others started with an idea; they then labored long and carefully over their work.
9. Beethoven was busy with his *C Minor Symphony* for over five years, and it took Brahms over twenty-five years to write his great symphony.
10. It is a fact that each composer works in his or her own way.

Compound-Complex Sentences

A compound-complex sentence is a sentence that has two or more independent clauses and one or more subordinate clauses.

In the following examples, the independent clauses are underlined once, the subordinate clauses twice.

> The bicycle, which I repaired myself, had better work, for I certainly cannot afford a new one. (The subordinate clause interrupts the first independent clause.)

> When the ice melted, heavy rains began, and the streets flooded.

Sentence Diagraming For information on diagraming compound-complex sentences, see page 360.

Exercises

A Write the following compound-complex sentences. Underline each independent clause once and each subordinate clause twice.

1. Divers sometimes explore the sunken ships under Lake Superior, but they must be careful, because these wrecks can be dangerous.
2. The clown looked everywhere for his trumpet; since it was in his back pocket, he couldn't find it.
3. After the beaker was broken, spilled liquid extinguished the flame, and the Bunsen burner wouldn't work.
4. Richard Burbage, who was the son of an actor, played the first Hamlet; moreover, he was a shareholder in Shakespeare's theater.
5. While the captain and the first mate were below, a violent storm arose, and the whalespotter noticed a waterspout in the distance.
6. There are very few tickets left, but you can see the concert provided that you don't mind sitting in the second balcony.

7. Gauguin painted palm trees of orange and purple; nevertheless, many European critics agreed that his work showed genius.
8. We enjoyed the jousting at the Renaissance Fair; however, the madrigal singers, who were among the best we've ever seen, put on an even better show.
9. The White Rabbit, who wore a waistcoat and a pocket watch, scurried by, and Alice gasped in amazement.
10. It was a still night, and we heard a loon that nested by the lake.

B Application in Literature Make four columns with the headings *Simple, Compound, Complex,* and *Compound-Complex*. Read the passage. List the numbers of the sentences that fit under each heading.

(1) One day after school, twenty-five years ago, several of us were playing with a football in the yard at Randy Shepperton's. (2) Randy was calling signals and handling the ball. (3) Nebraska Crane was kicking it. (4) Augustus Potterham was too clumsy to run or kick or pass, [and] so we put him at center, where all he'd have to do would be to pass the ball back to Randy when he got the signal.

(5) It was late in October and there was a smell of smoke, of leaves, of burning in the air. (6) Nebraska had just kicked to us. (7) It was a good kick too—a high, soaring punt that spiraled out above my head, behind me. (8) I ran back and tried to get it, but it was far and away "over the goal line." (9) It hit the street and bounded back and forth with that peculiarly erratic bounce a football has.

From *The Child Tiger* by Thomas Wolfe

Checkpoint Part 6

A On your paper, write the following sentences. Underline each independent clause once and each subordinate clause twice. Then identify each sentence according to its kind: *Simple, Compound, Complex,* or *Compound-Complex.*

1. The ski resorts upstate will lose money unless it snows soon.
2. Cockroaches feed on plant and animal remains, but they also come indoors in search of food or even wood.
3. Since the monkey house opened, attendance at the zoo has increased, and peanut sales have skyrocketed.
4. The saraband, a slow, graceful dance, originated in Spain.
5. Before he reached the age of twenty-five, John Updike had published many articles; moreover, he had also written a novel.

B On your paper, write the following sentences. Underline each independent clause once and each subordinate clause twice. Then identify each sentence according to its kind: *Simple, Compound, Complex,* or *Compound-Complex.*

1. Aquaculture is the finny future of high-tech fish farming.
2. An Aquacell at the University of Arizona provides an ideal environment for raising fish and other aquatic animals.
3. The fish are raised both as a subject for study and as a food source that is high in yield.
4. Because conditions must be carefully controlled, a computer checks oxygen levels and food consumption, and computer readings are taken each morning.
5. Scientists know more about warm-water species than they do about cold-water fish.
6. Eels are included in the study, but not as a food source.
7. Eels have a terrible feed conversion ratio; eight pounds of food produces only one pound of eel.
8. Catfish, which outstrip their closest rivals, are the number-one fish in U.S. aquaculture, and their popularity is growing.
9. Paddlefish, which produce fine meat and are an excellent source of eggs for caviar, are also under study.
10. The world has many mouths to feed; perhaps aquaculture holds the answer to the food shortage.

Linking
Grammar & Writing

Think of an activity that you do well. It could be anything from bicycle repairing to studying for a test. Then think of a simple process that you go through as part of this activity. For example, you might use a warm-up and stretching routine to get ready for football or ballet. You might also follow a series of specific steps when you practice guitar or piano or when you prepare dinner. Write one or two paragraphs that explain this process. In your explanation, use adverb, adjective, and noun clauses.

Prewriting and Drafting First visualize the process that you have chosen to explain. List all the steps involved. If possible, read your list to someone who is familiar with the process and ask for suggestions. Add any steps you may have forgotten. Then write your draft using your list as an aid. Include transition words such as *first, next,* and *after* to connect the steps. Remember that your reader will know only what you tell him or her. Make your explanation so clear and easy to follow that the reader could repeat the process.

Revision and Proofreading As you revise, consider the following questions:

1. Does the explanation that you have written include all the steps that are part of the process?
2. Are the steps in your process arranged in the order in which they will be performed?
3. Do the transition words connect the steps in a logical way?
4. Is each step clear and easy to understand?
5. Did you use adverb, adjective, and noun clauses where appropriate? Did you use them correctly?

Additional Writing Topic You have just thought of an invention that the whole world is waiting for. You want to sell your marvelous idea to a respected manufacturer so that production can begin on a large scale. Write a few paragraphs to the president of the company explaining why he or she should buy your invention. First try to write an interesting and persuasive letter using only simple sentences. Then expand your letter using complex, compound, and compound-complex sentences. Notice how variation in sentence structure creates a more interesting letter.

Navaho

T hough many Native American languages have been supplanted by English, the Navaho language continues to play an important role in the lives of the Navaho people. More than 100,000 people speak Navaho, principally on the sprawling Navaho Reservation covering fourteen million acres of Arizona, New Mexico, and Utah.

The Navaho language differs from English in many ways. It is a "tone" language, one in which the pitch used to pronounce a word helps determine its meaning. In addition, nouns are classified as either animate or inanimate, and words associated with active things have feminine gender while static things have masculine gender. Some verb forms change depending upon their direct object. For example, the verb form used to say *holding a ball* is different from the verb form used for *holding a stick*.

Instead of borrowing words from English, the Navaho adapt existing Navaho words and phrases to suit new needs. A car, for example, is a *chidi,* named after the noise a car makes when it starts. A car's headlights are "the eyes of the chidi," its wheels "the legs of the chidi," and its tires "the moccasins of the chidi."

Although many Native American languages are disappearing due to the dominance of English, the Navaho people are steadfastly holding on to their linguistic heritage.

Chapter 3
Application and Review

A Identifying Phrases On your paper, underline the phrases in the following sentences. Identify each phrase as *Prepositional, Participial, Gerund,* or *Infinitive.* Tell if each infinitive phrase is functioning as a *Noun, Adjective,* or *Adverb.* Tell if each prepositional phrase is functioning as an *Adjective* or *Adverb.*

1. *Moby Dick* is a book to be read slowly and carefully.
2. Mrs. Ling will be happy to show you her prize-winning orchids.
3. Ralph Waldo Emerson believed the only way to have a friend is to be one.
4. Hunted almost to extinction, the American buffalo is now protected in zoos and preserves.
5. Mr. Aldridge always wanted to see the spectacular geysers spouting in Yellowstone Park.
6. Climbing "El Capitán" will require training and perseverance.
7. Arachne was famous for weaving beautiful tapestries.
8. Hiking in the mountains helped William O. Douglas overcome a lung ailment.
9. Riding his bike, Alan can reach Jonesboro in two hours.
10. The ground, having become too dry, began to crack.
11. Finally the scuba diver emerged on the port side of the boat.
12. Having written several gothic novels, Mary Stewart is an author known to many.
13. Rosebushes of that kind need careful tending.
14. At the street fair, we enjoyed watching the mimes.
15. Shoppers laden with packages bustled here and there.

B Identifying Clauses Indicate whether each group of italicized words is an *Independent Clause* or a *Subordinate Clause.* For each subordinate clause, tell whether it is an *Adjective, Adverb,* or *Noun.*

1. *When you are shopping for winter clothes,* you should consider warmth as well as price and fit.
2. William Pitt was a statesman of great intellect, but *his physical health was poor.*
3. A history play on the career of Henry VIII was the last known work *that Shakespeare wrote.*
4. Our newspaper endorsed the candidate *who is the most qualified.*

5. *What career you pursue* will depend upon your interests.
6. *When the referee blows the whistle,* leap for the ball.
7. Although Francis Drake's treatment of Spanish ships sometimes amounted to piracy, *the Queen of England permitted and encouraged his activities.*
8. The family that you are born into and the people *that you meet* help shape your social behavior and attitudes.
9. Do you know *who wrote the biography of Carrie Chapman?*
10. While the band was playing, *several guards stood in front of the stage.*
11. Mark Twain said *that cauliflower is just a cabbage with a college education.*
12. A crampon is one of the tools *that a mountain climber uses.*
13. Ever since she read about Mark Twain's life, *she has wanted to ride on a riverboat.*
14. *Because some germs have become resistant to antibiotics,* it may be getting harder to fight disease.
15. *Can you tell* which mushroom is edible?

C Identifying Sentence Types
Identify each sentence as *Simple, Compound, Complex,* or *Compound-Complex.* In addition, find each subordinate clause and tell what kind it is—*Adjective, Adverb,* or *Noun.*

1. Blane demonstrated how she weaves cloth on a loom.
2. The owl screeched as it captured its prey.
3. Black and white photographs can be very dramatic.
4. Did a court jester juggle, or did he just tell jokes?
5. A pilot must consider temperature, wind, and visibility.
6. Darryl dropped the bag that contained the two dozen eggs, and then he slipped and dropped the bottle of milk.
7. Since she was very young, Bernice has collected hats.
8. Some shoppers hurried through the aisles, but others browsed.
9. While the band members marched, they formed designs on the field.
10. Bert fed the horse oats, and then he placed a blanket on its back while Laura untangled the bridle.
11. The popular play *Cats* was based on a series of poems that T.S. Eliot wrote about cats.
12. What annoys Mr. Berman most is tardiness.
13. The Chicago Fire of 1871 destroyed much of the city.
14. If the ice caps melted, much of the earth would be flooded, and the temperature would change throughout the world.
15. Joshua wants to visit Russia, but he speaks only English.

4
Writing Complete Sentences

*T*ry to imagine what this picture would look like if it were complete. Could you have guessed that the girl in pink was actually holding a catcher's mitt? Could you have known that the boy in the red shirt had a hulahoop around his waist?

Whenever you have to guess at what is missing, you run the risk of guessing wrong. That is why writers try to express their ideas as completely as possible, rather than in fragments. One way they do this is by writing in complete sentences.

In this chapter you will learn to write in complete sentences as well as to recognize and revise sentence fragments and run-on sentences. This will lessen the possibility that your meaning will be mistaken.

Part 1

Sentence Fragments

A sentence fragment is a group of words that is only part of a sentence.

As you learned in Chapters 2 and 3, a sentence must express a complete thought and must have at least one subject and one verb. Many sentence fragments lack either a subject or a verb.

Fragment   Will begin at 7:30 A.M. on Saturday. (What will begin? The subject is missing.)

Sentence   *The crew race* will begin at 7:30 A.M. on Saturday.

Fragment   Eight boats in the race around Manhattan. (What about the race? The verb is missing.)

Sentence   Eight boats *are competing* in the race around Manhattan.

Sometimes a fragment lacks both a subject and a verb.

Fragment   Under the Brooklyn Bridge. (Who or what is under the bridge? What is happening there?)

Sentence   *The boats will pass* under the Brooklyn Bridge.

As you will see in the discussion that follows, fragments often result from incomplete thoughts or incorrect punctuation.

Fragments Because of Incomplete Thought

You can think much faster than you can write. Many sentence fragments occur, therefore, because your mind has raced ahead of your hand. As a result you may find yourself writing a second thought before you have completed the first. In other cases you may discover that you have left out a key part of a sentence. Suppose, for example, that you wrote the following passage:

> In 1215 King John was presented with the Magna Carta. His nobles and churchmen forced him to sign the document. Establishing the principle that even the king must obey the law.

The third group of words in the paragraph above is not a sentence because it does not express a complete thought. The reader can only suppose that you meant to say that the Magna Carta established the principle described.

Exercises

A On your paper, write *S* for each group of words below that is a sentence. Write *F* for each sentence fragment. Then add words to change the fragments into sentences.

1. In a corner of the garage, the missing box of kitchen utensils.
2. Not a word appeared in the newspapers about the burglary.
3. Anyone who returns the valuable jewelry.
4. Huge trucks rolling along the nation's highways all night long.
5. Mr. Walters, one of the oldest residents of the nursing home.
6. Most of the classics are available in inexpensive editions.
7. Unfortunately a program just like several others.
8. Whenever she stays up too late.
9. A broad band of showers arriving from the southeast.
10. Several ambulances and police cars at the scene of the accident.

B Three of the groups of words in the following paragraph are sentences. The rest are fragments. On your paper, rewrite the paragraph, adding words to make the fragments into sentences.

(1) Ghost towns all across the country. (2) Pithole, Pennsylvania, one of the most famous. (3) It flourished for ten years. (4) For a time more than twenty thousand people in the town. (5) However, everyone left after the oil dried up. (6) Elsewhere, ghost towns in timber country. (7) Modern ghost towns in the iron mining regions of Minnesota. (8) The best-known in the mining sections of the West. (9) Houses full of furniture and offices with papers still in the desks. (10) Wherever the resources gave out, there are ghost towns.

Ghost town near Cody, Wyoming.

Fragments Because of Incorrect Punctuation

Sentences begin with a capital letter and end with a period, a question mark, or an exclamation point. Many fragments occur because the writer inserts end punctuation and a capital letter too soon.

Fragment   We will leave. *As soon as the dishes are done.*

Sentence   We will leave as soon as the dishes are done.

Fragment   *Before signing the bill.* The President congratulated the cosponsors.

Sentence   Before signing the bill, the President congratulated the cosponsors.

Exercises

A Each pair of word groups below contains one fragment and one sentence. Write each fragment on your paper. Then join each pair of word groups into one complete sentence by changing the punctuation and capitalization.

1. Once again the sirens wailed. Because of another accident.
2. Everyone liked my taco casserole. And the green bean salad.
3. The delegation arrived in Los Angeles. Just before midnight.
4. Mr. Wilkins Micawber was a character in *David Copperfield*. Who always felt that something would turn up.
5. Please send in your subscription. As soon as possible.
6. To improve her speaking skills. Linda joined the debate team.
7. Kim teaches yoga and aerobics three days a week. From 9 A.M. to 10:30 A.M.
8. The average American teen-ager watches television. More than twenty hours a week.
9. At the beginning of this century. Motoring was an adventure.
10. The team was still in the huddle. When time ran out.

B On your paper, write five complete sentences by combining a sentence in the left column with a fragment in the right column. Capitalize and punctuate your sentences correctly.

1. Did you finish your project?   A. Singing the theme from *Fame*
2. My cousin sold his bike.   B. At the band audition
3. The manager hired more ushers.   C. To work during the concert
4. Leo played effortlessly.   D. And bought a new tape recorder
5. Susan danced across the floor.   E. In time for the deadline

c *Proofreading* On your paper, rewrite the following paragraph, correcting the sentence fragments. Also correct any other errors in punctuation, spelling, and capitalization.

> The new Presidency. One of the last important issues at the Constitutional Convention. The resolution of this issue was largely due to the effort of james Wilson. An Immigrant from Scotland. James Madison had originally proposed that the President should be chosen by Congress. However, Wilson argued. That the President should draw his strength from a popular election. He would thus be accountabel directly to the people, further guaranteeing a genuine seperation of powers.

Part 2
Phrases and Clauses as Fragments

As you know, a **phrase** is a group of words that does not contain a subject and a verb. Therefore, a phrase cannot be a sentence; it can only be a fragment.

A common mistake occurs when a verbal phrase is mistaken for a complete sentence. This error occurs because verbals (gerunds, participles, infinitives) look like verbs and function somewhat like verbs. They are not verbs, however, and cannot be used as such.

The most troublesome verbals are those that end in *-ing*, such as *running* and *searching*. All gerunds and present participles end in *-ing*, and thus are often mistaken for verbs. You will avoid many sentence errors if you remember the following fact:

No word ending in *-ing* can be a complete verb unless it is a one-syllable word like *sing*, *ring*, or *bring*.

If an *-ing* word is preceded by *is, are, was,* or some other form of *be,* the words together are a verb: *is running, were searching.*

When you discover that a verbal phrase has been used as a fragment, you can correct it in one of two ways. Either add the verbal phrase to an already complete sentence or change the verbal into a verb and use it in a sentence.

The chart on the following page shows how different kinds of phrases, including verbals, can be rewritten as complete sentences.

Changing Fragments into Sentences

Participial Phrase	Covered with ice
Sentence	*Covered with ice*, the roads were impassable. (The phrase is added to a sentence.)
Sentence	The roads *were covered with ice*. (A subject is provided and an auxiliary verb is combined with the participle to make a verb phrase.)
Gerund Phrase	Canoeing across the lake
Sentence	I enjoy *canoeing across the lake*. (A subject and verb are added. The gerund becomes a direct object.)
Sentence	*Canoeing across the lake* is risky. (The gerund phrase becomes the subject of the sentence.)
Infinitive Phrase	To see the midnight sun
Sentence	Wendy and I have always wanted *to see the midnight sun*. (A subject and verb are added. The infinitive phrase becomes the direct object.)
Sentence	*To see the midnight sun* must be thrilling. (The infinitive phrase has become the subject.)
Sentence	It must be thrilling *to see the midnight sun*. (The infinitive phrase modifies *thrilling*.)
Prepositional Phrase	At the end of a long day
Sentence	Everyone enjoys relaxing *at the end of a long day*. (The phrase is added to a sentence.)
Sentence	*At the end of a long day*, Sheila takes a brisk walk. (The phrase is added to a sentence.)
Appositive Phrase	One a true story and the other fiction
Sentence	Both books, *one a true story and the other fiction*, were best sellers. (The phrase is added to a sentence.)

Series Fragments

Occasionally, items listed in a series may be so long or so compli-cated that they are mistaken for a sentence. This is especially true if the series is composed of verbal phrases. Series fragments may lack either a subject or a verb or both.

Series Fragment	Having hoped, having dreamed, and finally having won the trophy.
Sentence	*Having hoped, having dreamed, and finally having won,* Kimo clutched the trophy. (A subject and verb are added.)

Exercise

On your paper, correct each of the following sentence fragments by writing a complete sentence. Use one of the types of corrections shown in the chart on page 119.

1. The cymbidium, an Asian orchid of moderate size
2. A seventeenth-century scientist
3. Studying the ocean floor
4. About her bid for the Presidency
5. Soaking the rice paste, stirring the mixture, and finally making the rice paper
6. To become a skilled surgeon
7. Piled with books and papers
8. Starring my favorite singing group
9. Behind the hideous mask
10. Hippocrates, the Greek physician

Subordinate Clauses as Fragments

Unlike a phrase, a subordinate clause does have a subject and a verb. However, a subordinate clause does not express a complete thought and cannot be a sentence. Combine a subordinate clause with an independent clause to correct this kind of fragment.

Fragment   As soon as we saw the flames.
Sentence   *As soon as we saw the flames,* we dialed 911.

Another way to correct a fragment that is a subordinate clause is to rewrite the clause as a sentence.

Fragment   Trevor Library, which seemed like a stuffy old mausoleum.
Sentence   *Trevor Library seemed like a stuffy old mausoleum.*

Fragments in Conversation

Fragments often occur in conversation without harming communication. Tone of voice, gestures, and the presence of each speaker all help to add meaning and keep ideas clear.

Sentence   When is the canceled game going to be played?
Fragment   Probably Thursday.
Fragment   Morning or afternoon?
Fragment   After lunch, if it doesn't rain.

Professional writers sometimes use fragments when they want to create realistic dialogue, establish a certain mood, or achieve a particular rhythm in their prose. These professional writers know the rules of grammar but are consciously breaking these rules for a specific purpose.

Exercises

A On your paper, correct the fragments in each of the following groups of words.

1. To enhance the flavor of a dish, chefs often use the zest. Which is the outermost part of the rind of a lemon or an orange.
2. The tall figure of a man who appeared in the doorway.
3. Although James Michener's novel *Centennial* is unusually long. It is certainly worth reading.
4. The sky was blue and the sun shining. When we arrived at the lodge in Yellowstone Park.

5. To go on a photographic safari in Africa.
6. Just as he raised the camera. The animal disappeared.
7. India has over two hundred languages. And many religions.
8. Linda is studying forestry. Because she is concerned about the environment.
9. The rock collection that belongs to Dwayne's father.
10. The climbers carefully checked their pitons. Which are spikes used for climbing steep rock faces.

B Application in Literature Professional writers sometimes use fragments intentionally to establish a mood or to create realistic dialogue. List the fragments in the selection below. Rewrite each fragment as a sentence. Compare your sentences with the original. Be prepared to explain why you think Steinbeck chose to use fragments in this passage. (Notice that the author has also ignored some punctuation rules.)

(1) But most of the families changed and grew quickly into the new life. (2) And when the sun went down—
(3) Time to look out for a place to stop.
(4) And—there's some tents ahead.
(5) The car pulled off the road and stopped, and because others were there first, certain courtesies were necessary.
(6) And the man, the leader of the family, leaned from the car.
(7) Can we pull up here an' sleep?
(8) Why, sure, be proud to have you. (9) What State you from?
(10) Come all the way from Arkansas.
(11) They's Arkansas people down that fourth tent.
(12) That so?
(13) And the great question, How's the water?
(14) Well, she don't taste so good, but they's plenty.
(15) Well, thank ya.
(16) No thanks to me.
(17) But the courtesies had to be.

From *The Grapes of Wrath* by John Steinbeck

c *Write Now* Transcribe or tape record a short conversation that you hear during your day at school. Make a list of the fragments in the conversation. Rewrite the conversation changing all the fragments to complete sentences.

o much

last night all the buses had stopped running & slid on the ice and fell flat on my face

off I was

our mono job & my boots and had to

Part 3
Run-on Sentences

A run-on sentence is two or more sentences written as though they were one sentence.

In some run-on sentences the writer fails to use an end mark at the end of each sentence.

Run-on   The tide is out now the water is only a foot deep.
Correct   The tide is out. Now the water is only a foot deep.

In other run-on sentences the writer uses a comma instead of an end mark. This error is called the **comma fault** or **comma splice.**

Run-on   Don't worry about Joe, he can take care of himself.
Correct   Don't worry about Joe. He can take care of himself.

Correcting Run-on Sentences

There are several ways to correct run-on sentences. In both corrections above, the run-on sentence has been rewritten as two separate sentences. Sometimes, however, when the ideas expressed are closely related, it is preferable to join them into a single sentence.

You can join the sentences with a comma and a coordinating conjunction.

Run-on   The demonstrators were orderly, the mayor willingly listened to their complaints.
Correct   The demonstrators were orderly, **and** the mayor willingly listened to their complaints.

You can join the sentences with a semicolon.

Run-on   The demonstrators were orderly, the mayor willingly listened to
their complaints.

Correct   The demonstrators were orderly; the mayor willingly listened to
their complaints.

You can join the sentences with a semicolon and a conjunctive
adverb. (See page 38 for a list of conjunctive adverbs.)

Run-on   The demonstrators were orderly, the mayor willingly listened to
their complaints.

Correct   The demonstrators were orderly; **consequently,** the mayor
willingly listened to their complaints.

Grammar Note Each correct sentence above is a compound sentence with two independent clauses. (See pages 103–104 for more
about independent clauses and compound sentences.)

Exercises

A On your paper, correct each of the following run-on sentences by
(1) using end punctuation and capitalization to separate the sentences;
(2) joining the sentences with a comma and a coordinating conjunction;
or (3) joining the sentences with a semicolon or with a semicolon and a
conjunctive adverb. Do not correct every sentence the same way.

1. We flew to LaGuardia Airport then we took the shuttle to
Washington.
2. I try to practice the flute every day, I don't always have time.
3. Christy Brown overcame incredible handicaps, he became an
outstanding writer.
4. The marketplace was dusty and crowded, everywhere vendors hawked
their wares.
5. The small skiff edged carefully out of the harbor the wind changed
suddenly.
6. At the end of Hawthorne's *The Scarlet Letter,* Hester returned to Boston
Pearl remained in England.
7. My father is colorblind, he needs no help coordinating his ties, shirts,
and suits.
8. The contestant hesitated too long, the buzzer ended his turn.
9. Neal can try to make the Olympic team, he can turn pro.
10. The critic did not like the play, he wrote a scathing review.

11. Racehorses in the Northern Hemisphere have their official birthday on January first, in the Southern Hemisphere the date is August first.
12. Friendly Indians allowed wagon trains to pass through their hunting grounds, some even helped the pioneers.
13. John took a special class in computers he thought it would help him find a summer job.
14. Our bus broke down on the way to school, it broke down again on the way home.
15. It isn't a new dress, I wore it to homecoming last year.

B Copy this paragraph, correcting the run-on sentences.

Joseph William Turner was one of Britain's greatest painters. When he died in 1851, he willed all of his paintings to his beloved country, England this gesture, although generous, caused the government a great deal of trouble. Turner's family immediately set about to upset the will, claiming that the artist was not of sound mind when he

Slave Ship, J. W. Turner, 1840.

wrote it. Their efforts were unsuccessful Turner's work, finished and unfinished, was delivered to the National Gallery. The gallery, unprepared to accept such a volume of work, stored the canvases in the basement. In 1910, Turner's work was to be displayed it was to hang in the Tate Gallery, an annex of the National Gallery. Instead, the works went from one basement to another. The Thames River overflowed in 1928 many of the canvases were severely damaged. Now, 136 years after Turner's death, his works hang in a new gallery designed solely to display Turner's work finally the conditions of the will are fulfilled.

C *Proofreading* On your paper, write the following paragraph, correcting all the run-on sentences. Also correct any errors in spelling, punctuation, and capitalization.

> Many people agree that Wilt Chamberlain was the gratest player in the history of the National basketball Association, he still holds an incredible number of records. In one Season he played more on-court minutes than any other player. He led the league in scoring for seven strait years, and he has scored the most lifetime points his record is 31,419 points scored. In a game against New York in 1962, Chamberlain scored fifty nine points in one half, he ended up scoring one hundred points in the game. He was also a champion rebounder, he led the league in rebounds for eleven seasons, for a career total of 23,924. Chamberlain played for Philadelphia San Francisco and los Angeles all three teems wish they had him back.

Checkpoint *Parts 1, 2, and 3*

Rewrite the following fragments and run-ons as complete sentences.

1. The Union Pacific Railroad was completed in 1869. Linking the country from coast to coast.
2. The Siberian tiger is powerful the Indian tiger is more powerful.
3. The fossil which is sixty-five million years old.
4. To unlock the mystery of the Abominable Snowman.
5. Two bathrooms, a large sunny kitchen, and a two-car garage.
6. Guppies are easy to care for other fish provide color and variety in an aquarium.
7. Jupiter is a mystery. Because it is wrapped in clouds.
8. Eaves are part of the roof they protect the outside walls.
9. We like pizza with thin crust they prefer the thick variety.
10. Firecrackers, having originated in ancient China.
11. Nero ruled Rome wisely for a time. Then became obsessed by a fear that he would lose his ability to govern.
12. The hikers arose refreshed. After sleeping only a short time.
13. Tarragon is an herb it should be used sparingly.
14. There are three varieties of mangoes Hayden, turpentine, and pineapple.'
15. Since push buttons became popular, It has become more and more unusual to see a telephone with a rotary dial.

Linking
Grammar & Writing

Imagine that you are searching for a lost group of explorers in the Amazon jungle. You receive a radio communication from the explorers. However, the signal is faint, and you can only hear fragments of what is said. Read the fragments listed below. Then write a draft of the complete radio message by turning the fragments into sentences.

> . . . is Captain . . . not lost . . . located about three miles northeast of the village Quizotl . . . ten days . . . cannot move . . . explosion in our camp . . . Julio, of the Amazon exploration team . . . most of our party . . . quickly . . . medical supplies and blankets.

Prewriting and Drafting At the top of a page, make a column for each of the following questions: *Who? What? Where? When? How?* Place each fragment in a column that you think is appropriate. Then turn the fragments into complete sentences that help to explain what happened to the explorers. Your draft of the complete radio message should fully explain what happened.

Revising and Proofreading When revising your draft, consider the following questions:

1. Is the radio message complete and logical?
2. Can the reader easily follow the order of events?
3. Are fragments and run-on sentences avoided?

Additional Writing Topic Thumb through recent magazines or newspapers and look for sentence fragments in the headlines of advertisements. Turn the headline fragments into sentences that describe your personality or your current life. Then write a paragraph that connects your sentences and forms an interesting or humorous self-description. The following paragraph gives an example of this kind of description; the underlined phrases show the advertisement fragments.

> I feel better than ever, new and improved, and brighter and bolder. Now that I have a part-time job, I'm going to be all that I can be. I believe that, since you only go around once in life, you have to grab all the gusto you can. The best part is I can buy what I want at unbelievably low, low prices. I am definitely participating in part of the American dream.

Chapter 4
Application and Review

A Identifying Fragments, Sentences, and Run-ons Identify each of the following word groups as *F* (fragment), *S* (sentence), or *R* (run-on sentence). Then correct each fragment and run-on.

1. Researchers are trying to understand how memory works they are mapping where the brain forms and stores memories.
2. Because patients undergoing brain surgery do not need to be unconscious during the surgery. Patients can tell surgeons what they experience when parts of their brain are stimulated.
3. The cortex, which is the brain's wrinkled covering. Is the location of higher complicated thought activities.
4. The wrinkles and folds of the cortex. Increase its surface area.
5. Scientists compare tracing the pattern of memory in the brain to the myth of Theseus following the thread in the labyrinth of the Minotaur.
6. Memories-to-be enter the cortex and are analyzed then eventually they find their way deeper into the brain.
7. There, spouting chemical fountains. Which etch the item to be remembered into the brain somewhat like a picture is etched onto film.
8. Synapses are connections where a nerve impulse jumps from one brain cell to the next.
9. Synapses form patterns. Like spider webs throughout the brain.
10. In the future when researchers finally unlock the mysteries of synapse patterns.

B Correcting Fragments Correct the fragments in the following paragraph by connecting them to make complete sentences.

> Every year, people come from all over America. To gather in the little community of Bean Blossom, Indiana. And take part in the annual Bill Monroe Bluegrass Festival. The festival is a combination of old and new. A celebration of traditional and contemporary bluegrass music. It offers the finest in good old-fashioned, foot-stomping entertainment. Including music by some of the best bluegrass bands in the country. Visitors to the festival stroll up and down several acres of Indiana countryside. Listening to melodies like "Salty Dog" and "*T* for Texas." They can applaud the highly skilled musicians. Who play on instruments ranging from banjos and mandolins. To fiddles, autoharps, and guitars, both electric and acoustic.

C Correcting Run-on Sentences Correct each of the run-on sentences in the following paragraph. Use your judgment to decide the best way to correct the run-ons. For some run-ons, simply separate the sentences into two. For others, use commas with corresponding conjunctions, semicolons, or semicolons with conjunctive adverbs.

None of us could believe that Harry was guilty, he had never been known to do anything dishonest. He had always been careful to give customers the exact change, yet he was now charged with pilfering the cash register at his checkout counter. The manager himself usually picked up the extra cash twice a day, however, on Thursday evening he waited until the store closed for the night. He put Harry's cash in a separate bag, then he locked it up in the safe. When he counted it the next morning, it was ten dollars short. The manager accused Harry of pocketing the money, however, Harry denied the charge. He thought for a while, then he asked to count the money. The manager agreed, he stood beside Harry while he counted. Harry went through each stack of bills slowly, finally Harry found the ten dollars. Two ten-dollar bills had stuck together. The manager and his assistant apologized, they even let Harry pick up the cash from all of the other checkout counters in the store the next week to show that they trusted him. They never questioned Harry's honesty again.

D Correcting Fragments and Run-ons Rewrite the following paragraph, correcting all sentence fragments and run-ons. Use the methods you have learned in this chapter.

Theodore Roosevelt, the twenty-sixth president of the United States. He is remembered for his hunting trips although he believed that his most important achievement in public life was his effort to conserve forests and help wildlife. Roosevelt claimed that "The American had but one thought about a tree, and that was to cut it down." In order to preserve the beautiful forests of the United States. Roosevelt created the Forest Service in 1905, he set aside 150 million acres of forest reserves and formed a number of national parks.

The bespectacled New Yorker, who had been a sickly child. He traveled extensively. As a young man who enjoyed riding through the West. Here he saw that much of the wildlife of the country was disappearing. Such as buffalo, wild turkey, and elk. He established wildlife and waterfowl refuges. To protect many endangered species.

However the animal that Roosevelt did the most to "protect" is the bear, the "Teddy" bear was named after this president when he refused to shoot an old, almost-blind bear while on a hunting trip.

Cumulative Review

Chapters 3 and 4

A Identifying Phrases and Clauses Determine whether each group of italicized words in the sentences below is a phrase (*P*) or a clause (*C*). Then identify each phrase as *Prepositional, Appositive,* or *Verbal.* Identify each of the clauses as *Adjective, Noun, Adverb,* or *Independent.*

> Example   *Although he was born into poverty,* Gabriel García Marquez became a world-famous writer. *C, Adverb*

1. Many writers of great literature have had *to overcome physical or psychological adversity.*
2. The poet John Keats wrote some of his best-known works while suffering from tuberculosis, *a common disease of his era.*
3. The epileptic seizures of the Russian novelist Feodor Dostoevski were so severe that it took him days to recover; for much of his career *he was also overwhelmed with debts.*
4. *At various stages in her career,* Virginia Woolf experienced bouts of mental illness that prevented her from writing.
5. *John Milton wrote his most famous poem* after he had completely lost his sight.
6. The novelist Richard Wright overcame a childhood of hunger and prejudice, *and he became a powerful writer.*
7. Flannery O'Connor continued *writing short stories,* though she had an incurable disease which eventually took her life.
8. O. Henry, *who became a master of the short story,* began his writing career while in prison.
9. While *working as a hotel busboy,* Langston Hughes showed Vachel Lindsay his poems; soon a book of his poems was published.
10. The power *of Elie Wiesel's novels* can be traced to his childhood experience in concentration camps.
11. *After his father was imprisoned for debt,* the twelve-year-old Charles Dickens went to work in a factory.
12. Alice Walker was blinded in one eye as a child; *writing fiction* helped her escape from the taunts of her classmates.
13. *How the young orphan Jerzy Kosinski survived in war-torn Europe* became the subject for his highly praised novel.

14. *Katherine Mansfield spent her last years as an invalid,* yet during that time she wrote some of her best stories.

15. The Argentine writer Jorge Borges wrote many of his finest short stories *after he became totally blind.*

B Recognizing Sentence Structures Number your paper from 1–15. Describe the structure of each sentence in Exercise A as *Simple, Compound, Complex,* or *Compound-Complex.*

C Correcting Fragments and Run-on Sentences Rewrite the following paragraphs to correct all errors.

> The Old City of Jerusalem is a holy place to Muslims, Christians, and Jews. Containing within its walls the place from which Muslims believe that Mohammed ascended to heaven, the spot where Christians believe Jesus was killed and rose again, and the site where Jews believe Solomon's Temple once stood. The Old City makes up less than one percent of the modern city of Jerusalem, Israel's largest city is now the home of about 407,000 people.
>
> In A.D. 1099 Christian crusaders fought Jews and Muslims, established a kingdom in Jerusalem that lasted for about one hundred years. For the next six hundred years, the city was inhabited mainly by Muslims from Egypt, Syria, and Turkey. Until 1917, when a British army captured the city. After this, both Jews and Muslims flocked there. Jerusalem was a divided city until 1967, when Israel won control of the entire city. In the Six Day war.
>
> Today Muslims, Christians, and Jews live in the city, however, relations among them are sometimes stormy. Even violent. Despite the violence, Jerusalem continues to be holy land for three religions.

D Finding Misplaced and Dangling Modifiers Rewrite the following letter to correct problems with modifiers.

```
Dear Clyde,
    Answering your letter, my cow gave birth to a
beautiful calf. It was born while you were in Atlanta
bellowing for all the world to hear. I remembered
your letter soon after I first saw the calf in the
middle of dinner. I wanted to tell you only good news,
but I must also tell you that your goldfish died,
wishing you were here.
```

5
Using Verbs

E xaggerated actions, brightly colored costumes, and dramatic
makeup—these are the outstanding features of Japan's
kabuki theater. However, long after the costumes and
makeup have ceased to startle and delight the audience,
the action continues to captivate. Action tells the story
of the drama.

Similarly, readers rely on verbs to tell the story of a
sentence. In this chapter you will learn to use verb
tenses correctly and to differentiate between verbs that
are often confused. This will help you to communicate
more effectively and precisely.

Part 1
The Principal Parts of Verbs

Before you study the many forms of verbs, you may want to review some basic facts.

A **verb** is a word that expresses an action, a condition, or a state of being. Verbs are divided into two main categories. **Action verbs** describe a physical or mental action that someone is performing. **Linking verbs** do not express action. Rather, they serve as a link between the subject of the sentence and a word in the predicate that renames or describes the subject. For more information about verbs, see Chapter 1, pages 16–21.

Every verb has many different forms. All of these forms are made from the four **principal parts** of the verb: the **present infinitive** (usually called the **present**), the **present participle**, the **past**, and the **past participle**.

Present	Present Participle	Past	Past Participle
talk	(is) talking	talked	(have) talked
sing	(is) singing	sang	(have) sung
put	(is) putting	put	(have) put

In the examples above, notice that the present participle and the past participle are preceded by *is* and *have*. This is to show that these forms are always used with helping verbs. Also note that the present participle ends with *-ing*. This ending does not change; all verbs add *-ing* to the present to form the present participle. The endings of the past and the past participle, however, do change from verb to verb; the past and the past participle may be formed in several ways. These endings determine whether a verb is regular or irregular.

Regular Verbs

A regular verb is one to which *-ed* or *-d* is added to the present in order to form the past and the past participle. Most verbs are regular.

Some regular verbs change their spelling slightly when *-ing* or *-ed* is added to the present.

Present	Present Participle	Past	Past Participle
trip	(is) tripping	tripped	(have) tripped
spy	(is) spying	spied	(have) spied
picnic	(is) picnicking	picnicked	(have) picnicked

Exercise

On your paper, make four columns in which you list the principal parts of the following regular verbs.

1. grab	6. carry	11. clean
2. expel	7. disappear	12. admit
3. occur	8. regret	13. limit
4. narrate	9. move	14. receive
5. achieve	10. satisfy	15. omit

Irregular Verbs

An **irregular** verb is a verb that does not form the past and past participle by adding -*ed* or -*d* to the present. Irregular verbs form the past and past participle in a variety of ways.

There are approximately sixty commonly used verbs in this category. Several examples are given below.

Present	Present Participle	Past	Past Participle
put	(is) putting	put	(have) put
say	(is) saying	said	(have) said
tear	(is) tearing	tore	(have) torn
ring	(is) ringing	rang	(have) rung
throw	(is) throwing	threw	(have) thrown
go	(is) going	went	(have) gone
freeze	(is) freezing	froze	(have) frozen

Because the principal parts of irregular verbs are formed in a variety of ways, you must either memorize these parts or refer to a dictionary. The dictionary will list the principal parts of all irregular verbs. Remembering the parts of irregular verbs will be simpler if you break them down into the five groups that follow.

Group 1 The easiest of the irregular verbs to remember are those that have the same form for the present, the past, and the past participle.

Present	Present Participle	Past	Past Participle
burst	(is) bursting	burst	(have) burst
cost	(is) costing	cost	(have) cost
cut	(is) cutting	cut	(have) cut
hit	(is) hitting	hit	(have) hit
hurt	(is) hurting	hurt	(have) hurt
put	(is) putting	put	(have) put
set	(is) setting	set	(have) set
shut	(is) shutting	shut	(have) shut

Group 2 The irregular verbs in this group have the same form for the past and the past participle.

Present	Present Participle	Past	Past Participle
bring	(is) bringing	brought	(have) brought
catch	(is) catching	caught	(have) caught
fight	(is) fighting	fought	(have) fought
flee	(is) fleeing	fled	(have) fled
fling	(is) flinging	flung	(have) flung
get	(is) getting	got	(have) got
			or gotten
lead	(is) leading	led	(have) led
lend	(is) lending	lent	(have) lent
lose	(is) losing	lost	(have) lost
say	(is) saying	said	(have) said
shine	(is) shining	shone	(have) shone
		or shined	*or* shined
sit	(is) sitting	sat	(have) sat
sting	(is) stinging	stung	(have) stung
swing	(is) swinging	swung	(have) swung
teach	(is) teaching	taught	(have) taught

Usage Note Both *got* and *gotten* are standard usage. However, *got* is more common. Both *shone* and *shined* are standard usage, but *shone* is used when there is no direct object.

Beginning duck.

Exercises

A On your paper, write the past or the past participle form of the verb given in parentheses. Keep in mind that the past participle is used with a form of the auxiliary verb *have*.

1. Of all of Sherlock Holmes's cases, "The Adventure of the Speckled Band" (teach) me not to jump to conclusions.
2. A young woman named Stoner (sit) in Holmes's study.
3. She (say) that lately she had (put) some rather strange facts together.
4. Her stepfather had (bring) a cheetah and a baboon from India and had not (shut) them up, but had let them run loose.
5. Suddenly the nervous visitor (flee) from Holmes's study.
6. Holmes (lead) and I followed to the young lady's estate.
7. The moon (shine) brightly across the lawn.
8. We (catch) sight of a baboon who (swing) down from a tree.
9. I (fight) back thoughts that I had (lose) my mind.
10. We entered the house, where things (get) even more curious.
11. Ms. Stoner's sister Julie had mysteriously died, and rumors had (got) around about the cause of her death.
12. The stepfather had (lend) the use of Julie's bedroom to Ms. Stoner.
13. Each night a strange whistle had been heard, and a light (shine) from the middle window.
14. One night we watched and then (burst) into the bedroom.
15. There, in Ms. Stoner's bed, was a deadly Indian swamp adder; fortunately it had not (hurt) Ms. Stoner.

Scene from the film *The Adventures of Sherlock Holmes.*

B Find the verb that is used incorrectly in each sentence. Write the correct form on your paper. If a sentence has no verb errors, write *Correct*.

1. Mr. Chin brang out his collection of jade carvings.
2. The rookie quickly reached up and miraculously catched the hard-hit line drive.
3. The Cheshire cat set in a tree and grinned at Alice.
4. Robert Graves sayed that love is a universal headache.
5. At the finish line, the cyclists bursted through the ribbon.
6. Jellyfish have stinged many unsuspecting swimmers.
7. As the motor launch approached, the dolphins fled.
8. A careless motorist flinged a bag of litter from the car.
9. Carleen must have lended the lawnmower to the Johnsons.
10. The small passenger plane must have losed its way in the mysterious Bermuda Triangle.
11. Mack shut one eye and spied through the keyhold.
12. The aerialist swinged gracefully through the air.
13. Spanish conquistadors leaded many expeditions in hopes of finding the legendary land of El Dorado.
14. In medieval times spices costed a great deal of money.
15. Extensive vaccination programs have bringed an end to smallpox in the United States.

C *Proofreading* Rewrite the paragraph correcting errors in spelling, punctuation, capitalization, and verb forms.

As I sayed to that agriculture expert who came down here from the capitol, the kudzu's not a plant—its a green monster. Now, you may think Im exaggerating, but you should have seen what happened to that agriculture man when he tried to show the farmers around hear how to get rid of this pesky weed. If he had been smart, he would have fleed Instead, that so-called Expert getted out a can of weedkiller. I guess he figgered that plant was just going to lie there while he sprayed it. That old kudzu certainly teached him a lesson! It was a site! The vine catched him, swinged him right off the ground and putted him down in the top of a sycamore tree. well we called the volunteer fire department, and they brung ladders to get him down. When that vine herd the sirens, though, it grabbed him again and flang him up until his head bursted through the underside of a cloud. I guess he would have starved to death if I hadn't lended the fire department my shotgun so they could shoot biscuits up to him. I tell you, that kudzu's mean. So far, everyone that's fighted it has losed.

Group 3 The irregular verbs in this group form the past participle by adding *-n* or *-en* to the past.

Present	Present Participle	Past	Past Participle
bear	(is) bearing	bore	(have) borne
beat	(is) beating	beat	(have) beaten
bite	(is) biting	bit	(have) bitten *or* bit
break	(is) breaking	broke	(have) broken
choose	(is) choosing	chose	(have) chosen
freeze	(is) freezing	froze	(have) frozen
speak	(is) speaking	spoke	(have) spoken
steal	(is) stealing	stole	(have) stolen
swear	(is) swearing	swore	(have) sworn
tear	(is) tearing	tore	(have) torn
wear	(is) wearing	wore	(have) worn

Usage Note Both *bitten* and *bit* are standard. *Bitten* is more common.

Exercises

A On your paper, write the past or the past participle form of the verb given in parentheses.

1. The Guatemalan dancers (wear) elaborately embroidered costumes.
2. The council president has already been (swear) into office.
3. A test tube of the sulphuric compound (break) during the experiment, and a terrible stench filtered through the lab.
4. During the night, thieves (steal) the most precious painting from the collection at the museum.
5. The school board has (choose) an architect to design the new library.
6. The trapper's fingertips had almost (freeze) in the bitter cold.
7. Yesterday I (speak) to the manager about my job application.
8. The child had been (bite) by an unleashed dog.
9. She (bear) yesterday's bad news surprisingly well.
10. The championship team has (break) most of the school's track records.
11. The suspect (swear) he had been home reading poetry at the time the robbery was committed.
12. The wreckers (tear) down the abandoned hotel two weeks ago.
13. No one has ever (beat) Mr. Alvarez at backgammon.
14. Walden Pond had (freeze) solid by early November.
15. The general claimed that the rebel army (break) the truce first.

16. Poverty has not (beat) their resilient spirit.
17. Erosion and constant wind (wear) away the topsoil and created the great Dust Bowl of the 1930's.
18. I have (speak) in public often, but I still get nervous.
19. Gale-force winds have (tear) doors off hinges, turned over cars, and toppled telephone poles.
20. The aging athlete may have (steal) his last base.

B Find the verb that is used incorrectly in each sentence. Write the correct form on your paper. If a sentence has no verb errors, write *Correct*.

1. I would like to know who stealed the radio in my locker.
2. Her top rival has not beat her in the last seven matches.
3. During dessert I thought I had bit into a piece of metal, but it was a nutshell.
4. Has the relentless heat broke any records this summer?
5. Elizabeth I of England had many suitors chose for her, but she never married any of them.
6. In last year's blizzard the car door freezed shut.
7. Ms. Hernández has spoke to school groups about the needs of the elderly.
8. The stowaways must have stolen onto the ship at night.
9. The defenders of the Alamo had swore to fight to the last man.
10. Someone has tore two pages out of this month's *National Geographic* magazine.
11. My father has worn the same rumpled hat for five years.
12. The natives beared the wounded warrior back to their camp and took him to the hut of the *shaman,* or witch doctor.
13. Our team has soundly beat most of the other contenders for the league championship.
14. Our community has bore the full force of the tax hike, but services have not improved.
15. Have you spoke to your parents about using the car?
16. Most of our dishes broke when the moving van came to a sudden and unexpected stop.
17. The principal has chose Ramona to welcome the senator.
18. Dad has froze several containers of his tomato sauce.
19. Construction crews teared up most of the roadway along the East River.
20. Over the years wind, rain, and pollution have wore away the detailed carvings on many ancient Greek buildings.

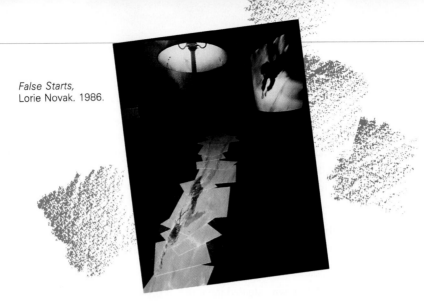

False Starts,
Lorie Novak. 1986.

C *Write Now* Fantasy stories often feature seemingly impossible circumstances or events, such as entering another dimension, traveling through time, or visiting another world. Let your imagination wander and create a fantasy story of your own. Use at least eight verbs from the lists on pages 134, 135, and 138.

Group 4 The irregular verbs in this group change a vowel to form the past and the past participle. The vowel changes from *i* in the present to *a* in the past to *u* in the past participle.

Present	Present Participle	Past	Past Participle
begin	(is) beginning	began	(have) begun
drink	(is) drinking	drank	(have) drunk
ring	(is) ringing	rang	(have) rung
shrink	(is) shrinking	shrank	(have) shrunk
sing	(is) singing	sang	(have) sung
sink	(is) sinking	sank	(have) sunk
spring	(is) springing	sprang *or* sprung	(have) sprung
swim	(is) swimming	swam	(have) swum

Exercises

A On your paper, write the past or the past participle form of the verb given in parentheses.

1. The French Revolution, which (begin) in 1789, was caused by unfair taxation of the lower classes and reckless spending by the nobility.
2. By the end of Hawthorne's story "Dr. Heidegger's Experiment," four aging friends had (drink) water from the Fountain of Youth.

3. A suspicious-looking stranger (ring) the doorbell.
4. Woody Guthrie wrote and (sing) hundreds of folk songs about social and political themes.
5. The orchestra had already (begin) the overture when we arrived.
6. My brand-new "non-shrink" sweatshirt (shrink) two sizes when I washed it for the first time.
7. Sandy promised he'd call, but the phone hasn't (ring) all afternoon.
8. In 1898 the U.S. battleship *Maine* (sink) in Havana's harbor, killing 260 people.
9. Greek soldiers (spring) from inside a great wooden horse and defeated the Trojans.
10. The marathon swimmer Diana Nyad has (swim) across Lake Ontario and around Manhattan Island.
11. As predicted, the snow (begin) to fall shortly after midnight.
12. The alto (sing) off key during rehearsal.
13. The philosopher Plato wrote that the city of Atlantis (sink) into the sea after an earthquake.
14. The exhausted hunters (drink) greedily from the mountain stream.
15. Since February the value of the dollar has (shrink) dramatically.
16. As the band played, the crowd (sing) the national anthem.
17. Bells (ring) out across the nation in celebration of the bicentennial of the Constitution.
18. My head (swim) when I thought about what the changes would mean.
19. Suddenly the announcer's voice (sink) to a whisper.
20. Greek myths say that the goddess Athena (spring) full grown from the head of Zeus.

B Find the verb that is used incorrectly in each sentence. Write the correct form on your paper. If a sentence has no verb errors, write *Correct*.

1. The senior choir sung patriotic songs at the special assembly.
2. Our coach thinks that we have began the debate season with an extremely strong team.
3. Yesterday, Andrea sank a hole in one.
4. The crowd looked skeptical when the rabbit springed from the magician's hat.
5. The horses had already swum to the opposite bank.
6. Meghan drunk soda water with lemon juice before she sang.
7. The trained dogs rung a bell for food.
8. Troubadours of the twelfth and thirteenth centuries went from castle to castle, where they sung poems about love and war.

9. The Russian submarine had sank beneath the surface.
10. "I think this boat has sprang a leak," said Carolyn.
11. We suddenly begun to see what Mom was getting at.
12. Either my new jeans have shrank, or I ate too much dinner.
13. The cashier had already rang up the grocery order when I realized I didn't have enough money.
14. Have you ever drank fresh coconut milk or papaya juice?
15. The spectators shrunk back in fear as the orange car spun wildly out of control.
16. Schools of fish swam under the glass-bottom boat.
17. My sister begun classes last week at Kenyon College.
18. The damaged Liberian freighter sunk off the California coast.
19. My dad has sang in the "Do-It-Yourself-Messiah" in Philadelphia for the last three years.
20. Private investigator Jerome Jackson sprung up and answered the phone on the second ring.

Group 5 The irregular verbs in this group form the past participle from the present—often by adding *-n* or *-en*. In the list that follows, note the similarity between the present and the past participle forms.

Present	Present Participle	Past	Past Participle
blow	(is) blowing	blew	(have) blown
come	(is) coming	came	(have) come
do	(is) doing	did	(have) done
draw	(is) drawing	drew	(have) drawn
drive	(is) driving	drove	(have) driven
eat	(is) eating	ate	(have) eaten
fall	(is) falling	fell	(have) fallen
give	(is) giving	gave	(have) given
go	(is) going	went	(have) gone
grow	(is) growing	grew	(have) grown
know	(is) knowing	knew	(have) known
ride	(is) riding	rode	(have) ridden
rise	(is) rising	rose	(have) risen
run	(is) running	ran	(have) run
see	(is) seeing	saw	(have) seen
shake	(is) shaking	shook	(have) shaken
slay	(is) slaying	slew	(have) slain
take	(is) taking	took	(have) taken
throw	(is) throwing	threw	(have) thrown
write	(is) writing	wrote	(have) written

Exercises

A On your paper, write the past or the past participle form of the verb given in parentheses.

1. Several ships (blow) off course during the storm.
2. People have (come) from miles around to attend the auction.
3. My parents (do) their best to discourage me from quitting.
4. As usual, the Rose Bowl game (draw) a capacity crowd.
5. During the subway strike we (drive) into Manhattan every morning.
6. Moths have (eat) a hole in my best jacket.
7. Live power lines had (fall) across the road.
8. Mom has (give) an ultimatum: clean up your room or else!
9. Josh has (go) to Israel for the summer to work on a kibbutz.
10. As the yearbook deadline approached, we (grow) panicky.
11. When I was little I (know) all the names of the state capitals.
12. If you have ever (ride) a unicycle, you know how difficult it is.
13. Two deer (run) across the road in front of our car.
14. The governor has (shake) hands with several hundred well-wishers.
15. Sir Gawain had (slay) the dragon with one blow of his sword.
16. Someone had (take) down the stop sign.
17. Jeff (throw) out the receipt for his jacket, and now the store refuses to let him return it.
18. Have you (write) for your entry blank?
19. The bread dough has (rise) in twenty minutes, but the recipe said it would take an hour.
20. Hundreds of people claim to have (see) Bigfoot, or Sasquatch, as he is sometimes called.

Time Passing, Paul Leith, 1984.

B Find the verb that is used incorrectly in each sentence. Write the correct form on your paper. If a sentence has no verb errors, write *Correct.*

1. A vendor come down the street selling bags of roasted chestnuts.
2. Scientists have did studies showing that salmon use their sense of smell to find their way back to their birthplace to spawn.
3. The pandas have already ate their daily portion of bamboo shoots.
4. Mr. Cobb had driven into the rest area off the highway because he was too sleepy to continue.
5. The empty house has fallen into disrepair.
6. Austrian archduke Maximilian had went to Mexico to establish an empire for Napoleon III, but the Mexicans refused to accept him.
7. Andrew must have growed four inches in a year.
8. We should have knowed that the banks would be closed today.
9. The marchers had rid a bus all night to attend the rally.
10. Hundreds of lemmings runned across the beach and into the sea.
11. The detective feared that the lawyer had slew his partner.
12. The road crews throwed sand and salt on the icy highways.
13. Fortunately for us, Clare has wrote ahead for reservations.
14. A cloud of moths rose from the old wool rug when we moved it from the attic.
15. Many normal, ordinary people claim that they have saw UFO's.

c *Proofreading* Proofread the following anecdote for errors in verb usage as well as other errors in spelling, punctuation, and capitalization. Then on your paper write the anecdote correctly.

> Young Henry martin was sitting on a large branch that had fell from an old Oak tree. He was watching the waters, of a nearby River, that had rised and were flooding the road. A passing moterist seen the water, slammed on his brakes, swang his car to the side of the rode, and drawed up next to the boy.
>
> "Has the water became too deep to cross?" he asked.
>
> "No sir. Go right ahead," Henry replied.
>
> After the motorist had drove partway through the water. his car sunk up to it's hood. He clumb out of the car, swimmed to dry ground, and begun to rant and rave. "Are you crazy? I almost drownd!" he shouted. "You certianly gived me some bad advice you must have knowed the water was too deep to cross."
>
> Young Henry shaked his head in amazment. "Thats funny," he said as he putted his hand too inches from the ground. "The water only comed up to hear on the ducks!"

Part 2

Verb Tenses

All verbs change form to show the time of the action they express. These changes in form are called **tenses.** English verbs have three simple tenses (present, past, and future) and three perfect tenses (present perfect, past perfect, and future perfect). You use these tenses to show whether something is happening now, has happened in the past, or will happen in the future. The six tenses are formed by using the principal parts that you have just studied and combining them with certain auxiliary verbs such as *be* and *have*.

Scene from the
film *Back to the Future.*

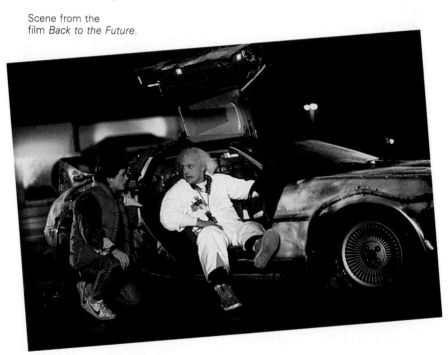

Verb Conjugation

A verb **conjugation** is a list of all the forms used in the six tenses of a verb. A verb conjugation also shows changes in form for the first, second, and third persons and for the singular and plural.

When you study the simple and perfect tenses of verbs on pages 147–148, refer to the conjugation of the regular verb *call* that is shown on the following page.

Principal Parts

Present	Present Participle	Past	Past Participle
call	(is) calling	called	(have) called

Simple Tenses

	Singular	Plural
Present Tense		
First Person	I call	we call
Second Person	you call	you call
Third Person	he, she, it calls	they call
Past Tense		
First Person	I called	we called
Second Person	you called	you called
Third Person	he, she, it called	they called
Future Tense (*will* or *shall* + the present form)		
First Person	I will (shall) call	we will (shall) call
Second Person	you will call	you will call
Third Person	he, she, it will call	they will call

Perfect Tenses

Present Perfect Tense (*has* or *have* + the past participle)		
First Person	I have called	we have called
Second Person	you have called	you have called
Third Person	he, she, it has called	they have called

Past Perfect Tense (*had* + the past participle)		
First Person	I had called	we had called
Second Person	you had called	you had called
Third Person	he, she, it had called	they had called

Future Perfect Tense (*will have* or *shall have* + the past participle)		
First Person	I will (shall) have called	we will (shall) have called
Second Person	you will have called	you will have called
Third Person	he, she, it will have called	they will have called

Using the Simple Tenses

The simple tenses include the **present, past,** and **future** tense.

The Present Tense To form the present tense, use the first principal part (the present form): *I go, we see.* Add *-s* or *-es* to the present form for the third person singular: *he goes, she sees.*

Use the present tense to show an action that (1) occurs in the present; (2) occurs regularly; or (3) is constant or generally true at any given time.

> There *goes* our bus! (action occurring in present)
> We *attend* band practice every Thursday. (action occurring regularly)
> The heart *pumps* blood. (constant action)

The **historical present tense** is used to tell of some action or condition in the past as though it were occurring in the present.

> The captain *orders,* "Abandon ship!" as the great vessel *lists* dangerously to starboard, its deck ablaze.

Note Use the present tense when writing about literature.

> In *Macbeth,* William Shakespeare *tells* the story of a Scottish king and his ambitious wife.

The Past Tense To form the past tense of a regular verb, add *-d* or *-ed* to the present form: *you smiled, they laughed.* If the verb is irregular, use the past form listed as one of the principal parts: *she went, we rode, they caught.*

Use the past tense to show an action that was completed in the past.

> Yesterday I *ran* around the reservoir.

The Future Tense To form the future tense, use the auxiliary verb *will* or *shall* with the present form. *Will* simply indicates future; *shall* usually implies an intention or obligation: *I will stay, we shall stay.*

Use the future tense for an action that will occur in the future.

> The test *will begin* at nine o'clock.
> I *shall* not *admit* latecomers.

Future time may also be shown by using the present tense in combination with an adverb or phrase that tells time.

> We *pick* up our bus passes next week. (The words *next week* indicate future time.)

Using the Perfect Tenses

The perfect tenses include the **present perfect,** the **past perfect,** and the **future perfect** tense.

The Present Perfect Tense To form the present perfect tense, use the auxiliary verb *has* or *have* with the past participle: *you have danced, she has slept.* Use the present perfect tense to show an action (1) that was completed at an indefinite time in the past or (2) that began in the past and continues into the present.

> He *has left* without his books. (action completed at indefinite time)
> We *have worked* here for ten years. (action continuing into the
> present)

The Past Perfect Tense To form the past perfect tense, use the auxiliary verb *had* with the past participle: *I had wondered, we had known.* Use the past perfect tense to show an action in the past that came before another action in the past.

> I *had* already *finished* when you called. (action preceding another past action)

The Future Perfect Tense Form the future perfect tense by using the auxiliary verbs *will have* or *shall have* with the past participle: *you will have eaten.* Use the future perfect tense to show an action in the future that will occur before another future action or time.

> By the time I meet Elena, I *will have bought* her birthday present—a new hat. (action occurring before another future action or time)

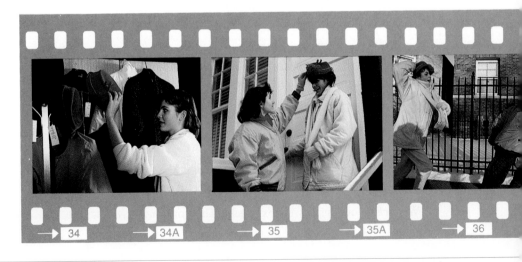

Exercises

A On your paper, write the verbs in the following sentences. Identify the tense of each verb.

1. The candidate had answers to most of the questions reporters asked at the press conference.
2. The workers on the demolition crew handled the explosives with care.
3. The world's largest crater, the Barringer, is 1,265 meters wide.
4. David Bushnell, an American engineer, built the first submarine in the 1700's.
5. Acid rain has taken its toll on many historic monuments.
6. Will the new classrooms have air-conditioning?
7. Amateur rock collectors have found many valuable gems.
8. By the end of the next century, scientists will have learned the language of whales.
9. Even the most loyal fans had begun to lose heart.
10. The party will begin at five o'clock in the old auditorium at the school.
11. I have taken the same bus every day for two years.
12. Have you ever ridden on a mechanical bronco?
13. In 1891 Marie Dubois discovered the bones of Java Man.
14. My car weighs about 2,000 pounds.
15. Little John had sworn his loyalty to Robin Hood.

B On your paper, write the verbs in the following sentences. Identify the tense of each verb. Then change the tense to the one given in parentheses.

> *Example*   Sonia came for a short visit. (future)
> came, Past
> Sonia will come for a short visit.

1. Elizabeth Blackwell lived in England as a child. (past perfect)
2. The guests ate French bread and *escargot* (snails). (future)
3. A new roller rink will open at the mall before Thanksgiving. (future perfect)
4. The girls' basketball team has won the state title. (future)
5. Cliff refuses any help with geometry. (past)
6. Martina Navratilova won the U.S. Open. (present perfect)
7. Tomorrow morning we will practice our mime routine on the small stage in the gym. (present)
8. The band played the grand finale. (past perfect)
9. The Detroit Symphony returned from Europe. (present perfect)
10. Debra played Juliet in *Romeo and Juliet*. (present perfect)

Part 3

Progressive and Emphatic Verb Forms

In addition to the six basic tenses, verbs also have other special forms. These include the progressive and emphatic forms.

Using the Progressive Forms

The **progressive forms** show ongoing action. They are made by using a form of *be* with the present participle; they always end in *-ing*.

> I *am calling* my brother. (present progressive)
> I *was calling* my brother. (past progressive)
> I *will (shall) be calling* my brother. (future progressive)
>
> I *have been calling* my brother. (present perfect progressive)
> I *had been calling* my brother. (past perfect progressive)
> I *will (shall) have been calling* my brother. (future perfect progressive)

Use the **present progressive** form to show an ongoing action that is taking place now.

> The tenants *are planting* a garden in the courtyard.

The present progressive form can also be used to show future time when the sentence contains an adverb or a phrase, such as *tomorrow* or *next week,* that indicates the future.

> We *are leaving* for Detroit tomorrow.

Use the **past progressive** form to show an ongoing action that took place in the past.

> I *was studying* all morning.

Use the **future progressive** form to show an ongoing action that will take place in the future.

> This summer we *will be visiting* all our relatives.

Use the **present perfect progressive** to show an ongoing action continuing in the present.

> My mother *has been taking* guitar lessons.

Use the **past perfect progressive** to show an ongoing action in the past interrupted by another past action.

> The car *had been running* smoothly until it was sideswiped.

Use the **future perfect progressive** to show a future ongoing action that will have taken place by a stated future time.

> By this time tomorrow, I *will have been wearing* this cast for six weeks.

Using the Emphatic Forms

The present tense and the past tense have **emphatic forms** that give special emphasis or force to the verb. To form the present emphatic, use the auxiliary verb *do* or *does* with the present form of the main verb. To form the past emphatic, use the auxiliary verb *did* with the present form of the main verb.

> They usually *practice* every day. (present)
> They usually *do practice* every day. (present emphatic)

> They really *won* twelve games in a row. (past)
> They really *did win* twelve games in a row. (past emphatic)

Usage Note When the emphatic form is used in negative statements or questions, there is usually no special emphasis intended.

> He *does*n't usually *forget* his appointments.
> *Do* you *think* this avocado is ripe?

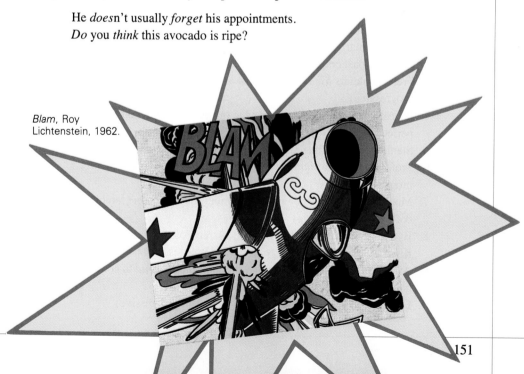

Blam, Roy Lichtenstein, 1962.

Exercises

A Write the verbs in the following sentences. Identify the tense of each verb and tell whether it is in the progressive or emphatic form, as shown in the example.

> *Example*   Dad did tell me about the flat tire.
> did tell, Past Emphatic

1. How have you been managing to get around?
2. These pre-Columbian figures do seem to be authentic.
3. We are now exploring new sources of energy.
4. The community had been hoping for a new sports and swimming complex for years.
5. CPR does save lives.
6. The lawyer will be filing her brief soon.
7. The patient really does seem better today.
8. Many scientists have been studying identical twins separated at birth.
9. Was anyone doing research for the project?
10. The principal did approve the student council's participation in the rally.

B On your paper, rewrite each of the following sentences, changing the italicized verb to the form given in parentheses.

1. Though not famous as a player, Mary E. Outerbridge *introduced* the game of tennis to the United States. (past emphatic)
2. The blue marlin caught by E. J. Fishman in 1968 really *weighed* 845 pounds. (past emphatic)
3. French soldiers *used* the crossbow as early as A.D. 851. (past progressive)
4. By August Jim *will have worked* at the pool for two months. (future perfect progressive)
5. Stanley *bowled* at the lanes every day after work. (past progressive)
6. Professor Pauling *studied* the aging process. (present perfect progressive)
7. Mocha was a little-known city in Arabia, but it *became* famous for its coffee. (past emphatic)
8. By the time he returned to Europe, Marco Polo *had worked* for Kublai Khan for seventeen years. (past perfect progressive)
9. Attendance has been falling, but the promoters *intend* to continue the concert through the weekend. (present emphatic)
10. I *register* for summer classes today. (present progressive)

Improper Shifts in Tense and Form

Use the same tense to show two or more actions that occur at the same time.

Within a paragraph or between sentences, do not shift tenses unless the meaning calls for a change. Use the same tense for the verbs in most compound sentences and in sentences with a compound predicate.

Incorrect	We *washed* the car, and then we *polish* it.
Correct	We *washed* the car, and then we *polished* it.

Incorrect	Chris *drafts* her letters and *corrected* them.
Correct	Chris *drafts* her letters and *corrects* them.

A shift in tense is not necessarily incorrect. There are times when a writer must use a tense shift to express a logical sequence of events or the relationship of one event to another. For example, to show one action occurring before or after another action, two different tenses are needed.

> Marcus *had solved* (past perfect) the problem before Mr. Weiss *explained* (past) how to do it.
> You *will have heard* (future perfect) the results by the time I *arrive* (present).
> I *see* (present) that you *have* already *finished* (present perfect) the book I *lent* (past) you.

Unnecessary or illogical shifts in verb tense are often made by inexperienced writers. Check your work carefully to avoid this type of error. Always be sure that your verbs express a consistent and logical time sequence.

Exercises

A On your paper, rewrite the following sentences. Correct improper shifts in tense by changing the tense of one verb to match the other.

Example   Louis XIV of France is crowned at age five
and continued to rule for seventy-two
years.
Louis XIV of France was crowned at age
five and continued to rule for seventy-two
years.

1. Coach called time out, and both teams dash for the sidelines.
2. The principal was walking purposefully to the front of the room when he is interrupted by a loud noise.
3. The aerialist climbed up the ladder and leaps onto the platform.
4. Carl hits a home run but neglected to touch third base.
5. Still invigorated by the day's adventure, we had already crossed Pennsylvania Avenue and head for the Washington Monument.
6. The writer Francisco Jiménez keeps a note pad and every day, without exception, had added the definition of an unfamiliar word.
7. A cloud of menacing grasshoppers swept from the sky and quickly destroy acres of wheat.
8. By the time she had finished her training, she will have studied with the finest musicians in the country.
9. In the moonlit garden the eyes of the cat glittered, and every hair on its body stands upright.
10. Angelo swam up behind me and dunks me in the frigid water.

B Application in Literature The following passages demonstrate how professional writers use the tenses and forms of verbs. Write the tense for each italicized verb below. Also tell if the verb is in the progressive or emphatic form. As you finish each passage, note how the author leads the reader back and forth through time by using various tenses and forms of verbs.

1. When enough years *had gone* by to enable us to look back on them, we sometimes *discussed* the events leading to his accident. I *maintain* that the Ewells *started* it all, but Jem, who *was* four years my senior, *said* it *started* long before that.   Harper Lee
2. I *had been reading* . . . of the Spanish influenza. At first it *was* far off. . . . Then the stories *told* of people dying in California towns we *knew,* and finally the [paper] *began* reporting the spread of the "flu" in our city.   Ernesto Galarza

3. "Harry, what *are* you *thinking* of?" Mrs. Oliver *asked* me. "*Don't* I *get* any change?" She *was laughing*. Albert Halper

4. In true quicksand a trapped pedestrian soon *sinks* to the depth of his knees and *will sink* further if he *stands* still or *struggles* wildly.

    Gerard H. Matthes

5. . . . I *like* to think that the flood *left* them a gift, a consolation prize, so that for years to come they *will be finding* edible mushrooms here and there about the house. . . . Annie Dillard

6. I *remember* the last time I *saw* him. It *was* early in September, and I *was sitting* on the gate. . . . Durango Mendoza

7. There *was* a commotion in Roaring Camp. It *could* not *have been* a fight, for in 1850 that *was* not novel enough to have called together the entire settlement. Bret Harte

8. But part of me is English, for I *love* England with a peculiar, possessing love. I *do possess* something of England. Pearl S. Buck

9. I *said* that writing *is* a craft, not an art, and the man who *runs* away from his craft because he lacks inspiration *is fooling* himself. He *is* also *going* broke. William Zinsser

10. "Oh, I *have had* such a curious dream!" *said* Alice, and she *told* her sister, as well as she could remember them, all these strange Adventures of hers that you *have* just *been reading* about; and when she *had finished,* her sister *kissed* her and said, "It was a curious dream, dear, certainly: but now *run* in to tea; it *is getting* late." Lewis Carroll

The Trial of the Knave of Hearts (from *Alice's Adventures in Wonderland*), Sir John Tenniel, 1865.

c *Write Now* Write a paragraph or two in which you describe how your attitude towards celebrating your birthday has changed over the years. You might want to focus on two or three birthdays, discussing your attitude, for example, at age five, age ten, and this year. Then discuss what you think your attitude will be at age fifty. Pay careful attention to how you shift tenses and forms of verbs.

Checkpoint *Parts 1, 2, and 3*

A On your paper, write the correct past or past participle form of each verb given in parentheses.

1. At the exhibit we (see) a skeleton of a brontosaurus.
2. I have (go) over my notes but cannot find the information.
3. Has Eric (give) you his entire coin collection?
4. If Columbus had (take) another route, America might have remained undiscovered for a long while.
5. After Alice (drink) the potion, she grew very tall.
6. Patriots had (ring) the Liberty Bell to proclaim our independence.
7. We (freeze) the leftovers after dinner.
8. The suspect's briefcase (burst) open, and money spilled out.
9. Gertrude Ederle (swim) the English Channel in 14 hours, 31 minutes.
10. Have you ever (take) the car ferry to Washington Island?
11. After Napoleon had (lose) at Waterloo, he went into exile.

12. Because the government had (break) the treaty of 1868, the Sioux fought for their land.
13. Mona has (lend) me a book about the penal colonies in Australia.
14. Mrs. Yoshida (teach) us origami, Japanese paper folding.
15. We have (write) for several copies of Garrison Keillor's article "How to Write a Personal Letter."
16. The light that (shine) from the North Star last night actually left the star 680 years ago.
17. Have you ever (bite) into a persimmon?
18. Confederate soldiers (sing) a song called "Eating Goober Peas."
19. Many runaway slaves (flee) to freedom on the Underground Railroad established by Harriet Tubman.
20. Have you (put) the car in gear or in neutral?

B On your paper, write the correct past or past participle form of each verb given in parentheses.

1. On May 30, 1889, the dam of the South Fork Reservoir at Conemaugh Lake about twelve miles east of Johnstown, Pennsylvania, (burst) due to heavy rains.
2. The owners of the dam had been warned about its flawed construction, but they had (choose) to ignore the warnings.
3. Due to the torrential rains in the last week of May, the Conemaugh River had already (rise) over its banks.
4. On the morning of May 30, messengers on horseback (ride) through the valley warning people that the dam could go.
5. At three o'clock came the awful cry, "The dam has (break)!"
6. People have (say) that they could hear the roar of the cataract for miles as it tumbled down the valley.
7. A wall of water forty feet high and a half mile wide (tear) through the valley.
8. The flood (bear) locomotives along like leaves.
9. It (fling) giant trees and boulders into the air.
10. It (take) with it bridges, houses, and hundreds of human lives.
11. In seven minutes the flood and the mountain of wreckage reached Johnstown, where it (hit) the Pennsy Bridge.
12. The bridge somehow resisted the impact, but the wreckage soon (catch) fire.
13. Many townspeople had (flee) in time.
14. However, over two thousand people (lose) their lives.
15. It (cost) over ten million dollars to repair the damage caused by the Johnstown Flood.

C On your paper, write the verbs in the following sentences. Identify the tense of each verb.

1. For her science fair report Margarite researched the development of the computer.
2. Susan's allergies have become worse this year.
3. In some people's opinion, Prime Minister Thatcher has borne the responsibilities of office well.
4. The debating team will go to the state meet next year.
5. The interpreter had learned Chinese in college.
6. Each year the Arctic tern migrates between the Arctic and the Antarctic, a round trip of 12,000 miles!
7. The members of the expedition will leave a flag at the summit.
8. In 2001 Australia will have been a nation for one hundred years.
9. Pablo Picasso, the famous artist, named his daughter *Paloma*, the Spanish word for "dove."
10. A famous piece of embroidery, the Bayeux Tapestry, illustrates the invasion of England by William the Conqueror in 1066.

D On your paper, rewrite the following sentences. Correct improper shifts in tense or form by changing the tense of one verb to match the other.

1. Marvin and Flo were painting their house flamingo pink while the neighbors had looked on in disbelief.
2. In 1932 more than fifteen hundred U.S. banks closed, and the depositors will lose 192 million dollars.
3. In 490 B.C. the Greek messenger Phidippides runs from Marathon to Athens and carried the news of an Athenian battle victory.
4. Since 1970 deaths due to heart disease have decreased 28 percent, and deaths due to strokes decrease 49 percent.
5. Medical research will become more sophisticated, and many diseases are cured in the future.

E On your paper, write the verbs in the following sentences. Identify each verb according to its form: *Progressive* or *Emphatic*.

1. Despite angry protests from citizens, the city council did approve the tax proposal.
2. In history we are studying the colonization of North America.
3. I do want your support in the upcoming student-council election.
4. William Thomson, the mathematician, was studying at Glasgow University at the age of ten.

5. By June my mother will have been working at the telephone company for fifteen years.
6. Your encouragement of my music really does make a difference.
7. The beekeeper was sowing clover near his hives to improve the flavor of his honey.
8. My sister will be completing her doctorate this year.
9. After the first performance of Igor Stravinsky's strange new music, the outraged Russian audience really did riot.
10. The quarterback and the wide receiver were practicing passes before the game on Sunday.

Part 4

Voice and Mood

You have already seen that verbs can take on many forms—the emphatic forms, the progressive forms, and the forms of the various tenses. The verbs change depending upon the purposes for which they are used. In addition to these common changes in verb form, there are other, more subtle forms that verbs can take. Writers use these verb forms to achieve special purposes.

Using the Active and Passive Voice

The **voice** of a verb tells whether the subject performs or receives the action of the verb. When the subject performs the action expressed by the verb, the verb is in the **active voice.** When the subject receives the action, the verb is in the **passive voice.** To form the passive voice, use a form of *be* with the past participle of the main verb.

Active Voice	The quarterback intentionally *threw* the ball out of bounds. (The subject *quarterback* performs the action of *throwing.*)
Passive Voice	The ball *was* intentionally *thrown* out of bounds by the quarterback. (The subject *ball* receives the action of being *thrown.*)
Active Voice	Liz *was cooking* dinner. (*Liz* performs the action of *cooking.*)
Passive Voice	Dinner *was being cooked* by Liz. (*Dinner* receives the action of being *cooked.*)

Notice that the verbs in the active voice above are transitive verbs; they have direct objects. When the verbs are changed from the active to the passive voice, the direct object becomes the subject. Only transitive verbs can change from active to passive. Intransitive verbs and linking verbs do not have direct objects. Therefore they cannot be in the passive voice because there is no word to become the subject.

Using Voice in Writing

In the passive voice, the subject does not act; it receives the action. Therefore, the active voice is usually more lively and more precise than the passive voice. For this reason, you should avoid writing long passages in the passive voice. You should also avoid mixing the passive and active voice in the same sentence or in related sentences.

On the other hand, do not hesitate to use the passive voice when you want to emphasize the person or thing receiving the action or when the person or thing performing the action is unknown.

> The performers *were given* a standing ovation. (The persons receiving the action are emphasized.)
> The concert *has been canceled* without notice. (The person performing the action is not known.)

Exercises

A On your paper, write the verbs in the following sentences. Identify each verb according to its voice: *Active* or *Passive*.

1. Within one hour every ticket to the concert had been sold.
2. In my dream last night, I had been invited by the Queen to Buckingham Palace.
3. My older sister has already chosen a career in cryogenics.
4. On the next pitch Dawson was hit by a curve ball.
5. That director does not understand the spy thriller genre.
6. Even with the new stadium lights only seventeen games have been played at night.
7. A new museum will be constructed on the site of the old Civil War battlefield.
8. The speaker told of her hair-raising adventures on Mt. Kilimanjaro in Africa.
9. Cynthia has bought a book entitled *Zen and the Art of Motorcycle Maintenance*.
10. That incredible flower-covered float was decorated by the people from the Botanical Gardens.

B Rewrite each sentence, changing all active verbs to passive and all passive verbs to active. Add words as needed.

1. The preface to the book was written by Isaac Asimov.
2. The mayor will dedicate the new bridge tomorrow.
3. The citrus crops were destroyed by the unexpected frost.
4. The sports celebrity will be introduced by the principal.
5. Scientists have identified more than one hundred elements.
6. Flu shots will be given by the school nurse.
7. The field trip to the arboretum was spoiled by the heavy rain.
8. A fire behind the stage interrupted last night's rock concert.
9. Jessica easily solved the mystery of the disappearing books.
10. The chef added leftovers to Monday's stew.

C *Write Now* Rewrite the following paragraph. Where appropriate, change passive verbs to active and make any other changes that might improve the description.

(1) On the night of April 12, 1865, the play *Our American Cousin* was seen by President Lincoln at Ford's Theatre. (2) The play was watched by the President and his wife from a special box. (3) The man who crept up behind him could be seen by no one. (4) The pistol was fired by him before anyone could protect the President. (5) The President's head was hit by the bullet, causing him to fall forward. (6) Down from the box jumped the man, breaking his leg; however, his escape was still managed. (7) The man, an actor and Southern sympathizer by the name of John Wilkes Booth, was later caught and shot.

Interior of Ford's Theatre.

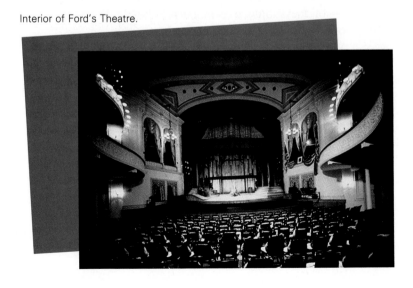

Understanding and Using Mood

The **mood** of a verb is the manner in which a verb expresses an idea. In English there are three moods: the indicative, the imperative, and the subjunctive. The **indicative mood,** which you use most of the time, states a fact or asks a question.

Indicative Mood   The killer whales in Puget Sound *were captured* for commercial exploitation.

Have you ever *seen* a herd of orca whales?

The **imperative mood** is used to give a command or make a request. This mood has only one tense (the present) and only one person (the second).

Imperative Mood   *Look* at this brochure about Big Sur, California.

Please *show* it to your teacher.

The **subjunctive mood** is used (1) to express a wish or a condition that is doubtful or contrary to fact or (2) to express a command or request after the word *that*.

Subjunctive Mood   I wish I *were* king. (expressing a wish)

If I *were* you, I would write that letter. (expressing a condition contrary to fact)

He asked that the books *be returned* promptly. (expressing a command or request after *that*)

We insisted that Fred *paint* the fence green. (expressing a command or request after *that*)

The forms of the subjunctive mood are identical to those of the indicative mood, with the following exceptions:

1. The *s* is omitted from the verb in the third-person singular.

Indicative   He *uses* safety belts.
Subjunctive   We asked that he *use* safety belts.

2. The present tense of the verb *to be* is always *be*.

Andrew asked that the order *be* canceled.

3. The past tense of the verb *to be* is always *were*.

If she *were* President, she would advocate programs to provide increased employment.

Usage Note The subjunctive mood is used mainly in formal contexts. It is seldom used in informal writing or speaking.

Exercise

Write the mood of each italicized verb below.

1. If I *were* rich, I would buy a major league baseball team.
2. The tennis instructor suggested that her student *hold* the racquet with both hands.
3. I wish I *were* a world traveler.
4. Please *help* me carry the amplifiers and drums.
5. How long *have* gondolas *been used* in Venice?
6. The Nez Percé asked that they *be allowed* to settle in Canada.
7. *Don*'t *trip* over those cables!
8. If we *were* never sad, we would not know how to be happy.
9. Though they *be* friendly, we shall remain wary.
10. We always *use* our safety belts.

Part 5
Commonly Confused Verbs

Three pairs of verbs are commonly confused: *lie* and *lay, rise* and *raise,* and *sit* and *set.* Because of the related meanings of each pair, it is important that you distinguish these meanings in order to use the verbs correctly.

Lie and Lay

Here are the principal parts of the verbs *lie* and *lay*.

Present	·Present Participle	Past	Past Participle
lie	(is) lying	lay	(have) lain
lay	(is) laying	laid	(have) laid

Lie is an intransitive verb that means "to rest in a flat position" or "to be in a certain place." *Lie* never has a direct object.

> Our cat always *lies* in the middle of the couch.
> Several books *were lying* on the floor of the closet.

Lay is a transitive verb that means "to place." *Lay* always has a direct object unless the verb is in the passive voice.

| **Active Voice** | The mayor *will lay* the cornerstone for the new gymnasium. (*Cornerstone* is the direct object.) |
| **Passive Voice** | After a long delay, the cornerstone *was* finally *laid.* |

Rise and Raise

Listed below are the principal parts of the verbs *rise* and *raise*.

Present	Present Participle	Past	Past Participle
rise	(is) rising	rose	(have) risen
raise	(is) raising	raised	(have) raised

Rise is an intransitive verb that means "to go upward." *Rise* does not take a direct object.

> The sun *will rise* in another hour.
> The water *has* already *risen* three inches.

Raise is a transitive verb that means "to lift" or "to make something go up." *Raise* always takes a direct object unless the verb is in the passive voice.

Active Voice   The custodian *raises* the flag every morning. (*Flag* is the direct object.)

Passive Voice   Every morning the flag *is raised*.

Sit and Set

Here are the principal parts of the verbs *sit* and *set*.

Present	Present Participle	Past	Past Participle
sit	(is) sitting	sat	(have) sat
set	(is) setting	set	(have) set

Sit is an intransitive verb that means "to occupy a seat." It does not take a direct object.

> Please *sit* next to me on the bus.
> The family *had been sitting* at the airport all night.

Set is a transitive verb that means "to place." *Set* always has a direct object unless the verb is in the passive voice.

Active Voice   The artist *set* a fresh canvas on the easel. (*Canvas* is the direct object.)

Passive Voice   A fresh canvas *was set* on the easel.

Exercises

A Write the correct verb form of the two given in parentheses.

1. Our dog won't (lie, lay) still.
2. The beautiful old chest had (laid, lain) in the attic for years.
3. New tennis courts have been (laid, lain) out in the field.
4. We (lay, laid) our towels on the beach and sat down.
5. The murder weapon was found in a drainage ditch, (laying, lying) in two feet of water.
6. Please (sit, set) those empty cartons in the hall.
7. A group of children were (setting, sitting) on the curb.
8. How long has this coffeepot been (setting, sitting) on the stove?
9. We (sat, set) down and waited for the play to begin.
10. You can (set, sit) the bag of ice in the cooler.
11. Please (raise, rise) the window a few more inches.
12. Their profits have (raised, risen) every year.
13. The dough should (raise, rise) by itself.
14. Someone was (raising, rising) a disturbance outside the election hall before the judges finished the ballot count.
15. Will the sales tax be (raised, risen) again this year?

B *Proofreading* Proofread the following paragraphs for errors in verb usage, as well as other errors in spelling, punctuation, and capitalization. On your paper rewrite the paragraphs correctly.

> In ancient Assyria books were wrote on tablets that were put in clay containers. In order to read the Contents, the containers were broke open with a chisel. Little is knowed about how the greeks

improved on this early method of bookbinding. It is commonly believed, however, that Athenians used a gluelike substance to hold together leaves of parchment or papyrus.

Regular bookbinding begun with the invention of printing. Unweildy containers gived way to covers made of leather. Kings and queens outdone one another in devising luxurious bindings. It become fashonible to emboss a cover with the owner's coat of arms. Sketches of birds and flowers were drawed and then tooled painstakingly onto the leather.

The French Revolution brung the art of bookbinding to a temporery halt. Ornate binding's and coats of arms were considered an insult to the citizenry. One literary revolutionist teared off offending covers and throwed them out the window.

In recent years reader's have chose paperbacks over hard-cover editions an inexpensive paperback can be lain open to hold one's place. It can be red while the reader is setting on a crowded subway or bus or laying on the beach. Nevertheless, their are still people who, once they have saw a beautifully bound book, cannot wait to own it.

Checkpoint *Parts 4 and 5*

A On your paper, write the verbs in the following sentences. Identify each verb according to its voice: *Active* or *Passive*.

1. The dispute was settled by the referee.
2. The annual awards banquet has always been catered by Luigi's Restaurant.
3. Her daily five-mile walk has made Gwen Clark, 95, a neighborhood legend.
4. We have owned the same car for six years.
5. The Youth Council has petitioned for a basketball court at the Community Center.
6. The film adaptation was written by Woody Allen.
7. More than 58,000 names are inscribed on the Vietnam Veterans Memorial in Washington, D.C.
8. The lost city of Troy was found by Heinrich Schliemann, a German archaeologist.
9. They will visit Balboa Park in San Diego.
10. Astronauts' helmets are sprayed with a thin film of gold.

B On your paper, identify the mood of each italicized verb in the following sentences: *Indicative*, *Imperative*, or *Subjunctive*.

1. Someone moved that the nominations *be closed*, but there were several objections from the delegates.
2. Yesterday the moon partially *obscured* the sun.
3. You sound as though your friend *were* the only player on the field today.
4. *Read* the book *Horsefeathers and Other Curious Words* before you write your report on word derivations.
5. Mother talks as if she *were planning* to take more courses in accounting.

C On your paper, write the correct verb form of the two given in parentheses.

1. Most of Alaska (lays, lies) below the Arctic Circle.
2. We wondered how long the expensive watch had (laid, lain) in the pile of leaves.
3. The British Army, under the command of General Cornwallis, (laid, lay) down their arms and surrendered to General Washington and the Continental Army at Yorktown.
4. Rainsford (laid, lay) awake all night plotting his escape from the island and the menacing General Zaroff.
5. (Lay, Lie) the spare tire and the flat on the grass and help me find the hubcap.
6. We (sat, set) the pot of water over the coals and waited for it to come to a boil.
7. We tried to (raise, rise) the cellar door ourselves, but it was too heavy for the two of us.
8. While waiting for the mail truck, we (sat, set) in the shade of an old apple tree.
9. The hikers (sat, set) down their packs and asked for directions to the camping grounds.
10. Dad was (setting, sitting) in the kitchen reading recipes for holiday breads.
11. At the meeting several merchants had (raised, rose) serious objections to the proposed parking meters.
12. As the music played, the snake's head began to (raise, rise) slowly from the basket.
13. Fortunately the water in the reservoir has (raised, risen).
14. I (raised, rose) from my bed at 7:00 A.M. sharp.
15. Have your garage doors ever (raised, risen) by themselves?

Linking
Grammar & Writing

The advent of the mini-cam has made up-to-the-minute and on-the-spot news coverage possible. In years past, people often did not learn of important and exciting events for days or even weeks after they happened. Imagine what it would be like to be a news reporter with a mini-cam crew at a famous event in history. Use one of the suggestions listed below or choose another event you find interesting and write an eyewitness report that describes the action taking place.

> The arrival of the first Conestoga wagon that crossed the country from
> St. Louis to Oregon
> The opening of the Panama Canal
> The sailing of the *Mayflower* from England
> The arrival of the Cherokee Indians in Oklahoma after their journey
> on the Trail of Tears
> The completion of one of the great pyramids of Egypt

Prewriting and Drafting To gather some details, you may wish to briefly research the event you have chosen. You might then prepare a list of active, interesting verbs that will help you to accurately capture the scene and "show" it to your readers. As you draft, remember that the time limit for mini-cam features is often short. Strive for an attention-getting opener and arrange details so that the action is covered both quickly and logically.

Revising and Proofreading Remember that you are reporting on-the-spot. Check to see that your verb tenses are appropriate and consistent. Can you make the action more forceful and direct by changing any passive voice verbs to active voice? Can you improve the order or number of details that you provide? Although the viewing audience will not read your report, a written copy must go to your news chief—a very demanding editor. Be sure spelling, capitalization, and punctuation are correct.

Additional Writing Topic In both speaking and writing we often confuse the words *lie*, meaning "to be in a horizontal position"; *lie*, meaning "to tell an untruth"; and *lay*, meaning "to put or place something." Test your knowledge of *lie* and *lay*. Compose a modern fable about a bricklayer who is given to telling untruths. Write the tale first in the present tense; then rewrite it in the past tense.

Word Blends

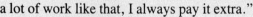

A fter Alice stepped into a new world in Lewis Carroll's *Through the Looking Glass*, she had a conversation with a famous language expert—Humpty Dumpty. "You seem very clever at explaining words, sir," said Alice. "Would you kindly tell me the meaning of the poem called 'Jabberwocky'?"

One by one, Mr. Dumpty explained the strange words in that nonsense poem. *Slithy*, for example, is a combination of *lithe* and *slimy*. *Mimsy* combines *miserable* and *flimsy*. "You see, it's like a portmanteau—there are two meanings packed up into one word," he said. A portmanteau is a large suitcase with two compartments. Humpty Dumpty's analogy has provided a common term for word blends—portmanteau words.

Blends have been a part of the language for centuries. Early examples include *glimmer*, a combination of *gleam* and *shimmer*, from the 1400's, and *clash* (*clap* plus *crash*) from the 1500's. Some of the blends Lewis Carroll contributed to English include *squawk* (*squeak* plus *squall*) and *chortle* (*chuckle* plus *snort*). More recent blends are *brunch* (*breakfast* and *lunch*), *smog* (*smoke* and *fog*), and *motel* (*motor* and *hotel*).

Just as more information can be packed into sentences by combining them, more information can be packed into words by creating blends. As Humpty Dumpty noted, however, "When I make a word do a lot of work like that, I always pay it extra."

Chapter 5

Application and Review

A Using Verbs Correctly Choose the correct verb form of those given in parentheses.

1. Juana has (gone, went) to the library to use the copying machine.
2. Years ago, automobiles (cost, costed) much less to produce.
3. The cat (torn, tore) a large hole in the newspaper.
4. That blister on my heel has (hurt, hurted) for days.
5. My parakeet must be sick; it hasn't (sang, sung) for a week.
6. Laura has (brought, brung) pumpkin pie for Thanksgiving dinner.
7. Our dog Zap has always (wore, worn) a collar.
8. Osaka has (broke, broken) the school record for diving.
9. A dinner bell was (rang, ringed, rung) to call the campers.
10. The candidate (shook, shaked) hands with everyone.
11. Tim (flung, flang, flinged) a dart at the target.
12. My new shirt (shrank, shrunk) two sizes in the clothes dryer.
13. Lost in the desert, Connors had (drank, drunk) no water for days.
14. We should have (knowed, known) that the weather would be bad.
15. A ten dollar bill (lay, laid) on the sidewalk.
16. An unexpected southwest wind (rose, raised) the temperature.
17. Please (lie, lay) your jacket on the couch so I can mend it.
18. The bricklayer (sat, set) the bricks in neat rows.
19. Ryan (sat, set) patiently in the dentist's chair.
20. Emily (rose, raised) her eyebrows in disapproval.

B Recognizing Verb Tenses and Forms Write the italicized verbs on your paper. Tell what tense each is. Also tell which verbs are in the progressive and emphatic forms.

1. Tim *will be helping* with the school directory.
2. Thousands of years ago, the Sahara *was* lush and green.
3. Lisa *tries* to write in her journal every day.
4. It *has been determined* that the first motorist ran a red light.
5. I *do want* to go with you, but I promised to wash my grandfather's car this afternoon.
6. It looked as though Miriam *had been waiting* for hours.
7. The United Nations *serves* as a forum for international opinions.
8. Steve *did rake* the leaves, but the wind has blown them all back into the yard again.

9. If you practice breathing correctly, your singing voice *will become* stronger.
10. Eating yogurt for breakfast *is getting* to be a habit.

C Understanding the Forms of Verbs
Rewrite the following sentences, changing the verb to the form shown in parentheses. Add or delete words as necessary.

1. Kareem Abdul-Jabbar constantly moved up and down the court. (present progressive)
2. Poachers have drastically reduced the black rhinoceros population in Kenya. (passive)
3. During the speech, no one applauded. (past progressive)
4. The astronauts spend many hours in a weightless environment. (future perfect)
5. The abusive football player was removed from the game by the frustrated umpire. (active)
6. I find chess more challenging than checkers. (present emphatic)
7. Karen and her brother are debating the issue. (past)
8. José's life was saved by Elise's knowledge of CPR. (active)
9. The linesman called the serve out of bounds. (past perfect)
10. The trains pick up new cars at the freight yards. (future)
11. Balboa the chimpanzee was often fed peanuts by visitors to the zoo. (active)
12. I think the critic was correct when he said that movie should be rated *R*. (past emphatic)

D Recognizing the Mood of Verbs
On your paper, identify the mood of each italicized verb in the following sentences.

1. *Stop* talking and listen to this weather bulletin.
2. If I *were* Marcia, I'd at least consider the suggestion.
3. The shape of the hair follicle *determines* whether a person has straight, wavy, or curly hair.
4. *Remember* to leave by 4:00 P.M. if you want to avoid rush hour traffic.
5. Andrew asked that the order *be canceled*.
6. When *did* you *discover* that your book bag was missing?
7. A British sea captain named Matthew Webb *was* the first person to swim across the English Channel.
8. Pandas *are* not actually bears.
9. He *requested* that Mary remove her car.
10. *Go* straight home and take care of that cold.

6

Subject and Verb Agreement

*Y*ou probably wouldn't try to squeeze three people into one pair of jeans. Similarly, good writers don't try to fit a compound subject with a singular verb because they know that this mismatch would result in a clumsy sentence that is difficult to understand.

In this chapter you will learn how to make subjects and verbs agree in number so that your meaning can be clearly understood.

Agreement in Number

The **number** of a word indicates whether the word is singular or plural. A word is **singular** in number if it refers to one person or thing. A word is **plural** if it refers to more than one person or thing. In English only nouns, pronouns, and verbs can change number.

The subject and verb of a sentence must agree in number.

If the subject of a sentence is singular, its verb must also be singular. If a subject is plural, then its verb must also be plural. This grammatical harmony between the subject and verb is called **subject-verb agreement.**

> The <u>kitten</u> (singular) <u>likes</u> (singular) catnip.
> The <u>kittens</u> (plural) <u>like</u> (plural) catnip.
>
> <u>Kate</u> (singular) <u>has</u> (singular) <u>been practicing</u> every day.
> The <u>girls</u> (plural) <u>have</u> (plural) <u>been practicing</u> every day.

The Number of Subjects and Verbs

The subject of a sentence is almost always a noun or pronoun. Determining the number of a noun or pronoun used as a subject is rarely a problem. By now you are familiar with the singular and plural forms of nouns and pronouns.

Except for *be,* the singular and plural forms of verbs should also cause little difficulty. Verbs show a difference between singular and plural only in the third person present tense. The third person singular present form ends in *s*.

Verb Forms

Singular		Plural	
I	sing	we	sing
you	sing	you	sing
he, she (Maria), it	**sings**	they (the twins)	sing

Grammar Note Nouns ending in *s* are usually plural, whereas verbs ending in *s* are usually singular.

Singular and Plural Forms of *Be* The verb *be* presents special problems in agreement because this verb does not follow any of the usual verb patterns. In the chart below, note that *be* has special forms for the singular and plural in both the present and past tenses and in all three persons.

Forms of Be

	Present Tense		Past Tense	
	Singular	*Plural*	*Singular*	*Plural*
First Person	I am	we are	I was	we were
Second Person	you are	you are	you were	you were
Third Person	he, she, it is	they are	he, she, it was	they were

Usage Note The most common errors involving the verb *be* are *you was*, *we was*, and *they was*. Avoid such nonstandard English in your speaking and writing.

Exercise

On your paper, write the form of the verb that agrees in number with the subject of each of the following sentences. Then tell whether the verb form is singular or plural.

> *Example*   Two dogs (has, have) climbed over the fence.
> have, plural

1. Francisco de Goya's later paintings (is, are) grotesque, satirical, and somber in color.
2. They (was, were) among the first to visit the prehistoric caves in southern France.
3. Halley's Comet (appears, appear) every seventy-five years.
4. Several dolphins (was, were) washed up on the beach.
5. We (has, have) always lived within an hour's drive of the ocean.
6. You (was, were) explaining the last geometry problem to me before the telephone rang.
7. My new record (was, were) melting on the radiator.
8. That umpire (need, needs) to have his eyesight checked.
9. Those German tourists (appear, appears) lost.
10. Those students (is, are) members of the new karate club.

Part 2
Words Between Subject and Verb

A verb agrees only with its subject.

Occasionally, a word or group of words comes between the subject and the verb. Even though another word may be closer to the verb than the subject is, the verb must still agree in number with its subject. When words come between the subject and the verb, identify the subject and make sure the verb agrees with it.

> The speakers on that car stereo are not working properly. (*Speakers*, not *stereo*, is the subject.)
>
> The plant with purple blossoms is an aster. (*Plant*, not *blossoms*, is the subject.)

The words *with, together with, along with, as well as,* and *in addition to* are prepositions. A phrase beginning with these prepositions does not affect the number of the subject.

> That country singer, along with his band, has been on tour for three months. (*Has* agrees with the singular subject *singer*.)
>
> The Prime Minister, together with her top aides, is visiting the United Nations. (*Is* agrees with the singular subject *Prime Minister*.)

Exercises

A On your paper, write the subject of each sentence. Then write the form of the verb that agrees in number with the subject.

1. The most poignant scenes in the play *Our Town* (occurs, occur) in Act Three.
2. The first clock to strike the hours (was, were) made in 1754.
3. Training, as well as courage, (is, are) needed to make an expert mountain climber.
4. The age of those huge sequoia trees (is, are) hard to believe.
5. The quarterback, as well as the offensive linemen, (is, are) planning an extra practice session.
6. The pilot, in addition to the crew, always (has, have) your safety and comfort in mind.
7. The high cost of repairs usually (comes, come) as a surprise.
8. Sir Edmund Hillary, along with Tenzing Norgay, (was, were) the first to climb Mt. Everest.
9. The decision of the umpires (was, were) loudly disputed.
10. Reports of flooding along the Ohio River (has, have) been exaggerated by the media.

B Rewrite the following sentences correcting all errors in subject-verb agreement. If a sentence is correct, write *Correct*.

1. The president of the company, along with her assistant, plan to fly to South Africa for meetings with the government.
2. Aid for the victims are being coordinated by the Red Cross.
3. The ultraviolet rays of the sun is widely known to have harmful effects on the skin.
4. The scientist's report, together with the photographs, is very convincing.
5. Several tenants in the apartment complex wants to know what to do in case of an earthquake.
6. The lights in the valley looks like distant stars.
7. Lee Iacocca, along with several other top business leaders, are speaking at the convention.
8. Our Doberman, along with her three pups, has been relocated in the basement.
9. The purpose of the Second Continental Congress in 1776 was to decide whether to declare independence from Britain.
10. In recent years the number of videocassette rentals have exceeded the number of books checked out from public libraries.

Part 3
Compound Subjects

Use a plural verb with most compound subjects joined by *and*.

> Both <u>aluminum</u> and <u>copper</u> <u>are</u> excellent conductors of heat.
> How <u>do</u> your <u>aunt</u> and <u>uncle</u> <u>like</u> living in Albuquerque?

Use a singular verb with a compound subject joined by *and* that is habitually used to refer to a single thing.

> <u>Macaroni and cheese</u> <u>is</u> a favorite dish in our house.

Use a singular verb with a compound subject that is preceded by *each, every*, or *many a*.

> Each <u>car</u> and <u>truck</u> in the lot <u>is</u> on sale this week.
> Every <u>student</u> and <u>teacher</u> <u>has been tested</u> for meningitis.

When the words in a compound subject are joined by *or* or *nor*, the verb agrees with the subject nearer the verb.

> Either my <u>mother</u> or my <u>father</u> <u>drops</u> me off at school in the morning. (The singular verb *drops* agrees with *father*, the subject nearer the verb.)
> A <u>novel</u> or two <u>plays</u> <u>meet</u> this semester's reading requirements. (The plural verb *meet* agrees with *plays*, the subject nearer the verb.)
> Neither the arresting <u>officers</u> nor the <u>commissioner</u> <u>wants</u> to make a statement to the press. (The singular verb *wants* agrees with *commissioner*, the subject nearer the verb.)

Exercises

A On your paper, write the form of the verb that agrees in number with the subject of each of the following sentences.

1. Neither the train nor the airlines (runs, run) on schedule during severe weather.
2. The chairs and the table (was, were) loaded with pumpkins just before Halloween.
3. Every man and woman voting in the election (has, have) an obligation to learn about the candidates.
4. Either Dad or Mother (has, have) left the front door open.
5. The horse and buggy (is, are) associated with an era that was slower-paced and less complicated.

6. (Is, Are) either pen or pencil acceptable on this application?
7. Two textbooks and a notebook (was, were) lying on the table.
8. A lifeguard or the swimming coach (is, are) always on duty.
9. Many a boy or girl (has, have) enjoyed books by Dr. Seuss.
10. Ham and eggs (is, are) my favorite weekend breakfast.

B On your paper, write the form of the verb that agrees in number with the subject of each of the following sentences.

1. During the 1970's Frank Shorter and Bill Rodgers (was, were) America's premier marathon runners.
2. An Olympic gold medal in 1972 and a silver medal in 1976 (was, were) Shorter's top achievements.
3. The Boston Marathon and the New York Marathon (was, were) the sites of Rodgers's finest victories.
4. Hard work and dedication (goes, go) into the making of a runner.
5. Two short, fast workouts or one long, slow run (makes, make) up the daily training routine of most competitive marathoners.
6. Neither inclement weather nor minor injuries (prevents, prevent) world-class runners from accomplishing their mileage quota—as much as twenty miles per day.
7. Every major marathon and small town race (poses, pose) the same challenge—to run as hard as possible for as long as possible.
8. High school track and field (is, are) where most marathoners get their start.
9. Many a young runner and future Olympian (has, have) been inspired by Shorter and Rodgers.
10. Today Shorter and Rodgers (continues, continue) to race; neither fame nor fortune (has, have) diminished their enthusiasm.

c *Write Now* Think of two athletes, teams, performers, movies, or authors that you can compare. Write a paragraph about the likenesses and differences between the two. In your comparison use some sentences with compound subjects. Begin at least one sentence with *either* or *neither* and one with *both*.

Checkpoint *Parts 1, 2, and 3*

A On your paper, write the form of the verb that agrees in number with the subject of each of the following sentences.

1. The curators at the museum (has, have) asked for funds.
2. Several paintings in the art gallery (is, are) being restored.
3. Neither wolves nor coyotes (lives, live) in this area.
4. Every player and coach (runs, run) ten laps after practice.
5. Either an agent or a business manager (advises, advise) a performer on every contract.
6. Jerry, together with his cousins, (is, are) buying a snowmobile.
7. The juice, along with the sandwiches, (is, are) in the basket.
8. Performers in a circus (works, work) long hours.
9. A doe and a fawn (was, were) grazing in the meadow.
10. Fish and chips (is, are) a popular snack in London.

B Rewrite the following sentences correcting all errors in subject-verb agreement. If a sentence is correct, write *Correct*.

1. Despite the law, several employees of the city lives outside the city limits.
2. Neither the audience nor the actors was aware of the mishap behind the stage.
3. Has the demand for more computer courses been met?
4. Plants in a shady area usually needs less water.
5. Tacos, my favorite food, is served every Wednesday.
6. The quality of these photographs are exceptionally good.
7. The boxer, as well as his trainers, live at the camp.
8. Three farmhands and the cook share the bunkhouse.
9. Neither the President nor his press secretary were responsible for the news leak.
10. Either the counselor or the coaches has been in touch with the college scouts.

Part 4
Indefinite Pronouns as Subjects

Some indefinite pronouns are always singular; some are always plural. Others may be either singular or plural.

Singular Indefinite Pronouns

another	either	neither	other
anybody	everybody	nobody	somebody
anyone	everyone	no one	someone
anything	everything	nothing	something
each	much	one	

Neither of the dressing rooms is available right now.
Everybody plans to attend the rodeo.

Plural Indefinite Pronouns

both	few	many	several

Use a plural verb with a plural indefinite pronoun.

Several in the class were excellent writers.
Both of the dancers were injured.

Singular or Plural Indefinite Pronouns

all	enough	most	plenty
any	more	none	some

These indefinite pronouns are singular when they refer to one thing. They are plural when they refer to several things.

Singular	Most of the ice cream <u>has melted</u>. (*Most* refers to one quantity of ice cream.)
	<u>Some</u> of the forest <u>was destroyed</u> by the fire. (*Some* refers to one portion of the forest.)
Plural	<u>Most</u> of the ice cream cones <u>are gone</u>. (*Most* refers to several ice cream cones.)
	<u>Some</u> of the trees <u>were</u> hundreds of years old. (*Some* refers to several trees.)

Exercises

A On your paper, write the subject of each of the following sentences. Then write the form of the verb that agrees in number with the subject.

1. Several of the station's disc jockeys (was, were) at the benefit for the homeless shelter.
2. Most of the programs on television (is, are) situation comedies.
3. Only one of the newspapers (has, have) covered the arson story.
4. All of the giant turkey (was, were) eaten in two hours.
5. Neither of the stock car racers (was, were) injured in the collision.
6. Both of the warring countries (has, have) finally come to the peace table in Geneva.
7. (Has, Have) either of the presidential candidates spoken about cuts in the defense budget?
8. Obviously, one of the witnesses (was, were) telling a lie.
9. This year some of the teams (has, have) new uniforms.
10. Many of the old houses in this block (is, are) being renovated.

B Rewrite the following sentences correcting all errors in subject-verb agreement. If a sentence is correct, write *Correct*.

1. Most of her jokes goes over like lead balloons.
2. Few of my friends knows the real me.
3. According to a recent study, one out of two defectors eventually return to his or her homeland.
4. Neither of these chemistry experiments have produced the desired effects.
5. One of the engines on the jet were smoking.
6. Each of the balloons carry scientific equipment.
7. Everyone in the wedding pictures are grinning happily.
8. Neither of these brands are the one I want.
9. Several of our listeners has called the radio station.
10. All of the workers have gone on strike.

c *Write Now* Your pep club is holding a recycled sporting goods sale to raise money for new basketball uniforms. The club has received piles of used gloves, skates, skis, balls, shoulder pads, and other equipment. You are to report to the club on the number and condition of some of the sale items. Write your report using indefinite pronouns as the subjects of several sentences. For example: We have fifteen footballs. A *few* of them are in good shape, but *many* have punctures and need patching. *Some* of these footballs are totally worthless and should be thrown away.

Part 5
Other Agreement Problems

There are several other situations where problems in subject-verb agreement may arise.

Inverted Sentences

Problems in agreement often occur in inverted sentences beginning with *here* and *there*; in questions beginning with words such as *why*, *where*, and *what*; and in inverted sentences beginning with a phrase.

Even when the subject comes after the verb, it still determines whether the verb should be singular or plural. Study the examples on the following page.

Incorrect	Here is the designs for the homecoming float.
Correct	Here are the designs for the homecoming float.

Incorrect	There is two *t*'s in "regretted."
Correct	There are two *t*'s in "regretted."

Incorrect	Who is those tall people in the parking lot?
Correct	Who are those tall people in the parking lot?

Incorrect	From out of the dark forest comes two hideous dragons.
Correct	From out of the dark forest come two hideous dragons.

Usage Note The contractions *here's*, *there's*, *what's*, and *where's* contain the singular verb *is*. Use them only with singular subjects.

Incorrect	There's my new golf clubs.
Correct	There are my new golf clubs.

Incorrect	What's the math assignments for next week?
Correct	What are the math assignments for next week?

Sentences with Predicate Nominatives

Use a verb that agrees in number with the subject, not with the predicate nominative.

Mother's main interest is computers. (*Interest* is the subject and takes a singular verb.)

Computers are Mother's main interest. (*Computers* is the subject and takes a plural verb.)

Running in the Olympics was her dream and her goal. (*Running in the Olympics* is the subject and takes a singular verb.)

Sentences with Don't *and* Doesn't

Use *doesn't* with singular subjects and with the personal pronouns *he, she*, and *it*. Use *don't* with plural subjects and with the personal pronouns *I, we, you*, and *they*.

Singular	Doesn't the bus stop at this corner?
	It doesn't run regularly on weekends.

Plural	Don't the buses run on Saturday?
	They don't stop here on weekends.

Grammar Note Remember that *not* and its abbreviation *n't* are adverbs—not part of the verb.

Exercise

On your paper, write the form of the verb that agrees in number with the subject of each of the following sentences.

1. Why (doesn't don't) he want to join the club?
2. There (was, were) many unusual exhibits at the new reptile house in the renovated zoo.
3. To the right of the entrance (was, were) a vending machine and a well-used video game.
4. (There's, There are) two gallons of cider in the refrigerator.
5. Here (comes, come) the best archers in the competition.
6. (Where's, Where are) the chopsticks I left on the counter?
7. (Doesn't, Don't) the wind sound especially wild tonight?
8. (Here's, Here are) the pamphlets you lent me for my report.
9. Down into the underwater cave (swims, swim) Jacques Cousteau and his assistant.
10. Their biggest drawback (is, are) their combination of inexperience and indifference.
11. Through this door (passes, pass) the lawmakers of our nation.
12. (Where's, Where are) the wigs and rubber noses for the skit?
13. The task of the expedition (was, were) to establish a base camp and to begin scientific observations.
14. In the middle of the garden (stands, stand) an ineffective scarecrow and a dozen hungry blackbirds.
15. (What are, What's) the weather predictions for this week?

Collective Nouns as Subjects

A **collective noun** names a group or collection of people or things: *family, choir, crew, herd, faculty.* Depending on its meaning in a sentence, a collective noun may take a singular or plural verb. If a collective noun refers to a group acting together as one unit, use a singular verb. If a collective noun refers to members or parts of a group acting individually, use a plural verb.

Singular   The team is the best in the history of our school. (acting as a unit)

Plural   The team were hurriedly dressing for the game. (acting individually)

Singular   The council has scheduled a meeting for Thursday. (acting as a unit)

Plural   The council have disagreed on the date. (acting individually)

Singular Nouns with Plural Forms

Some nouns are plural in form but are regarded as singular in meaning. That is, they end in *s* as most plural nouns do, but they do not stand for more than one thing: *news*, *mumps*, *mathematics*. Therefore, they take a singular verb.

> The stock market news was encouraging.
> Mumps is more serious for adults than for children.

Other nouns end in *s* and take a plural verb even though they refer to one thing or one unit: *scissors*, *pliers*, *trousers*, *congratulations*.

> Where are the pliers?
> Congratulations are in order.

Some nouns that end in *s* may be either singular or plural, depending on their meaning in the sentence: *ethics*, *economics*, *civics*, *politics*, *athletics*. When plural, these words are often preceded by a possessive form or a modifier.

Singular   Ethics consists of a set of values.
Plural   Their ethics are sometimes questionable.

The name of a country or an organization is singular even though it may be plural in form.

> The Philippines consists of thousands of islands and islets.
> The United Nations has televised most of today's sessions.

Titles and Groups of Words as Subjects

Use a singular verb with a title.

The title of a book, play, short story, article, film, TV program, musical composition, or work of art is singular even though it may be plural in form.

> *The Orphans* is the story of twins who attract misfortune.
> *David and Goliath* was painted for the King of France in 1295.

Use a singular verb with any group of words that refers to a single thing or thought.

> What we need is votes.
> "Because I said so" is a popular phrase.
> Canoeing down the Wolf River was definitely the highlight of my
>   family's summer.

Words of Amount and Time as Subjects

Words that refer to amounts are usually singular.

Use a singular verb with nouns or phrases that refer to a period of time, a weight, a measurement, a fraction, or an amount of money.

> Five <u>hours</u> <u>seems</u> a long time to wait.
> One hundred <u>pounds</u> of bird seed <u>is</u> in that container.
> Ten <u>yards</u> of material <u>is</u> enough for the backdrop.
> <u>Two-thirds</u> of the money <u>has</u> already <u>been raised</u>.
> A hundred <u>dollars</u> <u>is</u> too much for that jacket.

Use a plural verb when the subject refers to a period of time or an amount that is thought of as a number of separate units.

> Two <u>hours</u> <u>remain</u> before lift-off.
> Three <u>quarters</u> <u>were jingling</u> in my pocket.

Exercises

A On your paper, write the form of the verb that agrees in number with the subject of each of the following sentences.

1. Mowing her neighbors' lawns (was, were) Sue Ellen's summer job.
2. The relief party (was, were) nearly at the ledge when the rock slide began.
3. Last year home economics (was, were) offered as an elective.
4. The social dynamics in this big family (is, are) fascinating for an outsider to watch.
5. Two thousand (seem, seems) a low estimate for the number of spectators at the parade.
6. The East Indies (was, were) once an important source of European wealth.
7. "War of the Worlds" (was, were) written by H. G. Wells.
8. Two-thirds of the wheat crop (was, were) never harvested.
9. The jury (was, were) arguing over the final piece of evidence in the trial of the former governor.
10. Six quarts of milk (are, is) what we ordered; we received five.
11. Whatever you said to your sisters (is, are) forgiven now.
12. With its new strategy, the cycling team (has, have) been winning more consistently.
13. Genetics (has, have) become a controversial topic.
14. Three cockroaches (is, are) living in my locker.
15. The scissors (has, have) been left on top of the sewing machine.

B The following sentences contain many of the errors in subject-verb agreement that you have studied in this chapter. On your paper, rewrite those sentences correctly. If a sentence does not contain an error, write *Correct*.

1. Among the most famous of modern "monsters" are Nessie, who supposedly swims in the murky waters of Loch Ness in Scotland.
2. The Loch Ness Phenomenon Investigation Bureau, founded in the early 1960's, was established to keep track of information about Nessie.
3. The ethics of this organization is irreproachable.
4. To date, over three thousand sightings has been recorded.
5. Most of the sightings has taken place just before dawn.
6. Nessie's snakelike head, together with its camel-like body, have caused much speculation in the scientific community.
7. There's several theories about Nessie.
8. One scientific group believe that Nessie is a giant eel.
9. Chances of solving the centuries-old mystery has improved with the use of technology.
10. Recent studies, using underwater cameras and a special listening device, has detected moving shadows that are not identifiable.
11. The rewards offered for finding the elusive Nessie total nearly 2.6 million dollars!
12. One scientist, however, has said that he don't want to be there when the mystery is finally unraveled.

c *Proofreading* Proofread the following paragraphs. Rewrite them on your paper, correcting all errors. Pay particular attention to subject-verb agreement.

One man and his small son runs their fingers over the black wall, touching a name. Another kneel and bow his head. A family are placing flowers and a tiny flag at the base of the wall. The people are visitors at the Vietnam Veterans Memorial in Washington d.c.

Maya Ying Lin, chosen from 1421 entries in the contest to create a Vietnam War memorial, were only a 22-year-old architecture student at yale at the time. Maya Lin describes her design: "A rift in the earth, a long, polished black stone wall emerging from and receding into the earth." The Memorial are actually two walls, two leg's of a V, each 250 feet long. Over 57000 names—the killed and missing in the War—is carved in the black granite. The list of soldiers are arranged in the order of their deaths from 1959 to 1975. When the Memorial was dedicated in 1982, there was a public reading of all the engraved names, which took three days.

Politics were an everpresent factor in the controversial Vietnam War. Inevitably, the wall has been controversial also. Some doesn't like the Memorial and would prefer a more traditional statue Most has found it's simple design profoundly moving. The true meaning of the Memorial is clearly expressed by its creator, Maya Lin: "It does not glorify the war or make an antiwar statement. It is a place for private reckoning."

Part 6
Relative Pronouns as Subjects

A relative pronoun is sometimes the subject of an adjective clause (see pages 92–93). To determine whether to use a singular or a plural verb in the clause, you must first determine the number of the relative pronoun. A relative pronoun stands in place of its antecedent (the word to which it refers). If that antecedent is plural, the relative pronoun must be plural. If the antecedent is singular, the relative pronoun must be singular.

A relative pronoun agrees with its antecedent in number.

Singular   She is the candidate who has received the most votes. (*Who* refers to the singular antecedent *candidate*.)

Plural   Here is a list of candidates who have already conceded. (*Who* refers to the plural antecedent *candidates*.)

Singular   Ms. Greene is the only one of the coaches who has run in road races. (Only *one* has run races. *Who* refers to the singular antecedent *one*.)

Plural   Len is one of those people who are always coming late. (*People* are always coming late. *Who* refers to the plural antecedent *people*.)

The problem of agreement arises in the last two sentences because there are two words, either of which might be the antecedent of the relative pronoun. Remember that the verb in the relative clause will agree with the true antecedent of the relative pronoun.

Exercise

On your paper, write the form of the verb that agrees in number with the subject of the adjective clause.

1. Good running shoes are those that (has, have) firm support for the feet.
2. James is the only one who (has, have) finished.
3. Those are the fields that (produces, produce) the most oil.
4. This is the only one of his novels that (is, are) worth reading.
5. My cousin is one of those individuals who (is, are) always finding good in others.

6. Gib is one of the students who (notices, notice) everything going on in class.
7. The elderly gentleman was the only onlooker who (was, were) smiling at the mime.
8. Mr. Marin is the only teacher I know who (calls, call) the roll at the end of class.
9. Veterans Day is one of the holidays that (falls, fall) on Saturday this year.
10. Sarah is one of the drummers who (marches, march) in the band.
11. This is the only one of my teeth that still (aches, ache).
12. Here are two paints of the kind that (resists, resist) moisture best.
13. Joanne is the one person in the group who (is, are) willing to share her record collection.
14. He is the only one of the recently arrived refugees who (speak, speaks) English.
15. There are three members of our class who (has, have) consistently scored 100's on tests.

Checkpoint *Parts 4, 5, and 6*

A On your paper, write the form of the verb that agrees in number with the subject of the sentence.

1. All of the pigeons (gathers, gather) around that feeder.
2. Social studies (was, were) my best class last year.
3. Five dollars (are, is) a lot of money for a movie ticket.
4. *The King and I* (opens, open) this Saturday night.
5. Everyone (seems, seem) upset about plans to expand the airport.
6. Either of these novels (is, are) acceptable for the book report.
7. One out of four Americans (has, have) been on TV at some time.
8. (There's, There are) the new computers I told you about.
9. Visiting China and Tibet (was, were) Teresa's dream.
10. Black holes are objects in space that (doesn't, don't) emit light.
11. The committee (has, have) turned in their ballots.
12. Through the harbor in the glorious sunshine (sails, sail) replicas of the *Niña* and the *Pinta*.
13. (Who are, Who's) the winners of the athletic scholarships?
14. None of the active volcanoes (has, have) erupted this year.
15. Why (was, were) the tightwire performers working without a net?

B On your paper, write the form of the verb that agrees in number with the subject of each sentence.

1. The story of pizza (begins, begin) many hundreds of years ago in Naples, Italy.
2. *Moretum,* a work by the ancient Roman poet Virgil, (gives, give) a description of pizza.
3. This popular food (has, have) many appealing qualities, which (includes, include) convenience, affordability, nutritional value, and good taste.
4. There (is, are) now many regional varieties of pizza.
5. Some of these varieties (is, are) recognized by their distinctive toppings: in Nice, France—black olives; in Naples—mozzarella cheese made from water buffalo milk.
6. Neither of these pizzas, however, (is, are) quite like the Roman pizza, which (has, have) onions, but no tomatoes.
7. The first pizzeria in the United States (was, were) started in New York in 1905.
8. A booming business today (is, are) the pizza delivery services.
9. Over four billion dollars worth of pizza (is, are) sold each year.
10. Each day people in the United States (eats, eat) seventy-five acres of pizza!

Linking
Grammar *&* Writing

A famous Hollywood movie producer wants to film a documentary of a typical day in your life. You have been asked to write a schedule of your activities daily so that the director can prepare for filming. Write a schedule focusing on four typical "scenes" in your day. Describe what you will do and who will be with you in each instance. Make sure that your subjects and verbs agree.

Prewriting and Drafting Choose the day of the week that you want for the filming of the documentary. Then think of your activities on that day, consider the four "scenes" that best typify you, and identify the friends and family members who would be included. For each of your scenes, detail the happenings and note the time. Consider the following example:

> *3:30 P.M.* I come home about now, hungry as a bear. The camera should capture the relief on my face as I open the refrigerator and explore the leftovers.
> *3:45 P.M.* Now I have the radio blasting and I am phoning my friends at the same time. During my phone calls, my younger brother asks me who I'm talking with. He always asks, even though he knows how much it annoys me.

As you draft your schedule, remember to focus on typical activities, the kinds of things you often do, and to use the present tense.

Revising and Proofreading Consider these questions:

1. Do the activities in your schedule represent a typical day?
2. Have you described them in enough detail so that someone who does not know you can understand them?
3. Is the time sequence of your schedule clear and easy to follow?
4. Do all subjects and verbs agree?

Additional Writing Topic Sometimes schools, neighborhoods, communities, social groups, or teams have "personalities." Identify a group that has a very recognizable personality. Write about the people in this group. Discuss their beliefs, habits, behaviors, and attitudes. Write in the present tense, and use indefinite pronouns (*someone, everyone, none, almost, each, every, many, several*) where possible. Make sure that your subjects and verbs agree.

The Cowboy

What could be more American than the cowboys of the Wild West? Whether they are lassoing stampeding mustangs on the range or riding bucking broncos in the rodeo, these buckaroos seem to be American originals. Yet most of the words associated with their world are not original—they were borrowed from other sources.

Buckaroo is a corruption of the Spanish word *vaquero*, the name of the Spanish cattlemen and horse-traders the cowboys encountered on the trails of the West. Spanish is also the source of *lasso*, *stampede* (from *estampida*), *mustang*, *lariat* (from *la reata*), *bronco* (Spanish for "rough" or "unruly"), and *rodeo*.

Even *cowboy* was not born on the range. In England during the 1700's it was a term for boys who tended cattle. Its first use in America came during the Revolutionary War as a derogatory term for Tory soldiers who used cowbells to lure American soldiers and farmers into ambushes. During the Civil War, it was used to describe roustabouts who rustled cattle along the Texas-Mexican border. It also described teen-aged boys who served as drovers on long trail drives because older men had been pressed into service as soldiers.

Finally, after the Civil War, the cowboys of the great Western cattle drives earned their place in history and folklore. Over time, the other meanings have been forgotten, and what is remembered is *cowboy*'s rich and often romanticized connection to the American West.

His First Lesson, Frederic Remington, 1903.

Chapter 6

Application and Review

A Making Subjects and Verbs Agree Choose the correct form of the verb for each sentence.

1. Marc Chagall's intricate and colorful mosaic *Four Seasons* (was, were) installed in Chicago in 1974.
2. My backpack, together with its contents, (weighs, weigh) over twenty pounds.
3. Everyone who (thinks, think) that a reporter's life is romantic should spend time working on a newspaper.
4. There (is, are) some problems that can't be solved without the heip of others.
5. One of the new cars (gets, get) over sixty miles per gallon in highway driving.
6. Hawaii, like Japan, (is, are) actually several islands.
7. One-fourth of the goods that Americans buy (is, are) imported.
8. She (doesn't, don't) care whether anyone approves of her clothes.
9. Out of a mountain in the Black Hills (emerges, emerge) the gigantic sculptured figure of Chief Crazy Horse.
10. Two hundred years of democracy (has, have) made certain changes in the Constitution necessary.
11. His sunglasses (makes, make) him look mysterious.
12. The editor is the person who (decide, decides) which articles to print in each issue.
13. Compassion is one of the qualities that (are, is) necessary in a good leader.
14. Many of the people who (live, lives) in this neighborhood are of Polish ancestry.
15. Pneumatics (deal, deals) with the properties of air and other gases.
16. *A Tangle of Roots* (are, is) a thought-provoking story.
17. One hundred sixty pounds (are, is) the average weight of the players on the opposing team.
18. The lights at the end of the pier (are, is) easily seen at night.
19. A paramedic and a firefighter (was, were) hospitalized yesterday for their injuries.
20. Neither the governor nor her aide (was, were) interviewed on the local evening news.

B Solving Problems in Subject-Verb Agreement Choose the correct form of the verb for each sentence.

1. Salvaging autos (has, have) become a thriving business in the United States.
2. According to recent national figures, there (are, is) at least 29 million cars ten years old or older in this country.
3. Twenty-nine million (represent, represents) a considerable increase from just a few years ago.
4. Each of today's junkyards (has, have) its own personality.
5. Some of the junkyards (sell, sells) only parts for specific models; others (deal, deals) only in hubcaps.
6. Computers, which never would have been seen in a junkyard of old, (keep, keeps) track of the rapidly changing inventory in some newer junkyards.
7. Attractive showrooms, steam-cleaned parts, and the free use of power tools (is, are) offered by some junkyards.
8. At some fancier junkyards, neither couples on dates nor a well-dressed business person (is, are) a strange sight.
9. "The Riches of Wrecks," a recent magazine article, (tell, tells) about one "junkyard" that is contained within a six-story building.
10. Of course, many a junkyard still (has, have) the typical fierce-eyed mongrel keeping watch at the gate, guarding a mountain of rusty cars and old rubber tires.

C Correcting Errors in Subject-Verb Agreement The following passage contains several errors in the agreement of subjects and verbs. Rewrite the paragraph, correcting these errors.

(1) Charlie Brown is one of the characters created by Charles Schultz for his much-loved comic strip. (2) "Peanuts" have been around for over a generation now, and there is hardly anyone who don't feel compassion for the struggles of Charlie Brown. (3) Each of his readers, from children to adults, seem to identify with Charlie's tendency to fail. (4) One of the problems that Charlie often has are getting his kites to fly. (5) There's always trees in the way, and the kite invariably gets caught in one of them—on purpose, Charlie believes. (6) Then there is Charlie's inability to kick a football or win even a single baseball game. (7) Either the kite or sports give Charlie trouble in almost every strip. (8) Charlie's popularity has grown so much that "Peanuts" are now found on television. (9) He don't have to worry about being unloved. (10) Charlie Brown has millions of friends all over the world.

Cumulative Review

Chapters 5 and 6

A Identifying Verb Tenses and Forms Write the italicized verbs on your paper. Tell what tense each is. Also tell which verbs are in the progressive and emphatic forms.

1. By the time he *finishes* all of his schooling, he *will have been studying* for twenty-one years.
2. The young comedian *wanted* to know what *happens* to the socks that *are vanishing* every day in dryers across the country.
3. I *did know* that my shirt was on backwards; I *was* simply *trying* to determine if you *were* sharp enough to see the mistake.
4. Ever since we *moved* here, the bright red leaves of the sumac *have been brightening* the countryside in the autumn.
5. The slow, relentless movement of glaciers *had carved* out those hills centuries ago, long before the river *snaked* its way along the same path that *had been used* by the glaciers.
6. At this time tomorrow, the giraffe *will amble* once again to the feeder where it *will have found* its mid-morning snack.
7. Unicorns *have stirred* the imagination of poets for centuries.
8. If they *do build* the apartment complex, we *will be worrying* about what *will happen* to the current residents.
9. Renoir the artist *told* his son, who *became* a famous filmmaker, that to know people one *needs* to study their hands and faces.
10. "That girl *is* a winner," the admiring coach told her team; "she always *has been* a winner, and she always *will be* a winner."

B Changing the Voice of Verbs On your paper, rewrite the sentences below, changing all the italicized verbs from passive to active or active to passive. Add or change words as needed; you may create additional sentences if you wish.

1. The old maple tree by the courthouse on Vine Street *had been hit* by the stranger's car.
2. After he safely emerged from his car, the confused driver *told* the police his amazing story.
3. His car *had been driven* into the tree by a goblin who had taken control of the steering wheel.
4. The goblin *had entered* the car at a stoplight.

5. The man *was* quickly *pushed* from the steering wheel by the goblin, who seemed determined to drive.
6. After losing control of the steering wheel, the astonished man *stared* at the goblin; he *expected* disaster.
7. Surprisingly, no obstacles *were hit* by the car, because the goblin turned out to be a capable driver.
8. Then, the goblin *was* suddenly *distracted* by an ice-cream truck turning ahead at the corner.
9. The goblin *craved* ice cream, *looked* longingly at the truck, and *smashed* the car into the tree.
10. Discouraged but not hurt, the goblin *flew* after the truck, leaving the man alone to tell his story to the amused police.

C Recognizing the Moods of Verbs On your paper, identify the mood of each italicized verb in the following sentences.

1. If I *were* you, I would certainly call my parents right away to tell them about the errant pumpkin that *crashed* through the kitchen ceiling this afternoon.
2. *Tell* them the truth, even though it sounds like fiction.
3. When they ask that the whole story *be told,* simply recount the scene you *witnessed* when you returned from school.
4. If they do not believe you, have them call the police, who *said* they would explain everything to your parents.
5. They *have fined* the skydivers who *dropped* the pumpkin while playing catch two thousand feet above your house.

D Correcting Errors in Agreement Rewrite the following paragraph to correct all errors in subject and verb agreement.

Leonardo da Vinci, among all the artists of the Renaissance, represent the most diverse range of interests. His versatility has long amazed those admirers of his genius who has studied his work. All of his life's energies was devoted to understanding the world around him, and he did research in mathematics, architecture, music, optics, astronomy, geology, botany, zoology, hydraulics, aeronautics, and anatomy. In fact many seemingly modern inventions, such as the helicopter, was first developed by da Vinci. Even during those times when most of his attention were focused on a single project, he continued to study many different subjects. His work as artist, scientist, and inventor still command interest. If you visit a university today, you will find either art historians or an engineer who are engaged in the study of his work. His genius seems ageless and immortal.

7
Using Pronouns

*F*resh fish and a heaping plate of spaghetti—these dishes may look like the real thing, but look again. They're actually made of plastic. Such "stand-ins" are useful in situations where real food would quickly spoil. For example, in a restaurant-window display, a plate of polymer pasta continues to look appetizing long after real spaghetti would have lost its appeal.

Language has stand-ins too—pronouns. Pronouns take the place of nouns in sentences, yet they also function in specialized ways. In this chapter you will learn about the three cases that mark the specialized use of pronouns and about the relationship of pronouns to the nouns they replace.

The Cases of Pronouns

Pronouns are words that may be used in place of nouns. Pronouns change form, depending on their use in sentences. These changes in pronoun form are called changes in the **case** of the pronouns. There are three cases in English: the **nominative case,** the **objective case,** and the **possessive case.** The personal pronouns are classified below according to case, number (singular and plural), and person (first, second, and third).

Singular

	Nominative	Objective	Possessive
First Person	I	me	my, mine
Second Person	you	you	your, yours
Third Person	he	him	his
	she	her	her, hers
	it	it	its

Plural

	Nominative	Objective	Possessive
First Person	we	us	our, ours
Second Person	you	you	your, yours
Third Person	they	them	their, theirs

The pronouns *who* and *whoever* are classified below according to case.

Nominative	Objective	Possessive
who	whom	whose
whoever	whomever	whosever

Indefinite pronouns change form only in the possessive case. The nominative and objective cases are identical.

Nominative	Objective	Possessive
someone	someone	someone's
everybody	everybody	everybody's
no one	no one	no one's

The pronouns *this, that, these, those, which,* and *what* do not change their forms to indicate case.

The material in this chapter will explain when to use the various case forms of pronouns.

Exercise

Application in Literature List the italicized pronouns in the three passages below. Identify each personal pronoun as first, second, or third person; singular or plural; and nominative, objective, or possessive case. Write only the case for *who* and indefinite pronouns.

(1) Some boys taught *me* to play football. . . . (2) *You* went out for a pass, fooling *everyone*. (3) Best, you got to throw yourself mightily at *someone's* running legs. (4) Either you brought *him* down or you hit the ground flat out on *your* chin. . . . (5) Nothing girls did could compare with *it*.

(1) If in that snowy backyard the driver of the black Buick had cut off *our* heads, Mikey's and *mine,* I would have died happy, for nothing has required so much of *me* since as being chased all over Pittsburgh . . . by this sainted, skinny, furious redheaded man *who* wished to have a word with *us*. (2) *I* don't know how *he* found *his* way back to his car.

(1) *We* girls chafed, whined, and complained under our parents' strictures. (2) The boys waged open war on *their* parents. (3) The boys' pitched battles with *their* parents were legendary; the punishments *they* endured melted *our* hearts.

From *An American Childhood* by Annie Dillard

Past Lives,
Lorie Novak, 1987.

Part 2
Pronouns in the Nominative Case

Like nouns, pronouns can function as both subjects and predicate nominatives.

Pronouns as Subjects

The nominative form of the pronoun is used as the subject of a verb.

When a pronoun is a part of a compound subject, it is often difficult to decide on the appropriate form. To decide which form to use in the compound subject, try each part of the subject separately with the verb.

> Hal and (I, me) kayaked down the Brule. (Hal kayaked; I kayaked, *not* me kayaked.)

The plural forms *we* and *they* sound awkward in many compounds. They can be avoided by rewording the sentence.

Awkward   We and they planned to swim at dawn.
Better   We all planned to swim at dawn.

Pronouns as Predicate Nominatives

A pronoun that follows a linking verb is a **predicate pronoun.**

A predicate pronoun takes the nominative case.

It is often difficult to decide on the pronoun form to use after the verb *be.* Use the nominative case after phrases in which the main verb is a form of *be,* such as *could have been, can be,* and *should be.*

> It *was* **I** whom they called.
> It *must have been* **they** in the sports car.

When the nominative form sounds awkward, reword the sentence.

Awkward   The winner was she.
Better   She was the winner.

Usage Note In informal conversation and writing, it is acceptable to use the objective case after the verb *be* in the sentence *It is me.* For formal writing, however, use the nominative case.

Exercise

Write the correct form of the pronoun for each sentence. Choose from those given in parentheses.

1. Jeff and (I, me) are reporting on scientific explanations for UFO's.
2. At the center of the photo are Stalin, Churchill, and (he, him).
3. How many movies did Humphrey Bogart and (she, her) make?
4. Marty and (he, him) volunteered to fill sandbags.
5. The Warner brothers and (they, them) formed a film company.
6. The three dressed in togas were Pam, Ida, and (I, me).
7. Was it (he, him) who painted the stage set to look like stone?
8. (She, Her) and the officer were having a loud argument about which driver was at fault.
9. When Scott and (they, them) arrived at the South Pole, (they, them) found Amundsen's Norwegian flag already there.
10. We thought it was (he, him) in the clown outfit.

Part 3

Pronouns in the Objective Case

Like nouns, pronouns can also function as objects of verbs, objects of prepositions, or as part of infinitive phrases.

Pronouns as Objects of Verbs

The objective pronoun form is used for a direct or indirect object.

When a pronoun is part of a compound object, it is often difficult to decide on the appropriate form for the pronoun. The compound object may consist of pronouns or both nouns and pronouns.

To decide which pronoun form to use in a compound object, try each part of the object separately with the verb.

Direct Object	The principal wanted to see George and (I, me). (see George; see me, *not* see I)
	Jenny invited both (they, them) and (we, us) to the party. (invited them, *not* invited they; invited us, *not* invited we)
Indirect Object	The counselor gave Janet and (I, me) good advice. (gave Janet; gave me, *not* gave I)

Pronouns as Objects of Prepositions

The objective pronoun form is used as the object of a preposition.

When a pronoun is part of the compound object of a preposition, it is often difficult to decide on the appropriate pronoun form. To determine which form is correct, try each pronoun separately in the sentence.

> Will your sister be going with you and (I, me)? (with you; with me, *not* with I)

Use the objective pronoun forms after the preposition *between*.

> between you and him, *not* between you and he
> between him and me, *not* between he and I

Pronouns with Infinitives

The infinitive is a verb that is preceded by *to*. See pages 78 and 79 for more information about infinitives.

The objective form of the pronoun is used as the subject, object, or predicate pronoun of an infinitive.

> The referee asked *them to observe* the rules. (*Them* is the subject of *to observe*.)
> The team expected the MVP *to be her*. (*Her* is the object of *to be*.)

Exercises

A Write the correct pronoun from those given in parentheses.

1. The Friar secretly married Romeo and (she, her).
2. By working together, Mme. Curie and (he, him) discovered the element radium.
3. Marcus and (I, me) learned how to pack a parachute correctly.
4. (We, Us) did not expect to sit between Amy and (she, her).
5. Ray Bradbury gave Casey and (I, me) an interview.
6. The crowd would not allow (she, her) or (we, us) to speak.
7. The photographer met (he, him) and (I, me) at the finish line.
8. The moratorium gives the union representatives and (they, them) some time to think about further negotiations.
9. Holmes knew that the "ghost" would turn out to be (he, him).
10. Reservations were made for everyone except Russ and (we, us).
11. The voters know it was (they, them) who elected the mayor.
12. Just between you and (me, I), I am terrified of spiders.
13. Evan and (them, they) were feeling a bit squeamish about the dissection of the frog in biology class.
14. It was (him, he) who said that victory was bittersweet.
15. Jerry yelled for Marcia and (I, me) to take cover just as the hail started to fall on (we, us).

B Application in Literature Choose the pronoun that makes each of the following excerpts correct.

1. It was (she, her) who used to come between (I, me) and my paper when I was writing reviews. Virginia Woolf
2. (He, Him) and (I, me) both were afraid of me becoming a sissy—(he, him) perhaps more afraid than I. John Updike
3. We supposed (he, him) to be the leader, because he stood up in full view, swinging his big knife over his head. Rain-in-the-Face
4. The angels, not half so happy in Heaven,
   Went envying (she, her) and (I, me); . . . Edgar Allan Poe
5. Most of (we, us) in the camp were poor boys, or boys who were almost poor. Thomas Sancton
6. From childhood, my sister and (I, me) have had a well-grounded dislike for our friends the birds. Ruth McKenny
7. I had no reason to suppose that I'd see (her, she), or (her, she) (I, me) . . . in that hotel lobby. . . . Milton Mayer
8. Eileen and (me, I) didn't exchange a glance, but we loved each other now. Laurie Lee

c *Write Now* Think about a process that needs at least four people to complete, such as putting up a tent, playing a game, or moving a large piece of furniture or equipment. Then write an explanation of the process. Use at least ten pronouns, including five compound subjects or objects, two compound objects of prepositions, and two pronouns with infinitives.

Checkpoint *Parts 1, 2, and 3*

Write the correct pronoun form from those given in parentheses. Then tell the case of the pronoun you chose.

1. Inspector Clouseau questioned the butler and (they, them).
2. F.D.R. and (he, him) were both governors of New York.
3. The travel agent quoted (they, them) and (we, us) different prices for the same flight.
4. For Lee and (we, us) the fiesta was all work and no fun.
5. Was it (she, her) or her sister Charlotte Brontë who wrote *Wuthering Heights?*
6. We saw (they, them) and their bodyguards after the concert.
7. Neither (we, us) nor Canadians need visas for that country.
8. The party was a surprise for Grandpa and (she, her).
9. With Emily and (I, me), the marine biologist waited for high tide and the running of the small fish called grunion.
10. Just between you and (I, me), I'd love to conduct a symphony orchestra some day.
11. Later on our tour, (she, her) and (I, me) saw the Book of Kells.
12. It must have been (he, him); he was wearing one sequined glove.
13. Early election results indicated the winner would be (she, her).
14. The Clarks and (we, us) are going on a photographic safari.
15. The guide explained to (he, him) and (I, me) that the 3,200-year-old temple at Abu Simbel was built for Ramses II.
16. Do you know (who, whom) was the sculptor of Mt. Rushmore?
17. When will Andrew Wyeth and (they, them) exhibit their paintings?
18. Tom disagrees with Alice and (I, me) that the narwhal can be considered a unicorn.
19. Was it (he, him) who said "Honesty is the best policy"?
20. The drivers' education instructor taught (I, me) and (he, him) how to parallel park.

Part 4
Pronouns in the Possessive Case

Personal pronouns that show ownership use the possessive case. Possessive pronouns can be used to replace nouns or to modify nouns.

The possessive pronouns *mine, ours, yours, his, hers, its,* and *theirs* can be used in place of nouns, as in the following sentences: That is *mine. Yours* is blue.

My, our, your, his, her, its, and *their* are used to modify nouns: That is *my* sweater. *Your* sweater is blue.

You will notice that *his* and *its* are used in either situation.

Punctuation Note Never use an apostrophe with possessive pronouns. Spellings such as *it's* and *he's* indicate a contraction.

Possessive Pronouns Modifying Gerunds

The possessive form of the pronoun is used when the pronoun immediately precedes a gerund.

> *His running* has improved since the last track meet. (*Running* is a gerund functioning as the subject. The possessive form *his* modifies *running*.)

Remember that present participles, like gerunds, are verbals that end in *-ing*. However, the possessive case is not used before a participle. The nominative or objective case of a pronoun is used before a participle.

> We saw *him running* toward the finish line. (*Running* is a participle modifying *him*.)

To distinguish between a gerund and a present participle, remember this: if the *-ing* word is used as a noun, it is a gerund; if it is used as a modifier, it is a participle. It may also be helpful to ask yourself *Who?* or *What?* of the verb in the sentence.

> We dislike *their playing* the stereo at midnight. (What did we dislike? We disliked the playing. Therefore, *playing* is a gerund, the object of the verb *dislike*. The possessive pronoun *their* should be used.)
> We heard *them playing* the stereo at midnight. (What did we hear? We heard them. Therefore, *playing* is a participle modifying *them*.)

Exercise

Choose the correct pronoun from those given in parentheses.

1. (Him, His) giving up the throne for "the woman he loved" was totally unexpected.
2. Will you use Judy's ticket or (her, hers)?
3. I didn't like (him, his) sneaking in through the back door after curfew.
4. Is the tackle box (your, yours) or his?
5. If you like (me, my) cooking, please stay for dinner.
6. This is (their, theirs) listing of the property.
7. (Their, Them) exploring and mapping the northwestern United States in the early 1800's made Meriwether and Clark famous.
8. Mother doesn't want (you, your) talking and laughing to disturb the sleeping baby.
9. Parking your car in that restricted area will result in (you, your) getting a ticket.
10. (His, Him) dancing of the *Nutcracker* is almost as good as Baryshnikov's.

Part 5
Problems in Pronoun Usage

Certain situations involving pronouns often cause confusion.

Who *and* Whom *in Questions and Clauses*

The pronouns *who* and *whom* are used to ask questions or to introduce clauses.

To use *who* and *whom* in questions, it is necessary to understand how the pronoun is functioning in the question.

Who is the nominative form of the pronoun. It is used as the subject of the verb or as a predicate pronoun.

Whom is the object form of the pronoun. It is used as the direct object or as the object of a preposition.

> *Who* wrote this novel? (*Who* is the subject.)
> *Whom* will you choose? (*Whom* is the direct object of *choose.*)

The pronouns *who, whoever, whom, whomever,* and *whose* may be used to introduce noun or adjective clauses. These pronouns also have a function within the clause.

Who and **whoever** are nominative case pronouns and can act as the subject or predicate pronoun in a clause.

Whom and **whomever** are in the objective case and can act as the direct object or the object of a preposition in a clause.

The following steps and examples can help to eliminate confusion about the use of *who* and *whom* in subordinate clauses:

1. Isolate the subordinate clause.
2. Determine how the pronoun in question is used in that clause.
3. If the pronoun is used as a subject or predicate pronoun, choose *who* or *whoever*. If the pronoun is used as an object, choose *whom* or *whomever*.

> Galileo Galilei is the scientist *(who, whom)* invented the thermometer.
> 1. The adjective clause is *(who, whom) invented the thermometer*.
> 2. The pronoun is acting as the subject within the clause.
> 3. *Who* is in the nominative case and the correct choice.

> Pearl Buck is an author *(who, whom)* I admire.
> 1. The adjective clause is *(who, whom) I admire*.
> 2. The pronoun is acting as the direct object within the clause.
> 3. *Whom* in the objective case is the correct choice.

> A medal was given to *(whoever, whomever)* finished the race.
> 1. *(Whoever, Whomever) finished the race* is the noun clause acting as the object of the preposition *to*.
> 2. The pronoun is acting as the subject within the clause.
> 3. The nominative pronoun *whoever* is the correct choice.

***Whose* functions as the possessive pronoun within a clause.**

This is the artist *whose painting I bought.* (*Whose* is a possessive pronoun modifying *painting* in the clause.)

Exercises

A Write the correct pronoun from those given in parentheses.

1. (Who, Whom) knows how to figure skate well enough to do a Mohawk turn?
2. The student (who, whom) found the watch that I lost yesterday turned it in at the office.
3. Chris is the gymnast (who, whose) specialty is the rings.
4. For (who, whom) does Jeff baby-sit on Thursday nights?
5. Perry, (whoever, whomever) taught you how to trim a sail deserves a medal.
6. The President (who, whom) initiated the New Deal was Franklin Roosevelt.
7. Only the judges know (who, whom) the winner will be.
8. Ask (whomever, whoever) you want.
9. With (who, whom) will you travel?
10. The police asked everyone in the neighborhood (who, whom) the troublemakers were.
11. (Whoever, Whomever) needs advice should talk to a friend or guidance counselor.
12. (Who, Whom) was your report about?
13. Persephone was the woman (who, whom) Hades carried away to the underworld.
14. No one (who, whom) was in the audience will ever forget the singer's farewell performance.
15. Doug, (whom, whose) father repairs stereos, has volunteered to fix the speakers in the auditorium.

B Write the correct pronoun from those given in parentheses.

1. The inventor (who, whom) got movies off to a roaring start was Thomas Edison.
2. It was Edison, (who, whom) we now consider a genius, who introduced the kinetoscope in 1894.
3. With this instrument, (whoever, whomever) had a nickel could watch a film by peering through a viewer and turning a crank.
4. Two years later, the Lumière brothers, (who, whom) worked in Paris, invented a projector.

5. Consequently, theater owners, (whom, whose) main objective was making a profit, could collect ticket money from (whoever, whomever) they could crowd into their theaters.
6. It was Warner Brothers (who, whom) presented the first all-sound film in 1923.
7. Many actors (whom, who) starred in silent films faced a dilemma.
8. Actors (whom, whose) voices didn't match the audience's expectations were out of jobs.
9. For example, silent screen heartthrob Rudolph Valentino, (who, whom) was worshiped by millions of fans, quickly lost his popularity when women heard his high, thin voice.
10. Lillian Gish was one actress (whom, who) audiences loved in both silent films and "talkies."

Rudolph Valentino and Vilma Banky in the 1926 film *Son of the Sheik.*

Pronouns with Appositives

The pronouns *we* and *us* are often followed by an appositive, a noun that identifies the pronoun. Phrases such as *we students* or *us players* can cause confusion when you are trying to choose the correct pronoun. To decide whether to use the nominative case *we* or the objective case *us* in this type of construction, drop the appositive, or noun, and read the sentence without it.

(We, Us) girls can bring the lunch. (We can bring the lunch, *not* Us can bring the lunch.)
The problem was easy for (we, us) girls. (for us, *not* for we)

Exercise

Write the correct pronoun from those given in parentheses.

1. (We, Us) Americans can learn a great deal from other cultures.
2. The law guarantees the rights of (we, us) students.
3. Do you think that (we, us) two will have the same class?
4. There is no such thing as a junk car to (we, us) antique auto enthusiasts.
5. Only (we, us) two were asked to read the part of Macbeth.
6. The pianist played warm-up scales for (we, us) newcomers.
7. (We, Us) fans were not surprised by the Bears' record.
8. There is a private rehearsal for (we, us) flute players.
9. Did you know that (we, us) twins are taking part in a nationwide study on inherited versus acquired learning?
10. The candidate who won the mayoral election was grateful to (we, us) loyal supporters.

Pronouns as Appositives

You have learned how to use pronouns correctly when they are followed by appositives. Now you will see how to use pronouns when they, themselves, are appositives.

The form of a pronoun used as an appositive is determined by the use of the noun to which it is in apposition.

> The delegates, *Tony* and *I*, want your support. (*Tony* and *I* are in apposition to *delegates*, which is the subject of *want*. The nominative form *I* is required.)
>
> For the two producers, *Margo* and *him*, the show was a hit. (*Margo* and *him* are in apposition to *producers*, which is the object of the preposition *for*. Therefore, the objective form of the pronoun, *him*, is required.)
>
> We gave the neighbors, *Toby* and *her*, a housewarming gift. (*Toby* and *her* are in apposition to *neighbors*, which is the indirect object of *gave*. Therefore, the objective form of the pronoun, *her*, is required.)

To determine which form of the pronoun to use in apposition, try the appositive by itself with the verb or preposition.

> Her friends, Jackie and (he, him), were always calling. (Jackie and he were, *not* Jackie and him were.)
>
> The flowers are from two of your friends, Sally and (I, me). (The flowers are from me, *not* from I.)

Pronouns in Comparisons

Comparisons can be made by using a clause that begins with *than* or *as*. Notice the use of pronouns in the comparisons below.

> Fred is better at chess *than he is.*
> You have as many A's *as she has.*

The final clause in a comparison is sometimes **elliptical,** meaning that some words have been omitted. The use of an elliptical clause can make pronoun choice more difficult.

> Fred is better at chess than he.
> You have as many A's as she.

To decide which pronoun form to use in an elliptical clause, fill in the words that are not stated.

> Herb plays the trumpet better than (I, me). (Herb plays the trumpet better than *I play.*)
> Betty was expecting Paul rather than (she, her). (Betty was expecting Paul rather than *Betty was expecting her.*)
> We can sing as well as (they, them). (We can sing as well as *they can sing.*)

Exercises

A Write the correct form of the pronoun from those that are given in parentheses.

1. Write to your representatives, Mr. Owen and (he, him), to express your opinion about the proposed tax increase.
2. Bill is much better at budgeting than (I, me).
3. The performers, Brad and (she, her), were dressed in bright pink wigs and shiny black costumes with sequins.
4. The class would rather have you for president than (he, him).
5. No one was more upset over the test scores than (she, her).
6. After the concert we gave the soloists, Jenny and (she, her), bouquets of flowers.
7. The violin section is tuning up earlier than (they, them).
8. We were expecting someone at the zoning board meeting who had more information than (he, him).
9. At the end of the competition, the judges gave two speakers, Barry and (I, me), first place honors.
10. Would you mind if I asked my cousins, Loretta and (she, her), to go with us?

B Rewrite the following sentences, correcting any errors in pronoun usage. If the sentence contains no errors, write *Correct*.

1. Us hikers should always pay attention to the weather.
2. Our trail guides, Mario and him, told us to dress appropriately, but some of us didn't listen.
3. Guess whom was wearing a heavy sweater and slacks on what turned out to be the hottest day of the year?
4. The other hikers, who arrived in shorts, T-shirts, and light jackets, were obviously better informed than me.
5. After panting and sweating along the trail for hours, I decided I would never make this mistake again.

Reflexive Pronouns

A pronoun such as *myself, herself,* or *ourselves* is used reflexively when it refers to a preceding noun or pronoun.

A reflexive pronoun cannot be used by itself; it must have an antecedent in the same sentence.

Incorrect	Jean and myself carried it up the stairs. (There is no antecedent for *myself*.)
Correct	Jean and I carried it up the stairs.
Incorrect	The coach spoke to Tom and myself.
Correct	The coach spoke to Tom and me.

The words *hisself* and *theirselves* are nonstandard.

Incorrect	The boys washed the clothes theirselves.
Correct	The boys washed the clothes themselves.

Exercise

Write the correct pronoun from those given in parentheses.

1. Sam can ski much better than (I, myself).
2. Arthur Miller (hisself, himself) went to China to direct his play *Death of a Salesman*.
3. We kept some of the fruitcakes for (us, ourselves).
4. The coach spoke to Evie and (me, myself) about team spirit.
5. During the garage sale, Kim and (myself, I) will be cashiers.
6. No one but (yourself, you) volunteered to sell refreshments during halftime.
7. I can't hear (me, myself) think!
8. This discussion is between (him, himself) and (myself, me).
9. Everyone in the class understood the biology assignment but (themselves, them).
10. The drivers (theirselves, themselves) realized the danger.

Checkpoint *Parts 4 and 5*

A Write the correct pronoun from those given in parentheses.

1. Unfortunately, Jim knew the answers to the trivia questions on science and history better than (I, myself, me).
2. Do you know (who, whom) became king after Henry VIII?
3. These can't be (my, mine); (my, mine) gloves are leather.
4. Will the concert manager allow (we, us) three backstage if we tell him that we're reporters for the school paper?
5. We tried to alert (whoever, whomever) might be in the burning building by pulling the fire alarm.
6. My parents were awakened by (us, our) enthusiastic but off-key caroling on the front porch.
7. The sandwich with lettuce only is for (he, him); (hers, her) has tomato and mayonnaise.
8. (Who, Whom) knows the name of the Norwegian playwright who wrote *A Doll's House?*
9. Lenny burned (hisself, himself) yesterday afternoon while trying to light the barbecue grill.
10. (Who, Whom) would have thought that (she, her) debating in school would eventually lead to a career in politics.

B Rewrite the sentences, correcting pronoun errors.

1. Doug Henning demonstrated some tricks that were even easy enough for we amateurs.
2. My father says me watching too much television may injure my grades as well as my eyes.
3. Whomever gets there first should scout out a good campsite.
4. Before we plan our trip, we should talk to someone whom has already traveled to the Yucatán peninsula.
5. The foundation was organized by Senator Sam Nunn and he.

Part 6
Pronoun-Antecedent Agreement

An antecedent is the noun or pronoun for which another pronoun stands and to which it refers.

A pronoun must agree with its antecedent in number, gender, and person.

Agreement in Number If the antecedent of a pronoun is singular, a singular pronoun is required. If the antecedent is plural, a plural pronoun is required.

The singular indefinite pronouns listed below often cause difficulty. When a singular indefinite pronoun is the antecedent of another pronoun, the second pronoun must be singular. Remember that a prepositional phrase following an indefinite pronoun does not affect the number of any other word in the sentence.

another	anything	everybody	neither	one
anybody	each	everyone	nobody	somebody
anyone	either	everything	no one	someone

Each (singular) of the boys brought *his* (singular) guitar.
No one (singular) has made up *his or her* (singular) mind.

Notice in the example above that the phrase *his or her* is considered singular.

The following indefinite pronouns are plural and are referred to by the plural possessive pronouns *our, your,* and *their.*

both   few   many   several

Both of the countries have improved *their* economies.
Few of us wanted *our* pictures taken.
Many of you do not have *your* eligibility slips.

The indefinite pronouns *all, some, any,* and *none* may take either a singular or plural pronoun, depending upon the meaning intended.

All the furniture was in *its* original condition.
All the students were taking *their* last examination.

Some of the cider has lost *its* tang.
Some of the children in the refugee camp have heard from *their* parents.

In all of the examples above, the indefinite pronouns are used as subjects. Note that the verb as well as any other pronouns referring to the subject all agree in number with that subject.

Incorrect	None of the singers *was* making *their* debuts.
Correct	None of the singers *were* making *their* debuts.
Correct	None of the singers *was* making *his or her* debut.

Two or more singular antecedents joined by *or* or *nor* are referred to by a singular pronoun.

Either Bob or Hank will let us use *his* car.
Neither the cat nor the dog had eaten *its* meal.

Use the noun nearer the verb to determine the pronoun for subjects joined by *or* or *nor*.

> Neither the cat nor the dogs had eaten *their* meal.
> Neither the dogs nor the cat had eaten *his* meal.

Collective nouns may be referred to by either a singular or plural pronoun. Determine the number from the meaning in the sentence.

> The track team *has its* new coach. (The team is thought of as a unified, singular whole.)
> The track team *have* worked out in *their* spare time. (Various members act individually.)

Agreement in Gender Masculine gender is indicated by *he, his, him*. Feminine gender is indicated by *she, her, hers*. Neuter gender is indicated by *it* and *its*. A pronoun must be of the same gender as the word to which it refers.

When a singular pronoun must refer to both feminine and masculine antecedents, the phrase *his or her* is acceptable. It is, in fact, preferred by some people who wish to avoid what they consider to be sexist language.

Correct   Each student should have *his* ticket ready.
Correct   Each student should have *his or her* ticket ready.

Agreement in Person A personal pronoun must be in the same person as its antecedent. The words *one, everyone,* and *everybody* are in the third person. They are referred to by *he, his, him, she, her, hers.*

Incorrect   *One* should always wear *your* seatbelt.
Correct   *One* should always wear *his or her* seatbelt.

Exercise

Find and correct the errors in agreement in these sentences. Write *Correct* if there is no error.

1. The student council has made their decision to support an assembly commemorating the bicentennial of our state.
2. Everyone in my class agreed to donate their time to put on a skit about the early history of the state.
3. Many of the students voted for Elaine and me to direct.
4. At first, no one seemed to know what they were doing.
5. Their experience was more hectic than you expected.

6. For example, each of the leading players had their own schedule.
7. Also, it seemed that someone always left your props at home.
8. For a while, not one of the stage crew expected to see his or her home again.
9. Another problem was caused by the fact that not everybody was able to supply their own costume.
10. Suddenly, many of the problems found its own solution.
11. Some of the girls decided that they could adapt their old dance costumes.
12. We also found that you could borrow props from a resale shop.

Part 7
Pronoun Reference

A writer must always be sure that there is a clear connection between a pronoun and its antecedent. If the pronoun reference is indefinite or ambiguous, the resulting sentence may be confusing, misleading, or even humorous.

Indefinite Reference

To avoid any confusion for the reader, every personal pronoun should refer clearly to a definite antecedent.

Indefinite   *It* says in the newspaper that a strike is likely.
Better   *The newspaper* says that a strike is likely.

Indefinite	Al is running for office because *it* is exciting.
Better	Al is running for office because *politics* is exciting.

Indefinite	Read what *they* say about headsets.
Better	Read what *this article* says about headsets.

The pronoun *you* is sometimes used when it is not meant to refer to the person spoken to. The effect is usually confusing.

Indefinite	In that course *you* have fewer exams.
Better	In that course *there are* fewer exams.

Exercise

Revise the sentences to remove all indefinite pronoun references.

1. It said on TV that the President plans to veto the bill.
2. During Prohibition, they made the sale of liquor illegal.
3. Andy wants to be a chef because it interests him.
4. The best show they broadcast is *Nova*.
5. In this school, they make you study a foreign language.
6. I missed Carl's birthday, and I'm sorry about it.
7. The temperature is dropping; it may force the orange growers to light smudge pots to keep the crop from freezing.
8. In Hawaii, they greet you with leis made of flowers.
9. I have never told a lie, and it makes people trust me.
10. You visit three European capitals in three days on that tour.

Ambiguous Reference

The word *ambiguous* means "having two or more possible meanings." The reference of a pronoun is ambiguous if the pronoun may refer to more than one word. This situation arises whenever a noun or pronoun falls between the pronoun and its true antecedent.

Ambiguous	Take the books off the shelves and dust them. (Does this mean dust the books or dust the shelves?)
Better	Dust the books after you take them off the shelves.

Ambiguous	The hounds chased the foxes until they were exhausted. (Were the hounds or the foxes exhausted?)
Better	Until the hounds were exhausted, they chased the foxes.

Ambiguous	Before I could hit the mosquito on your arm, it flew off. (Did the mosquito or the arm fly off?)
Better	Before I could kill the mosquito, it flew off your arm.

Exercise

Rewrite the sentences below to remove all ambiguous pronoun references.

1. When I put the candle in the candelabra, it broke.
2. Sara told Tanya that she really should try out for track.
3. There's an orange in this lunch bag, but it isn't mine.
4. Allison put the plant in the wagon after she bought it.
5. Before you wash them, separate the clothes from the towels.
6. Tom explained to Fred that his car needed to be overhauled.
7. Julie told Kate that her drawing won an award.
8. Take the tennis rackets out of the presses and check them.
9. Joan took the belt off her dress and sent it to the dry cleaners.
10. Although I keep my books with my notebooks, I always lose them.
11. Ellen told Kay that she had made a serious mistake by not paying more attention in class.
12. As the designer talked to the model, she smiled.

Checkpoint *Parts 6 and 7*

Rewrite the sentences, correcting any errors in pronoun usage.

1. In most ads, they never tell you the price.
2. Neither of the people who complained would give their name.
3. Nobody showed up after the raffle to collect their prize.
4. When the traffic officer spoke to Mom, she frowned.
5. I think it is difficult to stay on a diet.
6. Take the saddle off the horse before you polish it.
7. Each of the players promised that they would sell ten raffle tickets by next Friday.
8. Nobody turned their outline in on time.
9. The butcher knew it was time to sharpen his knife.
10. Did either your father or grandfather change their name?
11. We found that you could hear well even in the last row.
12. Ana told Kim that her painting looked professional.
13. Some of the team have his equipment on wrong.
14. Either the principal or the class advisers must give his or her approval in writing.
15. I saw the picture in a magazine, but now I can't find it.

Linking
Grammar & Writing

You have just found out that plans are being made to construct a twenty-story building just four feet from your house or apartment. Write a letter to the editor of the local newspaper in which you give your opinion about whether or not the building should be built. In your letter, use pronouns in all three cases.

Prewriting and Drafting Think of the effects that such a large building would have, especially on you and your family. List all the positive effects that you can think of. Then list all the negative effects. Read through your lists and decide if you are for or against the building. Write one sentence that states your position. Then think of reasons that support your position.

When you draft your letter, begin by stating your purpose. Explain your point of view and the reasons behind it, using facts and details. Conclude with a sentence that summarizes your ideas.

Revising and Proofreading Use the following questions to help evaluate and revise your letter:

1. Is your position clearly expressed?
2. Have you given convincing reasons to support your position?
3. Have you used facts and details to explain your reasons?
4. Are the reasons arranged in an effective order?

Additional Writing Topic Write a two-paragraph description of yourself and one other person. In the first paragraph, describe your similarities. In the second, describe your differences. Use pronouns, and be certain that the antecedents are clear.

Chapter 7
Application and Review

A Choosing Pronouns Correctly Choose the correct form of the pronoun.

1. Was it really (they, them) singing or was it a lip-sync?
2. Except for my sister and (she, her), no one else saw the light.
3. (Who, Whom) does Inspector Holmes suspect?
4. The chef trained Britt and (he, him) as assistants.
5. Neither Hall nor David would budge from (his, their) point of view on arms control.
6. It was Gilbert and Sullivan (who, whom) created comic operettas such as *The Mikado* and *The Pirates of Penzance*.
7. No one understands the situation better than (I, me), and no one dislikes it more than (I, me).
8. Will you go to the air show with Marcus and (I, me)?
9. I really enjoyed (you, your) singing those Civil War ballads.
10. The flight attendant told (they, them) that (they, them) must be able to speak a foreign language.
11. The captain awarded (I, me, myself) a trophy for sportsmanship.
12. Everyone must provide (his or her, their) own transportation.
13. Sondra asked the ushers, Miguel and (she, her), for directions to the kinetic sculpture display.
14. Between (he, himself, him) and (I, myself, me), we managed to make a mess of the entire kitchen.
15. The "glamorous" passenger in the limousine was (I, me)!

B Correcting Pronoun Errors Rewrite the sentences, eliminating pronoun errors. If there are no errors, write *Correct*.

1. The proud owner of the dirt bike was myself.
2. Everyone left the debate feeling pleased with their performance.
3. If you could spend a day with a famous person from history, who would it be?
4. His playing in the band was a source of satisfaction to Brian's grandfather.
5. Max and me are trying to produce a program for cable television.
6. You made as many errors adding the figures as me.
7. The contest was between Frank and myself.
8. No one wants to give their free time to the project.

9. Whomever touches the wet paint will leave fingerprints on the doorknob.
10. The main attractions were her and the ventriloquist.
11. Every doctor should attempt to keep their medical knowledge up to date.
12. To whom did you want this message delivered?
13. Although you were shorter than Danny last year, you are now two inches taller than he.
14. Gina always peeks at the books' endings; I am more patient than her.
15. Neither my dad nor my uncle George can fit into their old World War II Army uniform.

c *Proofreading* Rewrite the following paragraphs. Correct all errors in pronoun usage as well as any errors in spelling, capitalization, or punctuation.

Sir Kay looked around and said, "Who took my sword?" A knight cannot be seen at a jousting tournament without their sword!"

Wart piped up, "I know where you sord is; I forgot to bring it from camp."

Sir Kay sputtered, "Didn't you hear my reminding you not to forget anything when Father and myself were leaving?"

"Yes," said wart pleasantly, "but you and him also asked me to water you're horses, and I did that first. Don't worry. I'll run back to camp and get your sword.

As Wart dashed threw the town square, he noticed a stone with a sword protruding from it. Wart glanced around to see who it could belong to, but no one was there. As he approached, Wart could see that the sword was inscribed, "Whomever pulls this sword from this stone shall be king of England.

"Oh, well," Wart said to hisself, "I'll just borrow it for the tournament and hope that whoever owns it will understand."

As soon as Wart pulled the sword from the stone, bells rang and a mystical lite appeared. Excited people came running from all directions, asking, "Who pulled the sword from the stone?"

"Look! He holds the sword. It has to be he."

Another cautioned, "Not so fast! Make him do it again so we can be sure it was him."

So Wart, being an agreeable lad, replaced the sword and removed it again the Crowd cheered.

They say that a week later Wart was crowned Arthur, King of England.

8
Using Modifiers

*A*n artist envisions a white horse
standing in a lavender garden,
creates it, and suddenly you see what before existed
only in the artist's mind. Amazing! Yet a writer can do
even more. Writers can convey not only what they see
but also whatever they hear, feel, taste, and touch.

In this chapter you will learn to use modifiers to
accomplish this feat by selecting and placing vivid
modifiers in your sentences as skillfully as artists mix
and use vivid colors in their compositions.

Part 1

Understanding Modifiers

An **adjective** tells *which one, what kind,* or *how many* about a noun or pronoun. An **adverb** tells *how, when, where,* or *to what extent* about a verb, adjective, or another adverb. To decide whether a modifier is an adjective or adverb, determine the part of speech of the word it modifies.

Garfield the cat is a character in a *popular* cartoon. (The word *popular* modifies the noun *cartoon. Popular* is an adjective.)

This feisty feline is quite *independent.* (The word *independent* modifies the noun *feline. Independent* is a predicate adjective.)

Garfield *always* fights for some of his owner's lasagna. (The word *always* modifies the verb *fights. Always* is an adverb.)

His owner, Jon, is *seldom* victorious. (The word *seldom* modifies the adjective *victorious. Seldom* is an adverb.)

Adjective and Adverb Forms

Adjectives cannot be recognized by any one form or ending. Adverbs, however, are often recognizable because most adverbs are formed by adding *-ly* to adjectives.

Adjective	Adverb
poor	poorly
careful	carefully
sudden	suddenly
excited	excitedly
happy	happily
inquisitive	inquisitively

A few adjectives and adverbs are spelled in the same way. In most of these cases, the adverb form does not end in *-ly*.

Adjective	Adverb
a *straight* course	thinks *straight*
a *hard* problem	works *hard*
a *high* note	soars *high*
a *long* journey	lasts *long*
a *late* flight	arrives *late*

Some adverbs have two forms, both of which are considered correct. One form is spelled with -*ly*. The other is not.

Come *quick!* Please, move *quickly*.
Drive *slow*. We must be careful and work *slowly*.
Stay *close!* Follow *closely* or you will get lost.

Usage Note The short form of the adverbs shown above is more likely to be used in informal speech or in short imperative sentences. The form ending in -*ly* is used in formal writing.

Modifiers That Follow Verbs

A word that modifies an action verb, an adjective, or another adverb is always an adverb.

Beyond the castle moat, a beast howled *dreadfully*. (*Dreadfully* modifies the action verb *howled*.)

The howl of this beast was *really* dreadful. (*Really* modifies the adjective *dreadful*.)

So dreadfully did the beast howl that the king sent a knight out to slay it. (*So* modifies the adverb *dreadfully*.)

Always use an adverb to modify an action verb. Be careful not to use an adjective to modify an action verb.

Incorrect The officer stepped *cautious* into the room.
Correct The officer stepped *cautiously* into the room.

Incorrect Two hot-air balloons rose *sudden* on the horizon.
Correct Two hot-air balloons rose *suddenly* on the horizon.

Incorrect The karate opponents bowed *polite* to each other.
Correct The karate opponents bowed *politely* to each other.

A linking verb, on the other hand, is usually followed by an adjective rather than an adverb. As you have learned, a predicate adjective follows a linking verb and modifies the subject of the sentence.

The plastic fruit in the bowl appeared *real*. (*Real* is a predicate adjective. It follows the linking verb *appeared,* and it modifies the subject *fruit.*)

A speaker or a writer rarely has a problem when a modifier follows a form of the verb *be,* the most common linking verb. Some linking verbs, however, may also be used as action verbs. When these verbs are used as action verbs, they can be modified by adverbs.

Verbs that can be used as both linking and action verbs include *look, sound, appear, grow, smell, taste,* and *remain.* Look at the examples below.

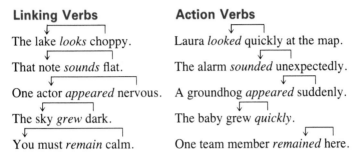

Linking Verbs	Action Verbs
The lake *looks* choppy.	Laura *looked* quickly at the map.
That note *sounds* flat.	The alarm *sounded* unexpectedly.
One actor *appeared* nervous.	A groundhog *appeared* suddenly.
The sky *grew* dark.	The baby grew *quickly*.
You must *remain* calm.	One team member *remained* here.

Exercises

A On your paper, write the correct modifier of the two given in parentheses. Then label it as an adjective or an adverb.

1. You can find the tollway (easy, easily) from here.
2. The young colt seems (unsteady, unsteadily) on its feet.
3. Both alarms sounded (simultaneous, simultaneously).
4. It rained (steady, steadily) for forty days and nights.
5. Can a small, pocket calculator process figures as (rapid, rapidly) as a computer?
6. The captain felt (uneasy, uneasily) about the approaching storm.
7. Harriet found the solution to the first problem and (quick, quickly) turned to the second.
8. Columbus thought he had (certain, certainly) found India.
9. Your voice sounds (different, differently) on the phone.
10. The detective looked (suspicious, suspiciously) at the fingerprints on the windowsill.

B Write the correct modifier of the two given in parentheses. Label it as an adjective or adverb. Then write the word it modifies.

> *Example*   Lasers appear very (bright, brightly) when compared with other lights.
> bright, adjective, Lasers

1. Scientists felt (confident, confidently) that they would be able to create the kind of superlight that was first described by Albert Einstein in 1917.

2. For fifty years, scientists worked (patient, patiently) to create this powerful light, which they called a *laser*.
3. In 1960, the first device for producing lasers was built (successful, successfully) by Theodore Maiman.
4. This rudimentary device was small enough to fit in one hand, yet it produced a beam of light stronger than any that had been produced (previously, previous).
5. Since Maiman's achievement, other scientists have used lasers (creative, creatively).
6. Some lasers produce beams so strong that they can cut (direct, directly) through steel.
7. Other lasers produce beams (precise, precisely) enough to be used in surgery.
8. Lasers are (remarkable, remarkably) in the ways they have improved surgical techniques.
9. Most laser surgery can be done (rapid, rapidly) without causing any bleeding.
10. Follow the development of lasers (careful, carefully); they are bound to be important in the future.

c *Write Now* In medieval times knights rode out to seek adventure and slay dragons. As protection, knights wore elaborate suits of armor. Do some brief research on the kinds of armor knights wore. Then use your imagination to write a description of what wearing a suit of armor would be like. First, describe the appearance of the armor. Then tell how it fits you and what it feels like as you move about. Use adjectives, predicate adjectives, and adverbs to make your description interesting and precise.

St. George and the Dragon, Paolo Uccello, circa 1450

Tom Swifties

Tom Swifties are word puns based on a comic relationship between an adverb and the main idea of a sentence.

Tom Swift, hero of a series of popular novels, was a youthful genius who invented such wonders as electric airplanes. The books are out of vogue now, but the punning word game named in Tom's honor is still going strong. These Tom Swifties will give you the idea [and, perhaps, lead you into creating your own].

"Pass the cards," said Tom ideally.

"I have the mumps," said Tom infectiously.

"You gave me two less than a dozen," said Tom tensely.

"I don't like wilted lettuce," said Tom limply.

"Our ball club needs a man who can hit sixty homers a season," said Tom ruthlessly.

"He's a young M.D.," said Tom internally.

"Gold leaf," said Tom guiltily.

"I'm out of cartridges for my starting gun," said Tom blankly.

"It's the maid's night off," said Tom helplessly.

"The thermostat is set too high," said Tom heatedly.

"The chimney is clogged," said Tom fluently.

"Golly, that old man is bent over," said Tom stupidly.

"Don't you love sleeping outdoors?" said Tom intently.

"I've been stung," said Tom waspishly.

"Let's invite Greg and Gary," said Tom gregariously.

"This boat leaks," said Tom balefully.

"Welcome to my tomb," said Tom cryptically.

"I just returned from Japan," said Tom disorientedly.

"I'll never stick my fist into the lion's cage again," said Tom offhandedly.

"I can't find the oranges," said Tom fruitlessly.

"I lost my trousers," said Tom expansively.

"Are you fond of venison?" said Tom fawningly.

"Here are my Tom Swifty entries," said Tom submissively.

"You've ruined my health," said Tom halfheartedly.

"Is there a quiz today?" asked Tom testily.

"It's just too early to get up," complained Tom mournfully.

"What's the angle?" asked Tom obtusely.

"Is that you?" asked Tom sheepishly.

"It's raining," reported Tom precipitously.

Willard R. Espy and others

Part 2
Comparison of Adjectives and Adverbs

Every adjective and adverb has a basic form, called the **positive degree.** This is the form of the word you will find in the dictionary. The positive degree is commonly used to describe individual things, groups, or actions.

Positive   Many microcomputers are *light*. Most of them can be transported *easily*.

The **comparative degree** of an adjective or an adverb is used to compare two things, groups, or actions.

Comparative   A portable computer is *lighter* than a desk-top computer. Most portables can be carried *more easily* than most desk-top computers.

When deciding whether the comparative is correct, be alert to phrases such as *the other one* that signal the comparison of two things.

When more than two things, group, or actions are compared, the **superlative degree** of an adjective or an adverb is used.

Superlative   A lap-top computer is the *lightest* computer. Of all computers now available, it can be transported the *most easily*.

To make comparisons correctly, remember that the comparative degree is used to compare only two things and that the superlative degree is used to compare three or more things. Specific numbers are not always given in a comparison. At times you must determine how many things are being compared. Would you use the comparative or the superlative form in the following sentence?

This is the (better, best) restaurant in the city.

You can infer that the comparison is between one restaurant and all the other restaurants in the city. Therefore, the superlative form, *best,* should be used. Now try this example.

Which is (better, best)—the French restaurant or the Italian one?

Since only two restaurants are being compared, the comparative form, *better,* should be used.

Regular Comparisons

Like verbs, modifiers may be regular or irregular. Most adjectives and adverbs are regular and form the comparative and superlative in one of two ways.

A one-syllable modifier forms the comparative and superlative by adding *-er* and *-est*. Some two-syllable modifiers also form the comparative and superlative in this way.

Positive	Comparative	Superlative
warm	warmer	warmest
close	closer	closest
soon	sooner	soonest
sad	sadder	saddest
funny	funnier	funniest

Spelling Note Most dictionaries list the comparative and superlative forms of modifiers in which there is a spelling change, such as the change from *y* to *i* in *funnier, funniest.*

Most modifiers with two syllables and all modifiers with three or more syllables use *more* and *most* to form the comparative and superlative.

Positive	Comparative	Superlative
helpful	more helpful	most helpful
precisely	more precisely	most precisely
optimistic	more optimistic	most optimistic
reliably	more reliably	most reliably

For negative comparisons, *less* and *least* are used before the positive form of the modifier.

Positive	Comparative	Superlative
careful	less careful	least careful
comfortable	less comfortable	least comfortable
eagerly	less eagerly	least eagerly
cautiously	less cautiously	least cautiously

Irregular Comparisons

A few adjectives and adverbs are irregular. Their comparative and superlative forms are not based on the positive form. Because irregular modifiers are used frequently, you should memorize their forms. Study the list of irregular modifiers on the next page.

Positive	Comparative	Superlative
bad	worse	worst
far	farther *or* further	farthest *or* furthest
good	better	best
late	later	latest *or* last
little	less	least
many	more	most
much	more	most
well	better	best

Usage Note *Farther* refers to distance, and *further* refers to an addition in time or amount: The distance to town is *farther* than I thought. I won't discuss it *further*.

Exercises

A Rewrite the following sentences. Correct all errors in the use of comparative and superlative modifiers.

1. Is solar energy the less expensive form of energy?
2. Of the three rowboats we rented, the yellow one was the leakier.
3. The worse experience of my life was forgetting my lines on stage.
4. Geoffrey has the stronger southern accent in the class.
5. Which is mightiest, the pen or the sword?
6. Malabar, a tropical plant, is least bitter than spinach.
7. The world's faster bird is named the swift.
8. Joe explained the problem patienter than I could have.
9. Which of these stereo speakers produces the best sound—this one or that one?
10. Fruit is most plentiful in summer than fall.
11. We all practiced the polka, but Jan did it more enthusiastically.
12. Of the horse and automobile, great-grandfather believed that a horse was safest.
13. Who among all those who auditioned for the ballet seemed the more promising?
14. Michelangelo's more famous masterpiece, the Sistine Chapel ceiling, took him four years to complete.
15. Housing is usually cheapest in rural areas than in the city.
16. That was the awfulest mistake I ever made.
17. Of the two candidates, Abernathy was the least qualified.
18. Which is the hardest substance, carbon or steel?
19. Try to think most positively about getting a college scholarship.
20. A rare metal called osmium is the heavier of all metals.

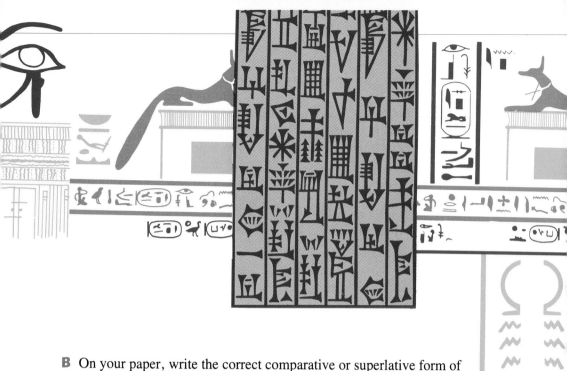

B On your paper, write the correct comparative or superlative form of the modifier given in parentheses.

1. About the same time that Egyptian hieroglyphics were fascinating European scholars, archaeologists in the Near East were uncovering another (mysterious) script.
2. Cuneiform, a wedge-shaped writing, had been in use much (early) than Egyptian hieroglyphics, but information about it had somehow been lost for a thousand years.
3. Of all the samples discovered, the (old) tablets were found in Mesopotamia.
4. The (good) way to describe cuneiform is to say that it looks like bird tracks left in wet mud.
5. Cuneiform writing was done by pressing a triangular-shaped stylus into a soft clay tablet; then the clay tablet was baked to make it (hard) and stronger.
6. Because it has (few) wedges than hieroglyphics, cuneiform is considered a (elementary) form of writing.
7. During the years it was used, cuneiform changed (little) than hieroglyphics.
8. Even though it is one of the (primitive) of all written languages, cuneiform does have a form of punctuation.
9. One mark that was clearly (small) than the others was used to separate words.
10. Some forms of cuneiform were (difficult) than others to read; it took scientists many years to decipher them.

c *Write Now* Imagine that you are a reviewer for your local newspaper. Your "beat" is either entertainment or special sports events. Your assignment this week is to attend two similar special events—for example, two rock concerts, two ballets, two tennis matches, or two ice-skating competitions. Write a review in which you compare the two performances. Use comparative adjectives and adverbs to describe and evaluate the events you have attended. Point out features of equipment (a *larger* racket, a *more elaborate* costume) and the actual performance (served *more powerfully,* spun the *most gracefully*).

Checkpoint Parts 1 and 2

A On your paper, write the correct modifier of the two modifiers given in parentheses. Then tell whether the modifier is an adjective or an adverb.

1. Press down (firm, firmly) so your signature comes through.
2. I type (more slowly, most slowly) than anyone else in class.
3. Of the twins, Kara is the (younger, youngest).
4. Which is (more far, farther) from Miami, Haiti or Bermuda?
5. Which are (funnier, funniest), old movies or sitcoms?
6. Eric's handwriting is the (elaboratest, most elaborate) imaginable.
7. The team felt (more confident, more confidently) after practice.
8. Of the two stations, PBS's coverage was (better, best).
9. Of all the squads, ours made the (fewer, fewest) goals.
10. Night descended (quick, quickly) on the valley.

B Correct any errors in the use of modifiers. If the sentence contains no error, write *Correct.*

1. This ice skate is the sharpest of the pair.
2. The fans have never cheered so enthusiastically.
3. The incoming waves are moving terribly fast.
4. The chimney must be cleaned regular to avoid fires.
5. Which is easiest to learn, knitting or crocheting?
6. Of all the basketball players, Lee dribbles the most skillfully.
7. Which did you feel was most suspenseful, the book or the movie?
8. The pollution from the factory smelled terribly all summer.
9. The charity drive is progressing steady toward its goal.
10. The coach was the better of the three banquet speakers.

Part 3

Using Comparisons Correctly

The following guidelines and examples will help you to use comparisons correctly.

Avoid Double Comparisons

The comparative form of a modifier is made either by adding *-er* or by using *more*. It is incorrect to use both.

The superlative form of a modifier is made either by adding *-est* or by using *most*. It is incorrect to use both.

Incorrect	My boat will go much more faster than yours.
Correct	My boat will go much faster than yours.

Incorrect	You should find it more easier to do.
Correct	You should find it easier to do.

Incorrect	It was the most fanciest house I'd ever seen.
Correct	It was the fanciest house I'd ever seen.

Avoid Illogical Comparisons

Illogical or confusing comparisons result if two unrelated items are compared or if something is compared with itself.

The word *other* or the word *else* is required in comparisons of an individual member with the rest of the group.

Illogical	Bill has won more trophies than any student athlete. (Bill is also a student athlete.)
Clear	Bill has won more tropies than any *other* student athlete.

Illogical	George is as tall as anyone on the school's basketball team. (George is also on the team.)
Clear	George is as tall as anyone *else* on the school's basketball team.

The word *as* or the word *than* is required after the first modifier in a compound comparison.

Illogical	Tim is as tall if not taller than Brad.
Awkward	Tim is as tall *as,* if not taller than, Brad.
Clear	Tim is as tall *as* Brad, if not taller.

| *Illogical* | Sue's grades are better or at least as good as Helen's. |
| *Clear* | Sue's grades are better *than*, or at least as good as, Helen's. |

| *Illogical* | The Dodgers' chances of winning the pennant are as good if not better than the Giants'. |
| *Clear* | The Dodgers' chances of winning the pennant are as good *as* the Giants', if not better. |

Both parts of a comparison must be stated completely if there is any chance of its being misunderstood.

Confusing	I miss her more than Sandra.
Clear	I miss her more than Sandra *does*.
Clear	I miss her more than I *miss* Sandra.

Confusing	Harvard beats Yale more often than Brown.
Clear	Harvard beats Yale more often than Brown *does*.
Clear	Harvard beats Yale more often than it *beats* Brown.

| *Confusing* | Rio is nearer the Equator than London. |
| *Clear* | Rio is nearer the Equator than London *is*. |

Exercises

A Find the errors in comparison in the following sentences, and rewrite the sentences correctly on your paper.

1. The work of a miner is more dangerous than a carpenter.
2. The letter *e* is used more frequently than any letter in the English language.

3. Joyce, the treasurer, is as informed as any member of the committee.
4. Strum your guitar a little more faster.
5. The rules of chess are more complicated than checkers.
6. Gardenias are as fragrant if not more fragrant than roses.
7. John Hancock signed his name more larger than usual.
8. Charles Lindbergh was more adventurous than any pilot.
9. I respect Betty Jean more than Chuck.
10. Spinach is as nutritious as any green vegetable.
11. The camera club enrollment is more bigger than ever this year.
12. The Colosseum in Rome is old, but the Parthenon in Athens is oldest.
13. Of all those in the contest, Tom's frog jumped the most highest.
14. Rye bread is as tasty if not tastier than pumpernickel.

B *Proofreading* The following paragraph contains errors in comparisons, spelling, capitalization, and punctuation. Rewrite the paragraph, correcting all errors.

> Have you noticed that billboard art is becoming even more bolder than in the past? Human figures are as large, if not larger than, the legendary giant Paul Bunyan. Some billboard people are raised from the background, they seem to pitch their product direct to each passerby. The most strikingest billboard I have seen shows a row of huge sneakers. It's colors are more vibranter than those in any billboard I have seen. Those sneakers would be to large even for Paul Bunyan!

Part 4
Special Problems with Modifiers

Certain adjectives and adverbs have forms that can be confusing. In the following section you will learn the correct use of adjectives and adverbs that are often used incorrectly.

This *and* These; That *and* Those

This and *that* modify singular words. *These* and *those* modify plural words. The words *kind, sort,* and *type* require a singular modifier.

Incorrect	*These* kind are the best.
Correct	*This* kind is the best.
Incorrect	*These* sort of gloves wear well.
Correct	*This* sort of glove wears well.

Them *and* Those

Those may be either a pronoun or an adjective. *Them* is always a pronoun and never an adjective.

Incorrect	Where did you get *them* statistics?
Correct	Where did you get *those* statistics? (adjective)
Correct	Where did you get *them*? (pronoun)

Bad *and* Badly

Bad is an adjective. When it is used after linking verbs, it modifies the subject. *Badly* is an adverb. It modifies action verbs.

I felt *bad*. (The adjective *bad* follows a linking verb and modifies the subject *I*.)

The team played *badly*. (The adverb *badly* modifies the action verb *played*.)

Good *and* Well

Good is an adjective. It modifies nouns or pronouns.

Zinnias are a *good* choice for a sunny garden.

Good can also be used as a predicate adjective with linking verbs. It then modifies the subject.

Dad always feels *good* after a brisk walk.

Well can be either an adjective or an adverb. As an adjective, *well* means "in good health," and it can follow a linking verb. As an adverb, *well* modifies an action verb. It tells how the action is performed.

The Vice-President looks *well*. (adjective)
Jake is sprinting *well* now. (adverb)

The Double Negative

Two negative words used together where only one is necessary is called a *double negative*. A double negative is incorrect.

Incorrect	He did*n't* have *no* energy left.
Correct	He did*n't* have *any* energy left.
Incorrect	She did*n't* know *nothing* about the Civil War.
Correct	She did*n't* know *anything* about the Civil War.

It is incorrect to use *hardly* or *barely* with a negative word.

Incorrect There was*n't hardly* a ticket left for the show.
Correct There was *hardly* a ticket left for the show.

Incorrect Terry could*n't barely* hit the ball.
Correct Terry could *barely* hit the ball.

Exercises

A On your paper, write the correct word of the two choices given in parentheses.

1. Anything that contains curry or thyme tastes (bad, badly) to me.
2. The bus that takes passengers to the terminal hasn't (never, ever) been so late before.
3. Be careful not to trip over (those, them) wires.
4. The lifeguard at the beach didn't say (anything, nothing) about an undertow.
5. The croton grew (good, well) even after being transplanted to the window box on the porch.
6. There (were, weren't) no socks left at the bottom of my drawer—they were all in the wash.
7. (Those, That) kind of elaborate theater costume requires many yards of brocade and lace.
8. The Prime Minister hasn't said (nothing, anything) that disagrees with our policy.
9. Secretaries should be able to type accurately, take dictation rapidly, and spell (well, good).
10. By midnight our family's Thanksgiving turkey (had, hadn't) barely begun to thaw out.

B On your paper, write the correct word of the two choices given in parentheses.

1. Until recently in India, there were hardly (any, no) tigers left in existence.
2. Hunting and the spread of civilization had destroyed three subspecies (quick, quickly), and the future of two more looked (bad, badly).
3. By (careful, carefully) studying the pugmarks, or tracks, of (those, them) cats that were left, conservationists learned where to establish a protected reserve.
4. Swampy areas south of Nepal were chosen because (these, this) kind of big cat is drawn to water.

5. Also, (this, these) areas aren't much good for (anything, nothing) else.
6. Tourists who haven't (ever, never) seen a tiger can visit the buffer zone around the park.
7. However, it is not (good, well) to go on foot.
8. For some reason, tigers won't do (nothing, anything) harmful to people mounted on elephants or riding in vehicles.
9. The big cat is doing (good, well) under protection.
10. (This, These) type of park may save tigers from extinction.

c *Proofreading* The following paragraph contains errors in the use of modifiers as well as other errors. Rewrite the paragraph correctly.

One can't hardly discuss the subject of inventers without mentioning Thomas Edison. The electric light, the storage battery, the phonographs, and the movie—all of them inventions are credited to Edison. Edisons impact on industrial America was great not only because he invented these kind of devices, but also because he revolutionized the businiss of invention. After Edison, the inventor was no longer an isolated individuel, instead, the inventor became a member of a scientific team. These new kind of team worked just as good, if not better than, inventors on their own.

Checkpoint Parts 3 and 4

A Rewrite the following sentences, correcting all errors in the use of modifiers.

1. Diamonds are much more harder than other gems.
2. Haven't none of the musicians arrived?
3. I telephone Louis more often than George.
4. We haven't scarcely begun to distribute our posters even though the concert is less than a week away.
5. In the upcoming season, the Knicks should play as good as any team in the division.
6. In full armor, some medieval knights couldn't hardly walk.
7. Saturn has as many satellites if not more than any planet.
8. Them cheeses are very high in cholesterol.
9. There isn't nobody else who writes such suspenseful stories.
10. The novels of Charles Dickens are more widely read than Jane Austen.
11. Please don't feel badly about the misunderstanding.
12. Grandfather is more active than anyone in the family.
13. The woodwind ensemble played so good that it received a standing ovation from the enthusiastic crowd.
14. These type of boots are fashionable but not practical for the cold, snowy winters of the Midwest.
15. The emcee pronounced the contestants' names bad.

B *Proofreading* Rewrite the following paragraph correcting all errors. Pay particular attention to the use of modifiers.

My brother and I needed money bad, so we convinced our nieghbor to let us paint her garage. We told her that we work good together and are not as slowly as professional painters. She agreed, and we headed to the hardwear store. A salesperson told us that we should use long-handled roller brushes so that we wouldn't have to climb no ladders. However, my brother told him, "We want to use these kind," and he pointed out some short-handled brushes. We bought them short-handled brushes and rented an eight-foot construction ladder. Our painting was going good when our neighbor came around to offer us something to drink. I turned toward her. And fell off the ladder! Them cans of paint and the brushes landed on top of me. It didn't hurt to bad, but I did get two black eyes and a coat of paint.

Linking
Grammar & Writing

The Guinness Book of World Records tells about a millionairess named Henrietta Green who had $95,000,000 when she died in 1916. She was a miser who saved scraps of soap and went to free clinics to avoid paying doctor bills. Write an interior monologue in which you put yourself into the mind of Henrietta Green and think her thoughts as she walks down the streets of New York City. Use adjectives and adverbs to make the impressions vivid and to show in concrete detail how the world's greatest miser saw life.

Prewriting and Drafting One way of writing an interior monologue is to imagine someone talking to himself or herself. Imagine, for example, what life would be like if you were a miser like Henrietta Green. What would you think about? How would you see the world around you?

As you draft your interior monologue, try to capture the unique personality of the miserly Henrietta. The following example shows one way of starting.

> Look at that broken bottle—a foolishly wasted penny that could have been wisely saved! Some poor fool will probably get hurt on the glass, and then there will be doctor bills, and medicine bills, and no end of trouble. How carelessly people throw money away these days! I'd suffer before I'd pay anyone good money.

Revising and Proofreading Read your draft aloud. Does it sound realistic and convincing, as if a real miser were talking? Have you used concrete details and vivid adjectives and adverbs to describe Henrietta's thoughts? Will your reader understand what Henrietta is seeing and sensing as she walks the streets of New York City?

After revising, carefully proofread your monologue. You may want to exchange monologues with a classmate.

Additional Writing Topic Imagine what our modern world would look like to a person from our country's past. What would Thomas Jefferson think of skyscrapers and digital watches? What would Emily Dickinson think of laser games and television commercials? Write a paragraph or two from the point of view of some historical figure seeing the modern world. Use comparative adjectives and adverbs to contrast the past and present worlds.

Weasel Words

T hink about the following advertising claims. As you read, notice the italicized modifier used in each one.

> Sudsos leaves dishes *virtually* spotless. (Since *virtually* means "practically," Sudso leaves spots on dishes.)

> Krumbles potato chips are made with 100 percent *natural* ingredients. (What would be *unnatural* ingredients?)

> Tum-Eez relieves *simple* indigestion. (What if your indigestion is not *simple*?)

Virtually, natural, and *simple* are examples of **weasel words**—words that seem forthright, but are actually evasive. Advertising slogans and political rhetoric are frequently accused of being filled with weasel words. The term was coined at the turn of the century by political commentator Stewart Chaplin. He was annoyed with the way politicians often used qualifying words that seemed to add emphasis, but, in fact, made statements weaker. "Why, weasel words are words that suck the life out of the words next to them, just as a weasel sucks the egg and leaves the shell," he said.

Chaplin's phrase became popular in 1916, when it was used by Theodore Roosevelt to describe misleading political statements. Today, weasel words may be used so that they have no meaning at all. Weasel words allow the user to weasel out of commitment.

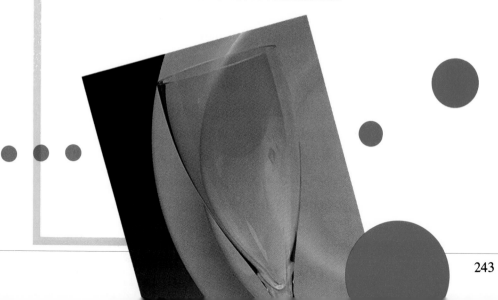

Chapter 8
Application and Review

A Choosing the Correct Modifier On your paper, write the correct form of the two choices given in parentheses.

1. That cartoonist draws her characters extremely (good, well).
2. The food that had been sitting out on the picnic table all day certainly smelled (bad , badly).
3. Would you bring me (them, those) pliers from the workbench?
4. I've never seen (this , these) kind of shoe.
5. Tooth enamel is one of the (hardest , most hardest) natural substances.
6. Jerry hadn't (never, ever) seen a television studio, so he was looking forward to the field trip.
7. Regina waited (nervous, nervously) for the results of her audition for the orchestra.
8. The radio announcer sounded (serious , seriously) when he explained that the interview had been canceled.
9. Of all reptiles on earth, the giant tortoise lives the (longer, longest).
10. Because of his cold, Eric (could , couldn't) hardly talk.
11. Eve types (accurate, accurately) enough to qualify for the word-processing position.
12. We developed both black and white and color film, but the color roll developed (faster , fastest).
13. The Library of Congress has more books than (any, any other) library in the nation.
14. The candidate's schedule of campaign activities doesn't allow (any , no) time for socializing.
15. Our mountain bike club traveled (more , most) miles on Monday than we did on Tuesday.
16. Anna's scheme for Student Council reelection sounds (foolish , foolishly).
17. Mark has been to more foreign countries than (anyone, anyone else) in his class.
18. The batter (had , hadn't) barely tipped the ball, yet still managed to get a base hit.
19. Tie-dyeing seems (easier , easiest) to do than making an intricate batik design.
20. The champion looked (intent, intently) at the chess board before making a move.

B Using Modifiers Correctly The sentences below contain errors in the use of modifiers. On your paper, rewrite each sentence correctly.

1. My little brother and my youngest cousin always play good together.
2. If you want to try a delicious fruit, try these kind of grapes.
3. The photographer moved silent around the sweetly sleeping children.
4. Dressed in her ballet costume, Felicia looked beautifully as she stepped into the spotlight.
5. Of all three debaters, Ricardo spoke the more persuasively in favor of stricter gun-control legislation.
6. We felt badly when we realized that our friends had been waiting at the theater for an hour.
7. The job will go more quicklier if you get a partner to help you address all these envelopes.
8. The rate of population growth in some countries is greater than the food .
9. We couldn't scarcely hear the weather report because of the thunder outside.
10. The painter Vincent van Gogh didn't have no idea that he would one day be famous.

c _Proofreading_ The following paragraphs contain errors in the use of modifiers as well as other mistakes. On your paper, rewrite the paragraphs, correcting all errors.

(1) Alfred Nobel left his mark on the world in too dramatically different areas. (2) It seems ironically that the person who invented dynamite would also bequeath a prize for world peace, but Nobel did just that.

(3) Nobel was born in Sweden in 1833. (4) His family was in the business of making explosives, and sometimes there were problems in controlling them dangerous substances. (5) Often, those kind of substances, such as nitroglycerin, would explode inside the Nobel factories. (6) To make the nitroglycerin more stabler , Alfred Nobel mixed it with another material. (7) He called his invention "dinamite ."

(8) In 1896, after dynamite and other inventions had made Nobel as rich, if not richer than, the wealthiest men in the world, Nobel wrote his will. (9) He didn't leave none of his fortune to his family. (10) Instead, his money was to go to men and women who would make outstanding contributions in the areas of literature, physics, chemistry, medicine, economics and world piece . (11) So it was that a pioneer in the feild of explosives became the founder of a peace prize.

Cumulative Review

Chapters 7 and 8

A Correcting Errors in Pronoun Usage Some of the following sentences contain errors in the use of pronouns. Rewrite these sentences, eliminating the errors. If there are no errors in a particular sentence, write *Correct*.

1. No one should lose their sleep worrying about that.
2. The lawyer asked the jury to find Ellen Anderson innocent, even though she had admitted her role in the crime of passion.
3. Long after other couples had grown weary, you could see their dancing with tireless enthusiasm as if the night had just begun.
4. You should let the neighbors know that my uncle and me will be hunting.
5. The coach gave Susan and me some invaluable tips during practice.
6. In a sprint, he can run faster than me , though he has trouble pacing himself for longer distances.
7. The decision is not mine alone to make; everyone in the club should have their say.
8. The faculty has officially approved their new contract.
9. No one had a better sense of what the audience liked than her .
10. Neither gusting, late-night winds nor the creaking of a floor in an empty house will frighten my sister or myself .
11. Who gave this elegant sapphire ring to you?
12. After we succeed in our lawn care business, the profits should be split evenly between you and I .
13. According to those two expert film critics, my mother and she , that new film is not worth the price of admission.
14. Someone had been throwing their trash in the river in defiance of the new clean water law.
15. Who will you vote for in the upcoming school election?
16. The police were still searching for whomever stole the school mascot from the display case.
17. The speaker at the assembly asked us to remember the sacrifices that previous generations had made for we young people.
18. Neither of the two players wanted to lose their role.
19. It was her whom you saw last night, supposedly lurking in the shadows; she was simply waiting for her ride to come.
20. Whom is the state's attorney general now?

B Correcting Errors of Pronoun Reference Revise the following paragraph to remove all indefinite and ambiguous pronoun references. You will need to rewrite some of the sentences.

> (1) Horatio Alger, Jr., wrote stories during the decades after the Civil War about poor boys who became rich through hard work, decency, and determination. (2) He wrote more than a hundred books about it, with titles such as *Making His Way*, *Strive and Succeed*, and *Struggling Upward*. (3) His stories of street urchins who became wealthy and virtuous business leaders gave you hope and inspired young people throughout the nation. (4) Though his books all followed similar plots, it was enormously influential. (5) It sent out the message to generations of young people that hard work and honesty would always be rewarded. (6) No matter how poor they were, Alger's stories gave millions of young Americans hope that a better tomorrow was possible. (7) It reinforced the image of the United States as a land where anyone could achieve material success, if only you worked hard enough.

C Using Adjectives and Adverbs Rewrite the following sentences, correcting any of the italicized modifiers that are incorrectly used. If a sentence has no errors, write *Correct*.

1. A tornado is a twisting, *powerfully*, and destructive wind storm, usually seen as a rotating, funnel-shaped cloud.
2. Though the dimensions of a tornado are far smaller than those of a hurricane, a tornado's destructive force is *greatest*.
3. Its winds reach speeds of three hundred miles per hour; they move faster than those found in *any* kind of storm.
4. Most of the world's tornadoes occur in the United States; of all its geographic regions, the West has the *fewer* tornadoes.
5. Tornadoes *frequently* strike Midwestern and Southern states; chiefly in spring and early summer.
6. Wherever a tornado touches down, it *immediate* poses a threat to any people or property in its vicinity.
7. Tornadoes can *quick* uproot trees, overturn railroad cars, and flatten entire homes.
8. After tornadoes, victims may have to search *careful* through debris to find remnants of their property.
9. Fortunately, the tornado warnings of the National Weather Service have worked *good*, saving countless lives over the years.
10. While nobody *can't* predict when a tornado will occur, scientists can identify weather conditions that may lead to one.

9
Capitalization

I magine the confusion that would result if everyone were simply called "person." Proper names enable you to distinguish the specific from the general. To indicate that a word is a specific name, or proper noun, and not just a label given to a category of things, or common noun, writers capitalize the first letter of that word.

In this chapter you will learn to use capitalization to distinguish proper nouns from common nouns so that you can efficiently and precisely refer to people, places, things, and ideas.

People, Personal Titles, Nationalities, and Religions

A **proper noun** is the name of a specific person, place, thing, or idea. A **common noun** names a general class of people, places, things, or ideas. Proper nouns are capitalized. Common nouns are not. A **proper adjective** is an adjective formed from a proper noun, and is, therefore, also capitalized.

Common Noun	Proper Noun	Proper Adjective
continent	Europe	European
queen	Queen Elizabeth	Elizabethan

Proper nouns and adjectives occur in many compound words. Capitalize only the parts of these words that are capitalized when they stand alone. Do not capitalize prefixes such as *pro-, un-,* and *pre-* attached to proper nouns and adjectives.

> pro-Leftist   un-American   pre-Civil War

The following rules will help you identify proper nouns and adjectives and capitalize them correctly.

Names of People and Personal Titles

Capitalize people's names and initials that stand for names.

> Elizabeth Dole   J.P. Morgan   Lyndon B. Johnson

Capitalize titles and abbreviations for titles used before people's names or in direct address.

> Reverend Jesse Jackson   **Ms**. Hudson   **Lt**. Harrison
> How often should I take this medication, Doctor?

The abbreviations *Jr.* and *Sr.* are also capitalized after names. In the middle of a sentence, these abbreviations are followed by a comma.

> Mr. Ralph Benson, **Sr.,** addressed the class.

In general, do not capitalize a title when it follows a person's name or is used without a proper name.

> The doctor wrote a prescription for Amy.

Capitalize a title used without a person's name if it refers to a head of state or a person in another important position.

the **P**resident and **V**ice-**P**resident of the United States

the **P**ope   the **P**rime **M**inister   the **C**hief **J**ustice

The prefix *ex-* and the suffix *-elect* are not capitalized when attached to titles.

ex-**P**resident Carter   the **P**rime **M**inister-elect

Family Relationships

Capitalize the titles indicating family relationships when the titles are used as names or as parts of names.

It's hard to believe that **A**unt **M**aria and **M**om are twins.

If the title is preceded by an article or a possessive word, it is not capitalized.

My uncle admitted that being a father can be difficult.

Races, Languages, Nationalities, and Religions

Capitalize the names of races, languages, nationalities, and religions, and any adjectives formed from these names.

Hinduism   **C**aucasian   **C**hinese cooking

French   **H**ebrew   **A**rabian horses

"Hold on there! I think you misunderstood—
I'm Al Tilley ... the bum."

© 1984 Universal Press Syndicate

The Supreme Being and Sacred Writings

Capitalize all words referring to God, the Holy Family, and religious scriptures.

the **L**ord	**A**llah	the **T**orah
Christ	the **G**ospel	the **K**oran
the **V**irgin **M**ary	the **O**ld **T**estament	the **T**almud

Capitalize personal pronouns referring to God.

They thanked the Lord for **H**is love and guidance.

Do not capitalize *god* and *goddess* when they refer to multiple deities, such as the gods and goddesses of various mythologies.

Isis was one of several Egyptian nature goddesses.
The Greek god Hades was ruler of the underworld.

The Pronoun I

Always capitalize the pronoun *I.*

I'll probably make the team if **I** improve my free throws.

Exercises

A On your paper, write the following sentences, using capital letters where necessary. If a sentence needs no capitals, write *Correct.*

1. Was henry kissinger secretary of state when ex-president ford was in office?
2. Last week rabbi kaplan, father ryan, and reverend anderson led a discussion on the role of god and his teachings.
3. My aunt said that her mother-in-law is the third member of their family to be elected a judge.
4. May i tell the vice-president that you're waiting, colonel?
5. During the Crusades, Christian armies fought to end arab rule in jerusalem.
6. Have father and cousin roger met lt. palermo?
7. Strong patterns of rhyme and rhythm are typical of scottish and english folk ballads.
8. Tomorrow sister bernadette's bible study group will discuss matthew and mark, the first two books of the new testament.
9. I told mr. arroyo that i'd invited mayor grant to the meeting.
10. The secretary of health, education and welfare met with representative-elect joseph p. kennedy, jr., to discuss federal policies.

Mahatma Gandhi addressing a crowd in New Delhi.

B Find the words that need capital letters in the following paragraphs. Write them correctly on your paper after the number of the sentence in which they appear.

(1) For centuries the indian people have been divided by struggles between the hindus and the moslems, two groups with vastly different religious beliefs. (2) The moslems, like christians and jews, believe in one god. (3) Founded by a prophet named mohammed, the moslem religion is based on the teachings of the koran, a sacred book similar to the bible. (4) Mosques are churchlike buildings where moslems worship their god, Allah.

(5) In contrast, hindus believe that the creator and his creations are one and the same, and can be worshipped in any form, including animals, water, planets, or stars. (6) Consequently, hindu temples are filled with statues of gods and goddesses—symbols of the faith's three-and-a-half million divinities. (7) The most important of these divine beings are brahma, shiva, and vishnu. (8) A hindu worships alone, searching for the perfect balance in life as taught in the vedas, four sacred books of scripture.

(9) On August 15, 1947, hindus and moslems joined together to form a unified indian nation, independent of british rule. (10) The two men most responsible for ending the country's internal struggle were the famous peace-loving hindu, mahatma gandhi, and viceroy of india louis mountbatten, the great-grandson of queen victoria.

Part 2
Geographical Names, Structures, and Vehicles

Certain nouns and adjectives that refer to geographical areas or topographical features are capitalized.

Geographical Names

In a geographical name, capitalize the first letter of each word except articles and prepositions.

Continents	**A**ustralia, **S**outh **A**merica, **E**urope, **A**sia
Bodies of Water	**L**ake **O**ntario, the **J**ordan **R**iver, **S**trait of **B**elle **I**sle, **C**ape **C**od **B**ay, the **A**driatic **S**ea, **S**t. **G**eorge's **C**hannel
Land Forms	the **P**yrenees, the **S**inai **P**eninsula, the **G**rand **C**anyon, the **S**yrian **D**esert, **M**ount **C**onstance, the **P**lains of **A**braham, **R**aton **P**ass, the **R**ocky **M**ountains
World Regions	the **O**rient, the **M**iddle **E**ast, the **F**ar **E**ast
Special Terms	the **N**orthern **H**emisphere, the **T**ropic of **C**ancer, the **N**orth **P**ole
Political Units	the **D**istrict of **C**olumbia, the **W**est **I**ndies, **S**an **F**rancisco, the **R**epublic of **T**exas
Public Areas	**G**ettysburg **N**ational **P**ark, **F**ort **N**iagara, the **B**lue **G**rotto, **M**ount **R**ushmore
Roads and Highways	**M**ain **S**treet, **R**oute 447, **W**est **S**ide **H**ighway, **V**an **B**uren **A**venue, the **O**hio **T**urnpike

Usage Note In official documents, words like *city*, *state*, and *county* are capitalized when they are part of the name of a political unit: *the County of Westchester, the City of Dallas*. In general usage, however, such words are not capitalized.

Capitalize the word modified by a proper adjective only if the noun and adjective together form a geographical name.

English **C**hannel	**E**nglish accent
the **I**ndian **O**cean	**I**ndian artifacts

Directions and Sections

Capitalize names of sections of the country or the world, and any adjectives that come from those sections.

> The Jennings moved from the **E**ast **C**oast to the **S**outhwest.
> Jane is from a **M**idwestern town, but she has an **E**astern accent.

Do not capitalize compass directions or adjectives that merely indicate direction or a general location.

> Drive south on Pine Street to the first stoplight.
> I spent my vaction on the western coast of Yugoslavia.
> The hurricane moved northward.

Bodies of the Universe

Capitalize the names of planets in the solar system and other objects in the universe, except words like *sun* and *moon*.

Neptune	Halley's **C**omet	an eclipse of the sun
Jupiter	the **B**ig **D**ipper	a phase of the moon

Capitalize the word *earth* only when it is used in conjunction with the names of other planets. The word *earth* is not capitalized when the article *the* precedes it.

> Mercury, Venus, Earth, Mars, and Pluto are known as the terrestrial planets because they resemble the earth in size, density, and chemical composition.

Structures and Vehicles

Capitalize the names of specific monuments, bridges, and buildings.

the Lincoln **M**emorial	**A**rch of **T**riumph
the **P**rudential **B**uilding	**T**ower **B**ridge
the **F**lat **I**ron **B**uilding	the **S**tatue of **L**iberty

Capitalize the names of specific ships, trains, airplanes, automobiles, and spacecraft.

Queen Elizabeth II	the *Denver Zephyr*
the *Spirit of St. Louis*	*R*eliant

Punctuation Note Underline the names of specific ships, airplanes, trains, and spacecraft, but not automobiles.

Exercises

A On your paper, write the following sentences, using capital letters where necessary. If no capitals are needed, write *Correct*. This exercise covers many of the rules you have studied so far in this chapter.

1. In 1909 american explorer robert e. peary led the first expedition to reach the north geographic pole, which lies near the center of the arctic ocean.
2. In the past two decades, many factories from the north have moved to the southwest.
3. The cayman islands, which belong to great britain, are located just south of cuba in the caribbean sea.
4. This bus goes down fifth avenue past central park to greenwich village and washington square.
5. The town of trier, on the mosel river in germany, was once an important city in the roman empire.
6. In 1976 a section of *viking I* landed on mars to conduct scientific experiments; it also returned the first television pictures from the martian surface.
7. The only german composers i could name were bach, beethoven, and brahms.
8. The winds near the equator move from east to west, but the prevailing winds in the upper latitudes move eastward.
9. One day on the slowly spinning planet mercury is equal to more than 58 days on earth.
10. In 1903 panamanians—supported by the united states—declared independence from the country of colombia and formed the republic of panama.
11. The elegant jefferson memorial in washington, d.c. is a circular structure built out of white marble; it was designed by the classical architect john russell pope.
12. In 1803 the united states purchased the louisiana territory, a parcel of land stretching from the gulf of mexico to the canadian border, and from the mississippi river to the rocky mountains.
13. In 1968 london bridge was dismantled and moved to lake havasu city, arizona.
14. The spanish explorer Juan Ponce de León was the governor of puerto rico until 1513, when he landed in Florida seeking the legendary Fountain of Youth.
15. In one of the most famous scenes in the original movie, king kong climbs up the empire state building; in the modern version of the film he scales the world trade center.

B Rewrite the following paragraph, supplying the necessary capitals.

(1) Few natural wonders in north america can compete with the majesty of niagara falls, which are located about halfway along the northward course of the niagara river. (2) Carrying the overflow of four of the five great lakes, the river plunges over a precipice between lake erie and lake ontario into the gorge on either side of goat island. (3) To the north of the small island is the nearly straight line of the american falls. (4) To the south and west, on the river's canadian side, is the graceful curve of horseshoe falls. (5) From rainbow bridge, which is just below the falls, one can observe arcs of color forming on the clouds of spray. (6) The most unusual view, however, is from a boat named *maid of the mist*, in honor of the legendary indian girl whose canoe tumbled over niagara. (7) Her ghostly image is said to appear occasionally in the foaming mist.

C *Write Now* Imagine that you appeared on a TV game show and won first prize—a two-week trip anywhere in the world. You have chosen your destination, and you are now on your way there. Write several journal entries describing your trip. Be sure to name the places you visit, the routes you travel, the structures you see, and the forms of transportation you take. You may need to research your topic before writing. Make sure to follow the rules of capitalization outlined in this chapter.

Part 3
Organizations, Historical Events, and Other Subjects

Several other commonly used words and phrases are capitalized. These are grouped into six major categories.

Organizations and Institutions

Capitalize the names of organizations and institutions.

Capitalize all words except prepositions and conjunctions in the names of organizations and institutions. Also capitalize abbreviations of these names.

Democratic Party	Central Intelligence Agency **(CIA)**
Sullivan High School	Securities and Exchange Commission
Lee Glass Company, Inc.	House of Representatives
First Methodist Church	Trans World Airlines **(TWA)**

Do not capitalize words such as *school*, *company*, *church*, *college*, and *hospital* when they are not used as parts of names.

Events, Documents, and Periods of Time

Capitalize the names of historical events, documents, and periods of time.

World War II	the Homestead Act
Bill of Rights	the Dark Ages
the Renaissance	the Battle of Bunker Hill

Months, Days, and Holidays

Capitalize the names of months, days, and holidays but not the names of seasons.

June   Tuesday   Memorial Day   winter

Time Abbreviations

Capitalize the abbreviations *B.C.*, *A.D.*, *A.M.*, and *P.M.*

Augustus ruled from 27 **B.C.** to **A.D.** 14.
The meeting begins at 9:30 **A.M.** and ends at 3:00 **P.M.**

Awards, Special Events, and Brand Names

Capitalize the names of awards and special events.

Nobel Prize for Peace   Super Bowl
Emmy Award   Michigan State Fair

Capitalize the brand names of products but not a common noun that follows a brand name.

Springtime air freshener   Golden Grain cereal

School Subjects and Class Names

Do not capitalize the general names of school subjects. Do capitalize the titles of specific courses and of courses that are followed by a number. School subjects that are languages are always capitalized.

biology   German
Home Economics 200   Introduction to Psychology

Capitalize class names only when they refer to a specific group or event or when they are used in direct address.

The juniors are selling tickets for the Junior Prom.
Every spring the Freshman Class holds a carnival.
Good luck, Seniors, as you graduate and begin new lives.

Exercises

A On your paper, write the following sentences, using capital letters where necessary.

1. The boston choral society will appear at the university of maine.
2. The new deal was a program designed to end the great depression.
3. In autumn, jewish people observe the holiday yom kippur.
4. During the spring semester, mr. otero will teach trigonometry as well as geometry II and algebra I.
5. Irreplaceable historical relics such as the rosetta stone and the magna carta are displayed in the british museum.
6. The oldest english company, javersham oyster fishery, has been in operation for over seven hundred years.
7. My european history class saw a film about the renaissance.
8. In 1975 the novelist saul bellow won the pulitzer prize for his novel *Humboldt's Gift.*
9. Opening day for springfield high school is the tuesday after labor day.

10. Theodore roosevelt led his famous Rough-Riders during the spanish-american war.
11. The senior class variety show will be presented to the freshmen, sophomores, and juniors on friday, may 3, at 7:30 p.m.
12. I ordered a plaid shirt and a pair of levi's jeans from carson, pirie, scott and company's christmas catalog.

B On your paper, write the following sentences, using capital letters where necessary and correcting improperly capitalized words. Refer to all the capitalization rules covered so far in this chapter.

1. In 1776 most americans were of dutch, french, swedish, scotch-irish, and english descent.
2. Citizens of the young Nation generally spoke english, worshipped as protestants, and shared a northern European heritage.
3. In the 1840's roman catholic irish immigrants crossed the atlantic to flee from Famine and harsh british laws.
4. Eastern europeans also hoped fo find a new homeland in america.
5. The armenians sought refuge from turkish oppression, while Italians and greeks hoped to overcome poverty.
6. Many polish people wished to escape Foreign rule in their divided country, and jews fled from russian persecution.
7. The Chinese arrived during the 1860's and 1870's to work on construction of the central pacific railroad.
8. Toward the end of the Century, however, the chinese and other newcomers who accepted lower wages were blamed for declining economic conditions.
9. The workingman's party in california urged the Government to pass laws discriminating against specific immigrant groups.
10. The sidewalk ordinance was one such law; it prohibited people who carried merchandise on poles from using sidewalks.
11. In later years, the United States congress restricted the numbers of immigrants from certain countries by creating laws such as the chinese exclusion act.
12. Many social reformers, however, tried to help Immigrants.
13. Jane Addams founded hull house, where newcomers could learn english and prepare for american Citizenship.
14. Industrialists such as carnegie steel company's Andrew Carnegie and standard oil company's John d. Rockefeller helped immigrants by funding Public Education Institutions.
15. In spite of the hardships, most immigrants improved their lives and made important Contributions to our diverse american culture.

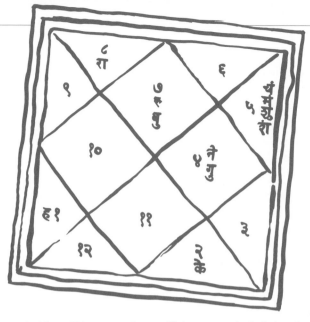

Left: an ox, a symbol from Chinese astrology.   Right: an astrological chart from India.

c *Proofreading* Rewrite the following paragraphs, correcting all errors in spelling, punctuation, and capitalization.

The origins of astrology date back to about 2,470 b.c., when the babylonians used Heavenly bodys to make predictions. By the middle ages astrology had spread throughout the World almost all the great Scholars were said to have studied it during the renaissance. Crime, disease, and catastrophes were "explained" using astrology.

Today there are several different astrologies—european, indian, and chinese. While some beleivers claim that astrology has roots in Science or Religion, most modern astrologists simply try to understand human behavior within the Universe. Do movements of the sun, moon, stars, and planets really affect our personalities. Researchers do not have answers to this question. In the meantime, however, people Worldwide continue to delight in relating themselves to the timeless elements of the Heavens.

Checkpoint Parts 1, 2, and 3

A Rewrite the sentences adding capital letters where necessary.

1. In a.d. 1263 john balliol and his wife, devorgilla, founded a college at oxford university.

2. I asked aunt maria to bring back some irish lace and english tea from her trip to the british isles.
3. According to a recent survey, thirty percent of all americans have visited yellowstone park.
4. Each summer over labor day weekend i sail our family boat, the *vagabond*, around the apostle islands in lake superior.
5. Could you tell me, dad, whether the cosmos computer company is located on ash street?
6. The orbit of halley's comet brought it close to earth in 1986.
7. Several french communities, such as st. louis, were founded in the midwest.
8. Because I scored 100 points on the test about the great depression, i received the student-of-the-month award in history class.
9. According to an ancient tale, rome was founded at 8:00 a.m. on april 21, 753 b.c., by the mighty chieftain, romulus.
10. Sarah ferguson became the duchess of york when she married prince andrew in westminster abbey on july 23, 1986.
11. Gold was discovered in the pike's peak region of colorado in the
12. The junior class of richmont high school sponsored a rock concert to raise money for unicef.
13. The strategic arms limitations talks (salt) stopped when the soviet union invaded afghanistan in 1979.
14. We flew to frankfurt on lufthansa airlines and then traveled through the night on the *komet*, a sleeper express train.

B Application in Literature In the following paragraph, some capital letters have been changed to lower-case letters, and some lower-case letters have been capitalized. Return the paragraph to its original, correct form by rewriting it and correcting all capitalization errors.

(1) San Francisco put on a show for me. (2) i saw her. . . from the great road that bypasses sausalito and enters the golden gate bridge. (3) The afternoon Sun painted her white and gold—rising on her hills like a Noble City in a happy dream. (4) A city on hills has it over flat-land places. (5) New york makes its own Hills with cran-ing buildings, but this gold and white acropolis rising wave on wave against the blue of the pacific sky was a stunning thing, a painted thing like a picture of a medi-eval italian city which can never have existed.

From *Travels with Charley* by John Steinbeck

Part 4

First Words and Titles

The first words of a sentence, a quotation, and a line of poetry are capitalized.

Sentences and Poetry

Capitalize the first word of every sentence.

The coach gave his players a pep talk.

Capitalize the first word of every line of poetry.

Whenever Richard Cory went down town,
We people on the pavement looked at him:
He was a gentleman from sole to crown,
Clean favored, and imperially slim.

From "Richard Cory" by Edward Arlington Robinson

Usage Note Sometimes, especially in modern poetry, the lines of a poem do not begin with capital letters.

Quotations

Capitalize the first word of a direct quotation.

Patrick Henry exclaimed, "Give me liberty or give me death!"

In a **divided quotation,** do not capitalize the first word of the second part unless it starts a new sentence.

"It's true," said Renée, "that appearances can be deceiving."
"It's true," said Renée. "Appearances can be deceiving."

Letter Parts

Capitalize the first word in the greeting of a letter. Also capitalize the title, person's name, and words such as *Sir* and *Madam*.

Dear Ms. Lopez   Dear Sir or Madam

Capitalize only the first word in the complimentary close.

Sincerely yours,   Very truly yours,

Outlines and Titles

Capitalize the first word of each item in an outline and letters that introduce major subsections.

    I. Entertainers
      A. Musicians
         1. Vocal
         2. Instrumental

Capitalize the first, last, and all other important words in titles. Do not capitalize conjunctions, articles, or prepositions with fewer than five letters.

Book	*To Kill a Mockingbird*
Newspaper	*Miami Herald*
Magazine	*Interview*
Play	*Much Ado About Nothing*
Television Series	*The Oprah Winfrey Show*
Work of Art	*The Last Supper*
Long Musical Work	*The Marriage of Figaro*
Short Story	"The Pit and the Pendulum"
Song	"We Are the World"
Chapter	Chapter 11, "The Rise of Islam"

The word *the* at the beginning of a title and the word *magazine* are capitalized only when they are part of the formal name.

    The New York Times   the *Springfield Courier*
    Audubon Magazine   *Time* magazine

Punctuation Note Titles are either underlined or put in quotation marks. See Chapter 12, page 322 for punctuation rules.

Exercises

A Rewrite the items below, capitalizing words where necessary. Underline any words that are italicized in the exercise.

1. "the only thing we have to fear," claimed Franklin Roosevelt in 1933, "is fear itself."
2. Robert Frost's poem, "stopping by woods on a snowy evening," speaks of fulfilling one's obligations in life.
3. dear sir:
   please send me audition information on your upcoming production of *sunday in the park with george*.
   sincerely yours,
alonzo m. sanchez
4. the ending of the short story "the lady or the tiger" is left to the reader's imagination.
5. i celebrate myself, and sing myself,
   and what i assume you shall assume,
   for every atom belonging to me as good belongs to you.
   Walt Whitman
6. "did you happen to see last night's episode of *who's the boss?*" asked kathleen.
7. we read and discussed chapter 6 in our biology text, entitled "the liver and its function."
8. I. literature
   a. fiction
      1. short stories
      2. plays
      3. novels
   b. nonfiction
9. the september issue of *smithsonian* magazine included an article entitled, "have you hugged a manatee today?"
10. yesterday in Humanities II we studied Cézanne's painting, *the basket of apples*.
11. "let's get tickets for *the barber of seville*," said Ron. "it's my favorite opera."
12. *the princess bride*, directed by rob reiner, is a modern movie adaptation of a classic fairy tale.
13. my dad subscribes to *the wall street journal*.
14. Bob Dylan's song "the times they are a-changing" expressed the social unrest of the 1960's.
15. "for my great books class," said Amy, "I read *crime and punishment* and *a tale of two cities*."

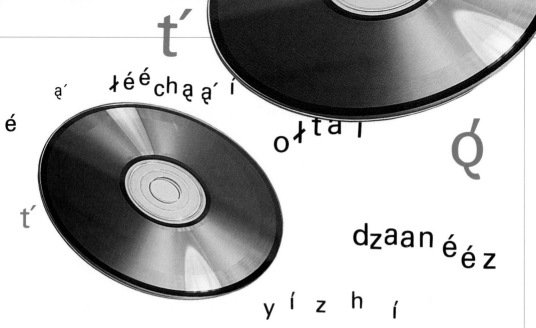

B Application in Literature In the following passage, some capital letters have been changed to lower-case letters, and some lower-case letters have been capitalized. Return the passage to its original, correct form by rewriting it and correcting all errors in capitalization.

(1) I've read that Navajo, a language related to that of the indians of alaska and northwest canada, has no curse words unless you consider "coyote" cursing. (2) by comparison with other native tongues, it's remarkably free of english and spanish. (3) a navajo Mechanic, for example, has more than two hundred purely navajo terms to describe automobile parts. (4) It might be navajo that will greet the first Extraterrestrial ears to hear from planet earth. (5) On board each *voyager* Spacecraft traveling toward the edge of the solar system and beyond is a gold-plated, long-playing record. (6) Following an aria from mozart's *magic flute* and chuck berry's "johnny b. goode," is a navajo night Chant, music the conquistadors heard.

From *Blue Highways* by William Least Heat Moon

c *Write Now* Briefly describe two works of art that have had a powerful effect on you. The works of art can include such things as books, movies, paintings, poems, songs, or musicals. In addition, explain what significance these works of art have for you. Use correct capitalization throughout, paying particular attention to titles.

Checkpoint *Parts 1, 2, 3, and 4*

A Rewrite the following sentences, correcting all capitalization errors.

1. success is counted sweetest
   by those who ne'er succeed.
   to comprehend a nectar
   requires sorest need.
   Emily Dickinson
2. amanda asked, "will you be marching with the veterans of foreign wars in the parade, grandpa?"
3. "my art History class," said kevin, "Will attend a lecture on *dancers in the wings*, a painting by french artist edgar degas.
4. the prime minister of australia will dine at the white house during his visit there on monday.
5. the *lusitania* was a british steamship that was torpedoed and sunk by a German Submarine off the Coast of ireland in may, 1915.

B On your paper, rewrite the following passage, using capital letters where necessary.

(1) born into a modest midwestern household on december 5, 1901, walter elias disney became one of the best-known creative geniuses of the twentieth century. (2) disney developed his interest in drawing while living on his family's Missouri Farm, and later he received a smattering of formal art education at the kansas city art institute. (3) his job at kansas city film ad company gave eighteen-year-old disney the experience in animation techniques that he needed to open his own animation company. (4) his animated versions of fairy tales such as "puss in boots" and "the four musicians of bremen" began a long and successful film career.

(5) four days before christmas in 1937, *snow white and the seven dwarfs* premiered in hollywood. (6) it was the first feature-length animated film. (7) during the next three decades, mr. disney entertained america with hundreds of cartoons and films—from *song of the south* and *alice in wonderland* to *the sword in the stone* and *mary poppins*.

(8) in addition to creating film entertainment, disney's dream of an amusement park for people of all ages became a reality when disneyland opened on july 17, 1955, in anaheim, california.

Linking
Mechanics & Writing

Imagine that your favorite celebrity (athlete, entertainer, politician, artist, or writer) has just won an award and that you are to interview this person for your local newspaper.

Prewriting and Drafting Begin by making a list of facts about the celebrity. Your list should include the name of the celebrity, the name of the award, and the reason this celebrity is getting the award. Also include a quote from the celebrity regarding the secret of his or her successful career.

Select the most interesting and relevant information on your list, organize your material into paragraphs, and write your first draft.

Revising and Proofreading As you revise your first draft, consider these questions:

1. Have you given a clear, specific picture of this person's life?
2. Have you included details of this person's achievements—titles of songs, literary pieces, movies, works of art, athletic competitions, or governmental posts?
3. Does your story follow a logical sequence?
4. Have you followed the rules for correct capitalization?

Additional Writing Topic Imagine that you are a famous anthropologist in A.D. 2110. You have just spent ten years studying a strange tribe in a remote region. Now you must report your findings. Include information about the region's geography, the tribe's social groups and leaders, tribal art, and literature.

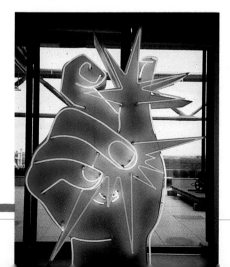

Chapter 9
Application and Review

A Using Capital Letters Correctly Write the following sentences, capitalizing words as necessary.

1. passing under the north pole, the *nautilus* was the first submarine to travel from the pacific ocean to the atlantic.
2. the gulf stream keeps winters mild along cape cod.
3. majorca is a spanish island resort in the mediterranean sea.
4. I. federal officials
      A. the president
      B. cabinet members
   II. state officials
5. the movie *a man for all seasons* recounts the story of sir thomas more, who was beheaded by king henry VIII for remaining loyal to the roman catholic church.
6. several western high schools are offering interesting courses in frontier history.
7. the first known photo of the "monster" in loch ness was taken by col. robt. k. wilson in 1933.
8. at the country kitchen cafe i had the italian minestrone and house salad with french dressing.
9. the tallest sandcastle ever built was created at treasure island, florida, and entitled "lost city of atlantis."
10. headquarters for the united nations are in new york city.
11. the wheel was invented in the tigris-euphrates valley by the sumerians in 3500 b. c.
12. "we ask, o lord," prayed rev. dixon, "that you bless this occasion."
13. let's welcome the freshman class to cooper high school.
14. my favorite song from the musical *my fair lady* was "i could have danced all night."
15. carlos, did your sister take european history or history 20 in her junior year?
16. the greyhound bus traveled east along route 3 until it arrived in jefferson city.
17. the tallest building today is sears tower on wacker drive in chicago.
18. on its way to mercury in february of 1974, the american spacecraft *mariner 10* took pictures of venus.

19. my uncle phil brought his kodak camera to the game at white sox park last saturday.
20. the longest sentence ever published was 2,403 words; it was written by jack mcclintock and appeared in the *miami herald* newspaper.

B Using Capital Letters Correctly Find the words in the following paragraphs that are capitalized incorrectly. On your paper, write the words and capitalize them correctly after the number of the sentence in which they appear.

(1) "a marathon," Says *webster's new world dictionary,* "Is any long-distance or endurance contest." (2) most runners know the story behind the word *marathon*—the legend of a fierce Battle on the plains near the greek town of marathon in 490 b.c. (3) the athenians caught the invading persian army by surprise, charged the enemy, and saved the greek empire. (4) a greek soldier, pheidippides, was ordered to run from the Battlefield to athens with news of the victory, a distance of twenty-two miles. (5) although pheidippides had no training in running, he managed to reach athens, exclaiming, "rejoice, we conquer!" (6) poor pheidippides promptly collapsed and died, but his name is remembered because his lengthy run is considered the first "marathon."

The marathon became an official event in the modern olympic games in 1896. (7) the present standardized marathon distance of 42,195 m was actually determined by an english princess in london. (8) a marathon was set up to begin at windsor castle and end at white city stadium. (9) her royal highness wished to view the start of the race from her castle window and then see the finish from her stadium seat—a 26 mile span. this distance has remained the same for every olympic marathon since that Summer day in 1908.

(10) the first marathon in the united states was run in new york city, but the best-known american marathon is held each year in boston. (11) thousands of runners have tested their endurance in this famous eastern race, but you might ask, "why would people subject themselves to such a grueling challenge?" (12) to answer this question, consider the case of carl eilenberg, who was ready to quit the 1975 boston marathon when he was halfway up heartbreak hill. (13) a former star runner from syracuse university, tom coulter, ran alongside, and gave carl some memorable words of encouragement. (14) "once you cross the finish line at boston," tom said, "there's nothing you can't do." (15) these words gave carl the strength to continue running and ultimately to finish the race.

10

End Marks and Commas

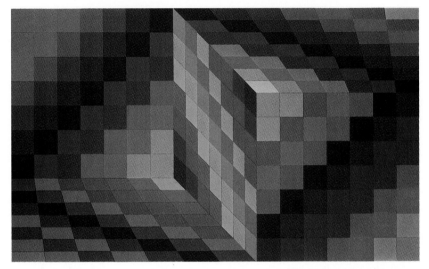

Piece from the Gestalt Series,
Victor Vasarely, 1968–1974.

*H*ow does this painting make you feel confused anxious do you know where it begins where it ends where it's going?

Unlike the preceding paragraph and the painting above, language has marks that punctuate its flow, pace the presentation of ideas, and indicate where one thought ends and another begins. In this chapter you will learn how to use periods, question marks, exclamation points, and commas to help you communicate clearly.

Part 1
End Marks

End marks are the punctuation marks that indicate the end of a unit of thought. The three kinds of end marks are the period, the question mark, and the exclamation point. The proper use of each end mark is described on the following pages.

The Period

Use a period at the end of all declarative sentences and most imperative sentences.

> More people speak Mandarin Chinese than any other language in the world.
>
> Please lock the door when you leave.

When an imperative sentence expresses strong emotion or excitement, an exclamation point, rather than a period, is used to end the sentence.

> Watch out!   Let's hurry!

Use a period at the end of an indirect question.

An **indirect question** indicates that someone has asked a question, but it does not give the reader the exact words of the question. (See page 318 for punctuation of direct questions.)

> Jeremy asked whether Amelia Earhart's airplane had ever been located.

Use a period at the end of an abbreviation or an initial.

Sen. Phil Gramm	Inc.	6:00 A.M. on Oct. 1
Gov. Martha L. Collins	Tues.	3 ft. 2 in.
Mr. John Williams, Jr.	Jan.	2 hr. 35 min.

For abbreviations of metric measurements, acronyms, and abbreviations that are pronounced letter by letter, periods are optional. Use your dictionary to check whether periods are required for the following abbreviations.

cm	ml	NATO	UNICEF	NFL	MIT	CIA
km	g	NASA	CARE	UFO	PBS	FBI
kg	L	HUD	NOW	TV	TWA	IRS

Use a period after each number or letter in an outline or a list.

Outline
I. Television programs
  A. Daytime
    1. Soap operas
    2. Game shows
  B. Evening

List
1. paintbrush
2. canvas
3. watercolors

Use a period between dollars and cents and to indicate a decimal.

$8.57   5.36

The Question Mark

Use a question mark at the end of an interrogative sentence or after a question that is not a complete sentence.

How many days does it take for Mars to orbit the sun?
Your cassettes? I think you left them in the den.
The date? It's the twenty-fifth.

Occasionally, writers may use a question mark to indicate that a declarative sentence is intended to be expressed as a question. In these cases the question mark is a signal to read the sentence with rising inflection.

Declarative
You've finished your homework.
These are yours.

Interrogative
You've finished your homework?
These are yours?

The Exclamation Point

Use an exclamation point at the end of an exclamatory sentence or after a strong interjection.

An **interjection** consists of one or more words that show feeling or imitate a sound.

What a great game!   That's unbelievable!
Oh no!   Crash!   Fantastic!   Yes!   Zoom!

When an interjection is followed by a sentence, the sentence may end with a period, a question mark, or an exclamation point.

Wait! I almost forgot my keys.
Wonderful! Will you play that song again?
Look! There's a truck heading toward us!

At the Porcupine Ball

Exercises

A Rewrite the following sentences, adding periods and other end marks as necessary. If you are unsure about punctuating abbreviations, consult a dictionary.

1. Mr Franz asked the company, Gilson's Inc, whether the bill for $749 was correct
2. In AD 79 the eruption of Mt Vesuvius destroyed Pompeii, an ancient city in Italy
3. Help I've been robbed
4. Rev Thomas ran through the J FKennedy Forest during his 6 5 (six and five-tenths) km race near downtown St Louis
5. I Federal agencies
    A Investigative
        1 CIA (Central Intelligence Agency)
        2 FBI (Federal Bureau of Investigation)
    B Economic
        1 SEC (Securities and Exchange Commission)
        2 IRS (Internal Revenue Service)
    II State agencies
6. The answer Ask me the question again
7. On Nov 5, at 9:00 AM, Dr J A Larson, Jr, will attend a nutrition conference in Washington, DC
8. Did UCLA beat MSU in the football game on Sat, Sept 8th
9. Are you serious Mrs James actually chose *me* for the leading role in the play
10. Look out Didn't you see that last step

B Rewrite the following paragraph, adding end marks as needed.

(1) At 10:42 AM Jas R Fox, Jr, began to panic (2) He had been running for 2 hrs and still had 3 km to go (3) He wondered whether he had the energy to cover the remaining 2 mi of the race (4) Would he make it (5) Buildings seemed to float past him as he continued down Ash St —Chas A Stevens and Co, F W Woolworth's, Bidwell's, Inc (6) Throat parched and head pounding, he spotted the finish line about 25 yds away (7) Straining, urging his exhausted limbs forward, he finally felt the rope hit his chest. (8) "I've made it" he exulted

Part 2
Commas: Series, Introductory Elements, and Interrupters

Commas can help you express your ideas by slowing down the rhythm of a sentence, showing a shift in thought, or adding clarity. The following rules explain the proper uses of the comma.

Commas in a Series

Use a comma after every item in a series except the last one.

A series consists of three or more items of the same kind.

Words	Benjamin Franklin was a politician, a writer, a scientist, and an inventor.
Phrases	Groups of children played behind the house, on the porch, and in the yard.
Clauses	The archaeologist explained where the dinosaurs lived, what they ate, and how they protected themselves.

Do not use a comma if all parts of the series are joined by the words *and, or,* or *nor*.

All summer we swam and fished and sailed.

Use commas after *first, second,* and so on, when they introduce a series. (Note also the use of semicolons [;] below. For more information on semicolons refer to pages 295–297.)

Our bus stopped at three streets: first, Clark Street; second, Johnson Avenue; and third, Main Street.

Use commas between coordinate adjectives that modify the same noun.

Raging, howling winds whipped the coastline.

To determine whether adjectives are **coordinate**—that is, of equal rank—try placing an *and* between them. If the *and* sounds natural, and if you can reverse the order of the adjectives without changing the meaning, then a comma is needed.

His loud (*and*) whining voice made the audience shudder. (The *and* sounds natural, and the meaning is not changed by reversing the order of the adjectives. Therefore, a comma is needed.)
His loud, whining voice made the audience shudder.

Maria is an experienced (*and*) subway rider. (The *and* sounds awkward, and the adjectives cannot be reversed. No comma is necessary.)
Maria is an experienced subway rider.

In general, it is safe to omit the comma after numbers and adjectives of size, shape, and age.

a big round moon   five tiny wafers

Equal rank.
Left: the insignia of a Master Chief Petty Officer in the U.S. Navy. Right: the insignia of a Chief Master Sergeant in the U.S. Air Force.

Exercises

A Rewrite the following sentences, placing commas where necessary. If no commas are needed, write *Correct*.

1. In the early 1900's jazz was introduced to the major cities of the United States by composers and performers such as W.C. Handy Bessie Smith Louis Armstrong Earl Hines and Joe Oliver.
2. All roads bridges and highways into the city have been blocked by the blinding driving snowstorm.
3. Suddenly, the commanding officer picked up a pen reached for my papers signed them and handed them across the desk to me.
4. The Himalayan Mountains extend across portions of China Nepal India and Pakistan.
5. In 1687 King Louis XIV gave a dinner party for a distinguished foreign guest in Paris that included the following: twenty-two "large" soups sixty-four "small" soups twenty-one main courses forty-four kinds of roasts sixty-three side dishes thirty-six salads and twelve sauces.
6. On weekends I usually bowl or see a movie or go to a party.
7. Princess Diana's engagement ring is a large oval sapphire surrounded by fourteen small diamonds.
8. The growling snarling dog stood behind the sturdy spiked gate in front of the house.
9. At basketball practice we worked on several skills: first dribbling; second passing; and third rebounding.
10. Carlos pulled on his old blue sweatshirt bounded down the stairs and devoured a bowl of hot creamy oatmeal.

B Application in Literature Some commas have been omitted from the following sentences. Write the word before each missing comma and place the comma correctly. Notice how commas help to clarify the writers' ideas.

1. He straightened his shoulders flipped the reins against the horse's shoulder and rode away.   John Steinbeck
2. The brother came with his plump healthy wife and two great roaring hungry boys.   Katherine Anne Porter
3. Mrs. Proudhammer knew very well what people thought of Mr. Proudhammer. She knew, too, exactly how much she owed in each store she entered how much she was going to be able to pay and what she had to buy.   James Baldwin
4. It was true we were at war, observing heatless meatless and wheatless days and conserving sugar.   Sterling North

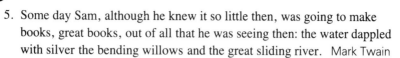

5. Some day Sam, although he knew it so little then, was going to make books, great books, out of all that he was seeing then: the water dappled with silver the bending willows and the great sliding river. Mark Twain

6. [Frederick] Douglass was then twenty-four years old six feet tall with hair like a lion and very handsome. Langston Hughes

7. The shaggy little creatures kicked bucked sprang into the air ran through our legs and even hurtled straight up the walls. James Herriot

8. Hours of wintertime had found me in the treehouse, looking over the schoolyard spying on multitudes of children through a two-power telescope Jem had given me learning their games following Jem's red jacket through wriggling circles of blind man's bluff secretly sharing their misfortunes and minor victories. Harper Lee

9. Tarzan ran his brown fingers through his thick black hair cocked his head upon one side and stared. Edgar Rice Burroughs

10. She was a lofty dignified conventional lady; and she smelled like an old dictionary among whose pages many flowers have been dried and pressed. Elizabeth Enright

C *Write Now* You are an eyewitness to a jewelry store robbery and are being questioned regarding details of the incident. Write a statement describing the crime as you saw it. Be sure to explain the robber's sequence of actions, as well as his or her specific appearance. Apply the rules for commas that you have just studied, so that your "police report" will be clear and precise.

Commas with Introductory Elements

Use a comma after introductory words, mild interjections, or adverbs at the beginning of a sentence.

Well, I think I can manage the job by myself.

Yes, I would like some watermelon.

However, the storm raged for two more days.

Nonetheless, I expect you and Christopher to be ready for next Saturday's car wash.

Use a comma after a series of prepositional phrases at the beginning of a sentence.

Before gaining independence in 1960, Nigeria was a colony of Great Britain.

A single prepositional phrase that begins a sentence may be set off by a comma if it is followed by a natural pause when read.

Because of heavy traffic, we missed half of the movie.

A comma is not necessary when there would be almost no pause in speaking, or if the phrase is very short.

By tomorrow I'll be rested.

Use a comma after verbal phrases at the beginning of a sentence.

Hoping for victory, the exhausted players pressed on.

To enhance your appearance, wear colors that complement your complexion.

Use a comma after adverbial clauses at the begining of a sentence. (For more information on verbals and adverbial clauses, see Chapter 3, pages 78–79 and pages 96–97.)

When the concert ended, the audience applauded wildly.

Use a comma after words or phrases that have been transposed; that is, moved to the beginning of a sentence from their normal position.

Call Serena for directions if necessary. (normal order)

If necessary, call Serena for directions. (transposed order)

The birthday card is obviously going to be late. (normal order)

Obviously, the birthday card is going to be late. (transposed order)

Commas with Interrupters

Use commas to set off nonessential appositives.

Nonessential appositives are words or phrases that add extra information to an already clear and complete sentence.

> The World Series, baseball's toughest competition, is held annually in the fall.
> *Growing Up*, a touching and humorous autobiography, was written by Russell Baker.

Essential appositives, however, are needed to make the sentence clear and complete. Do not use commas with essential appositives.

> The movie *The Color Purple* was based on a novel by Alice Walker.
> The Spanish monk Torquemada was responsible for the infamous Spanish Inquisition.

For further information about appositives, see Chapter 3, pages 75–76.

Use commas to set off words of direct address.

> Erika, please pass the pasta.
> I understand, Mr. Ames, that your hobby is woodworking.
> You've just won the drawing, Mario!

Use commas to set off parenthetical expressions.

Parenthetical expressions are words and phrases used to explain or qualify a statement. Since they interrupt the flow of thought in a sentence, they are set off by commas.

> Our car, I believe, is over there.
> You know, of course, that Mark Twain was a pseudonym.

The following expressions are often used parenthetically:

of course	consequently	for example
in fact	I believe	on the other hand
by the way	after all	nevertheless
however	moreover	therefore

Grammar Note When words and phrases such as *I believe* are used as basic parts of the sentence, they are not set off by commas.

> I believe our car is over there.
> We hope we'll get back in time for the meeting.

Conjunctive adverbs such as *nevertheless*, *therefore*, and *consequently* may be used parenthetically. Since they interrupt the flow of a sentence, they are set off by commas.

> The explorer, nevertheless, completed his hike up the mountain.
> The artist, therefore, has little need for a home computer.
> The rally, consequently, was attended by very few.

Occasionally, words like *however*, *therefore*, and *consequently* are used to modify a word in a sentence. As modifiers they are essential parts of the sentence and need no commas.

> Pat cannot arrive on time however hard he tries.
> The cast had performed the play the previous semester. They
>   therefore needed little rehearsal.
> Evening rehearsals were consequently eliminated.

For more information on conjunctive adverbs, see Chapter 1, page 38.

Exercises

A Rewrite the following sentences, placing commas where necessary. If a sentence needs no commas, write *Correct*.

1. Both Colin and Evan enjoy playing soccer a rough and tumble game.

2. The actor Henry Fonda won an Oscar for *On Golden Pond*.
3. Did you realize Joan that six American Presidents were born in October; moreover we have never had a President born in June?
4. After scoring six runs in the first inning the Mets let up.
5. Saving some of your money however is simply good sense.
6. My sister on the other hand is quite a spendthrift.
7. When we explored the campsite area we discovered a cave.
8. The oldest human-built structure a rough circle of piled lava blocks dates back to 1,700,000 B.C.
9. You are obviously the best candidate for this office Senator.
10. Yes as a matter of fact I walk the dog every morning for twenty minutes or more.
11. Politicians however sincere they may be are distrusted by many Americans.
12. Consequently the fate of Amelia Earhart remains a mystery.
13. Sally K. Ride the first American female astronaut was a member of the 1983 *Challenger* crew.
14. Off the coast of California we went deep-sea fishing.
15. To avoid muscle soreness or injury always warm up and cool down when exercising.

B Rewrite the following paragraph, adding commas where necessary.

(1) William Faulkner one of America's greatest writers grew up in Mississippi hearing tales of honor gallantry and defeat. (2) Although he dropped out of high school, he read widely traveled and wrote poetry and prose. (3) Encouraged by author Sherwood Anderson Faulkner published two novels by 1927. (4) Moreover he continually experimented with new writing techniques. (5) His long sentences were packed with images and detail and therefore allowed the reader to share the characters' innermost thoughts. (6) *The Sound and the Fury* many believe is the best example of Faulkner's unique style and his greatest contribution to American literature.

c *Write Now* You are trying to convince your parents to grant you some special privilege such as staying out later than is usually allowed. Write out this discussion, using introductory words and interrupters to indicate the opposing sides of the argument. For example:

Me: I'm old enough, in fact, to stay out past midnight. Letting me stay out would show that you really do trust me.
Parents: It isn't a question of not trusting you. However, we'll talk about it and let you know.

Part 3
Commas: Quotations, Compound Sentences, and Clauses

Use commas to set off the explanatory words of a direct quotation.

Explanatory words are statements that identify the speaker but are not part of the quotation. Use a comma after explanatory words when they precede the quotation.

> Mark said, "Drive east to the first stoplight."

When the explanatory words follow the quotation, a comma belongs at the end of the quotation inside the quotation marks.

> "Drive east to the first stoplight," Mark said.

In a divided quotation, use a comma within the quotation marks after the first part of the quotation and after the explanatory words.

> "Drive east," Mark said, "to the first stoplight."

Indirect quotations require no commas.

> Mark said to drive east to the first stoplight.

Commas in Compound Sentences

Use a comma before the conjunction that joins the two main clauses of a compound sentence.

A comma is not necessary when the main clauses are very short and are joined by the conjunctions *and*, *but*, *so*, *or*, or *nor*.

A comma does separate clauses joined by *yet* or *for*.

> You said you'd help, yet I finished the project myself.

There is no comma between the parts of a compound predicate.

> Eighty percent of Japan is covered with mountains and cannot be used for agriculture.

Exercises

A Commas have been left out of the following sentences. Number your paper from 1 to 10, write the word that comes before the missing comma, and place the comma correctly. Some sentences may need more than one comma. If no commas are needed in a sentence, write *Correct*.

1. We had not intended to stay up late for we had an early class.
2. "Few details are known"said Alexander "about William Shakespeare's life."
3. Glaciers on Greenland slide into the sea and break into icebergs.
4. "I've written some poetry I don't understand myself" said Pulitzer Prize-winning poet Carl Sandburg.
5. The principal said that the pep rally would be rescheduled.
6. New York ranks thirtieth in size but is second in population.
7. "The first woman champion at Wimbledon" said Ann "was Maud Watson."
8. "I'd better work on my science report today or I'll never have it finished by tomorrow" said Kate.
9. The catcher signaled and Viola threw the ball.
10. World War I began in 1914 and ended in 1920.

B Application in Literature Rewrite the following passage adding fifteen missing commas. You will use several of the comma rules you have learned so far in this chapter. Notice how the use of commas adds clarity and organization to writing.

(1) The doctor said "I was not in when you came this morning. (2) But now at the first chance I have come to see the baby."

(3) Kino stood in the door filling it and hatred raged and flamed in back of his eyes. . . .

(4) "The baby is nearly well now" he said curtly.

(5) The doctor smiled but his eyes in their little lymph-lined hammocks did not smile.

(6) He said "Sometimes my friend the scorpion sting has a curious effect. (7) There will be apparent improvement, and then without warning—pouf!". . . (8) "Sometimes" the doctor went on in a liquid tone "sometimes there will be a withered leg or a blind eye or a crumpled back. (9) Oh I know the sting of the scorpion my friend and I can cure it."

From *The Pearl* by John Steinbeck

c *Write Now* Writers of historical fiction must use their imagination when they write dialogue. Do some brief research about one of the situations below. Then combine this information with your imagination and write the dialogue that might have taken place. Vary your quotations to include explanatory words that precede, divide, and follow the speaker's words. Place commas correctly.

> Delegates to the Constitutional Convention discuss adoption of the Constitution of the United States.
>
> Columbus reports his discoveries to Queen Isabella.
>
> Queen Elizabeth and William Shakespeare talk about the opening of the Globe Theatre.

The Declaration of Independence, John Trumbull, 1786.

Commas with Nonessential Clauses and Phrases

Use commas to set off nonessential clauses.

A **nonessential clause** merely adds extra information to an already complete sentence. An **essential clause** is necessary to complete the meaning of the sentence; if it is dropped, the meaning changes. No commas are used with essential clauses.

Nonessential Clause	The Mississippi River, *which empties into the Gulf of Mexico,* is the setting of the musical *Showboat.* (Clause can be dropped.)
Essential Clause	The river *that empties into the Gulf of Mexico* is the Mississippi. (Clause cannot be dropped.)

Notice that *which* is used to introduce nonessential clauses, and *that* is used to introduce essential clauses.

Use commas to set off nonessential participial phrases.

A nonessential participial phrase can be dropped without making the meaning of the sentence incomplete.

An essential participial phrase is necessary to the meaning of the sentence. No commas are used with essential participial phrases.

Nonessential Participial Phrase	The man, *driving a Ford sedan*, headed down Fir Street at 25 mph. (Dropping the phrase does not change the meaning of the sentence.)
Essential Participial Phrase	The man *driving a Ford sedan* is my father. (The phrase identifies a specific man, so it cannot be dropped without changing the meaning of the sentence.)

Exercise

Rewrite the following sentences, adding the necessary commas. If no commas are needed, write *Correct*.

1. Lewis Carroll who wrote *Alice in Wonderland* was a British author and mathematics professor.
2. This is the house that we expect to buy.
3. The coach fearing overconfidence put the team through a rigorous practice session.
4. The Carlsbad Caverns which attract sightseers to New Mexico are the largest known underground caves.
5. The horse that is pawing the ground has not been fed.
6. Charles Hires who was a student at Jefferson Memorial College became the first manufacturer of root beer in 1866.
7. The movie now showing at the Tivoli Theater stars the popular actor Emilio Estevez.
8. The commuters agitated by a long delay climbed quickly onto the morning train.
9. Running for the bus Angela slipped and twisted her ankle.
10. The car that you just passed is a police car.
11. *On the Terrace* painted in 1881 is one of the most popular of Renoir's paintings.
12. Mount St. Helens which had lain dormant for 123 years erupted on May 18, 1980.
13. The tag sewn into the lining tells whose coat it is.
14. Walking in pairs the chorus members entered the auditorium.
15. The Chinese name Chang which belongs to at least 104 million people is the most common family name in the world.

Part 4
Commas: Other Uses

There are several other situations that call for the use of commas.

Commas in Dates, Place Names, and Letters

In dates, use a comma between the day of the month and the year. When only the month and year are given, no comma is necessary.

> October 1, 1948   November 16, 1980   May 1975

When a date is part of a sentence, a comma also follows the year.

> On July 5, 1835, there were snowstorms in New England.

Use a comma between the name of a city or town and the name of its state or country.

> Dallas, Texas   Paris, France   Sydney, Australia

When an address or place name is part of a sentence, it is necessary to use a comma after each item. Do not put a comma between the name of a state and the ZIP code, however.

> Please forward my mail to 3144 Camelback Road, Phoenix, Arizona 85016, where I will reside for two months.

Use a comma after the salutation of a friendly letter. (Use a colon after the salutation of a business letter.) Use a comma after the closing of a friendly letter or a business letter.

> Dear Angie,   Yours truly,

Commas to Avoid Confusion

Use a comma to separate words or phrases that might be mistakenly joined when read.

In some situations, commas are needed to separate words that may be mistakenly read together. The first situation occurs when the conjunctions *but* and *for* are mistaken for prepositions.

Confusing   I liked all the speeches but one was superb.
Clear   I liked all the speeches, but one was superb.

A second source of confusion is a word that may be an adverb, a preposition, or a conjunction at the beginning of a sentence.

Confusing   Below the earth looked like a quilt.
Clear   Below, the earth looked like a quilt.

A third source of confusion is a noun following a verbal phrase.

Confusing   While sleeping Di dreamed she was attacked by polka dots.
Clear   While sleeping, Di dreamed she was attacked by polka dots.

Use a comma to indicate the words left out of parallel word groups.

Detroit manufactures cars; Hollywood, dreams.
The day became warm, and our spirits, merry.

Commas with Titles and Numbers

Use commas when a name is followed by one or more titles. Also use a comma after a business abbreviation if it is part of a sentence.

I met with John Kane, Jr., regarding the fund-raiser.
My brother worked for Lane and Fox, Inc., for two years.

In numbers of more than three digits, use a comma after every third digit from the right, with the exception of ZIP codes, phone numbers, years, and house numbers.

An estimated crowd of 60,000 people thronged the stadium.

Exercises

A Rewrite the following sentences, using commas where necessary.

1. David Kunst walked 14500 miles around the world between June 10 1970 and October 5 1974.
2. My sister loves classical music; my brother jazz.
3. He stayed at 465 Turner Terrace Lexington Kentucky for a week.
4. Please send the payment to Barbara Snower D.D.S. by April 1 1989.
5. Beyond the residential section extends for miles.
6. Please write to me at 2367 W. Ash Street Earlham New York 11023.
7. John D. Rockefeller Sr. formed the Standard Oil Company in 1870.
8. My brother became angry, and my dad silent.
9. By the year 2000 there may be 6100 million people on our planet.
10. Phillip waited for he knew his friend would call soon.
11. Elizabeth II Queen of England was born in London England in 1926.
12. Inside the restaurant was beautifully lighted.
13. Edith Wharton wrote *Ethan Frome*; Doris Lessing *African Stories*.
14. Skip painted all the chairs but four needed repair as well.
15. After refueling the plane the pilot flew on to Des Moines Iowa.

B Rewrite the following letter, adding commas where necessary.

April 24, 19--

Dear Holly

Did you know I'm a celebrity? Before you answer look on page 23 of the April issue of Photographer magazine. Can you believe that a girl from Byfield Oregon could win a photo contest that had 2400 entries? Until I heard from the sponsor, Picture This Ltd. I didn't think I had a chance.

I will be spending the summer studying photography under Gregory Martin Jr. Write to me at L'Hôtel Marquis 73 rue Duret Paris France.

Sincerely

Connie

Checkpoint Parts 1–4

A Copy the following sentences, adding periods, question marks, exclamation points, or commas where they are needed. If the punctuation is correct, write *Correct*.

1. After fishing my sister cleaned the trout and fried them
2. All of the visitors spoke Spanish English and Portuguese
3. Marion Heid PhD was named the President's advisor to NATO
4. The time It's exactly 5:08 PM
5. Believe it or not Elvis Presley recorded eighty albums
6. After the discovery of gold many settlers came to Australia.
7. Wow Dave Winfield just hit a grand slam
8. The exotic island of Bora-Bora first described by Capt James Cook in 1769 has attracted travelers writers and film makers
9. November 25 1987 was a holiday. The library was therefore closed
10. The first baseball game in which one team scored more than 100 runs took place in Philadelphia Pennsylvania on October 1 1865
11. I Department stores
     A W T Grant
     B Fox and Co
     II Specialty shops
     A The Timepiece Inc
     B Video Etc
12. Muhammad Ali, one of America's most famous world-class athletes, won fifty-six fights and lost five.
13. The highest auction bid for Vincent van Gogh's *Landscape with Rising Sun* was $9900000
14. George Washington Carver as a matter of fact revolutionized agriculture by developing new uses for sweet potatoes and peanuts
15. "Karen please send my mail to my new address" said Josh "I will be living at 3476 N Rock Rd Ames Iowa 64978"
16. Yes our plane was forced to land in Columbus Ohio for the weather in Detroit was cold and wet and foggy.
17. Ed wondered why he owed $710. "The ten cents is tax" he asked.
18. Dear Jan
         The flight to Montreal was great. Below the clouds looked like snowy peaks. Give me a call soon
                                                    Yours truly
                                                    Lauren

19. Having won seven Olympic medals and setting twenty-six world records Mark Spitz might be considered history's most successful swimmer
20. "In 1987" asked Ralph "who won the World Series"
21. At 6:10 AM on January 19 1977 snow began to fall in West Palm Beach Florida
22. Chief Joseph whose American Indian name means "Thunder Traveling Over the Mountains" led his people the Nez Percé to within thirty miles of Canada before being captured

B *Proofreading* Proofread the following paragraph for punctuation errors. For each sentence, list any words that should precede a punctuation mark, and follow each word with the correct punctuation.

(1) *Commedia dell'arte* which is a form of comic theater was performed all across Europe between the years 1400 and 1600 (2) Unlike most actors of today performers of the *commedia* did not memorize written dialogue (3) Instead they improvised which means that they made up their lines as they went along (4) The actor who was most important in the *commedia* was the clown (5) He had to be very athletic since much of the humor in *commedia* performances came from his gymnastics (6) The clown who was very clever usually played tricks on the other characters (7) *Commedia dell'arte* was very popular; in fact an entire town would often turn out to watch a performance (8) Audiences for the most part could be counted on to fill the hat that was passed around after every show

Seventeenth-century *commedia dell'arte* characters.

Linking
Mechanics *&* Writing

Imagine you are from a remote island and are unfamiliar with common American pastimes, such as baseball games, movies, or skateboards. Write a composition that will explain several popular pastimes to the people of your island. Remember that most of what you describe will be unknown on your island, so you will have to use appositives and essential or nonessential phrases and clauses to explain these things.

Prewriting and Drafting Whether you live in a city, a suburb, or the country, entertainment is part of your life. Use clustering or brainstorming to gather ideas to write about. Then organize your information in a logical sequence and write a first draft. Remember that your point of view should be that of an outside observer.

Revising and Proofreading Review your draft as though you were someone who has never had this experience. Have you given enough information so that readers on your island will understand your descriptions? Have you used sensory words and active verbs to make the events come alive? Pay close attention to comma use when you proofread your draft.

Additional Writing Topic Advertisers often try to create a sense of excitement regarding very ordinary products that they are trying to sell. Write an ad to rent out your house or apartment, describing it as though it were a resort or vacation hotel. Use both questions and exclamations to let your readers know how exciting it would be to spend a week where you live. The following example may give you some ideas and help you get started.

> Do you want to spend a week in paradise? Come to 1223 Elm Street in Oceanside. Relax in luxurious surroundings, where you can enjoy all the wonderful comforts of home and then some:
> Picture-perfect color TV
> Great movies nightly!
> Gourmet cooking
> Hot stereo!
> Room overlooking quaint suburban street
> Off-street parking!
> Unlimited use of grounds

Chapter 10
Application and Review

A Using Punctuation Correctly Rewrite the following sentences, adding punctuation where necessary.

1. Traveling through space the astronaut radioed the information back to earth
2. Dornette did you go to Sacramento or did you stay in San Jose
3. Historically the objects that have served as money include stones shells furs fish ivory and precious metals
4. Dr Sayner who is the team doctor will undoubtedly tape your ankle
5. After the local band left the stage Whitney Houston appeared and the audience exploded in applause
6. My favorite Shakespearean play is *Hamlet*; hers *Othello*
7. The mammoth which is a kind of prehistoric elephant once roamed the region that is now Texas
8. Hooray Our team made the play-offs
9. Reptiles have several distinguishing characteristics: first they are coldblooded; second their skin is covered with scales; and third they lay eggs
10. Reaching its maximum speed of 1450 mph the *Concorde* flew from New York to London England in a record 2 hrs 56 min and 35 sec on January 1 1983
11. St Francis of Assisi a thirteenth-century friar was known for his humility reverence for nature and strong religious faith
12. The American inventor Thos A Edison demonstrated the first phonograph machine on December 7 1887
13. German shepherds are if I am not mistaken gentle animals
14. Oh no Did you see that lightning Mr Gordon
15. Above the sky was filled with thunderclouds
16. Marshall High School left the gym in victory, and Hoover High in defeat
17. All the girls went skating but Sue had to stay home.
18. "Did you know" asked Cindy "that you have to order tickets for *Phantom of the Opera* six months before the performance date"
19. At some time during the first century AD, the Romans created a stronger more durable type of concrete
20. Consequently the smaller less sporty car sells for around $6000 which makes it more affordable

B Finding Punctuation Errors Number your paper from 1 to 20. After each number, list any words that should be followed by a punctuation mark; then place the mark correctly.

1. Honestly we are not justified in complaining
2. When the tide went out we walked along the sandy beach
3. Watch out for that truck
4. Miss Jordan asked the class "Who knows the author of *Crime and Punishment*"
5. The ancient Egyptian Pharaoh Pepi II the longest reigning monarch is said to have ruled for ninety-four years
6. If possible make the appointment for Tuesday or Thursday
7. We visited Adams Library one of the oldest in America
8. "The oldest surviving fabric was found in Turkey" said Mr. Jarvis "It was radiocarbon dated back to 5900 BC"
9. Amy's favorite vegetable is corn; Jeremy's tomatoes
10. Never worrying Alex met each day with enthusiasm and energy
11. Juan Ramón Jiménez who wrote *Platero and I* received the Nobel Prize for Literature in 1956
12. Inside the calf was sleeping on a bed of coarse wet straw and its mother was resting nearby
13. "You look beautiful tonight Amanda" he said managing a smile
14. My Uncle Joe trying to lower his cholesterol level eats lots of salads fruits and whole grains
15. Would you like a cool refreshing dip in the pool

C Proofreading Rewrite the following passage, correcting errors in punctuation, spelling, and capitalization.

Are you a "chocoholic" Well your not alone my freind In fact chocolate has been making americans smile for four thousand years A product grown and used by the aztecs for centurys, chocolate was beleived by ancient peoples to have been brought down from the Garden of Life by the god Quetzalcoatl It was a consolation to people for having to live on earth In the afterlife it was expected to be served perpetually

The first north american chocolate was manufactured in boston in 1765 but America's most famous chocolate maker was milton hershey a Pennsylvania dutchman Another contribution to the american market was made by Domingo Ghirardelli who sent 600 lbs of his chocolate to San Francisco with a merchant heading west to the gold rush The Ghirardelli Chocolate Company located in San Leandro California is now one of the most successful businesses in the western US

11

Semicolons, Colons, and Other Punctuation

all ignorance toboggans into know
and trudges up to ignorance again:
but winter's not forever,even snow
melts;and if spring should spoil the game,what then?

From "All Ignorance Toboggans into Know"
by e. e. cummings

Without punctuation, this poem by e. e. cummings would plummet out of control like a runaway toboggan. Notice how the colon and semicolon link thoughts smoothly, perhaps even suggesting the rhythm of a sledder and of the changing seasons.

In this chapter you will learn how to use semicolons, colons, dashes, hyphens, and parentheses to express yourself knowledgeably and to make your own writing flow.

Part 1
The Semicolon

Like commas, semicolons separate different elements within a sentence. The semicolon, however, signals a more emphatic break than a comma does.

Semicolons Used with Commas

When there are several commas within parts of a compound sentence, use a semicolon to separate the parts. Use a semicolon between main clauses joined by a conjunction if the clause before the conjunction contains commas.

> Jim had done research, taken notes, and made an outline; but he
>   didn't feel ready to begin writing.
> We put out sandwiches, cider, raw vegetables, and potato salad; and
>   still we wondered if there would be enough to eat.

When there are commas within parts of a series, use a semicolon to separate the parts.

> Members of our class come from as far away as Leeds, England;
>   New Delhi, India; and San Juan, Puerto Rico.
> Maris was in charge of the scenery; Roy, the costumes; and Felipe,
>   the directing of the play.
> Eric called the dancers together; reviewed the opening number, solos,
>   and finale; and told them to be ready by seven sharp.

Semicolons Between Main Clauses

Use a semicolon to join the parts of a compound sentence if no coordinating conjunction is used.

A stronger relationship between the clauses is shown by a semicolon rather than by a conjunction such as *and* or *but*.

> Bonita is good at set shots, but I am not.
> Bonita is good at set shots; I am not.

> The cyclone struck with savage fury, and it demolished most of the
>   little coastal town.
> The cyclone struck with savage fury; it demolished most of the little
>   coastal town.

Remember that a semicolon may be used only if the clauses are closely related. Do not use a semicolon to join unrelated clauses.

Incorrect   José is a fine athlete; the school fields many teams.
Correct   José is a fine athlete; he has earned letters in three sports.

Semicolons and Conjunctive Adverbs

Use a semicolon before a conjunctive adverb or a parenthetical expression that joins the clauses of a compound sentence.

> Our treasury was nearly empty; accordingly, we began considering various fund-raising projects.
> Many of their talents complemented each other; for example, he played the piano and she sang.

Note that the conjunctive adverb or transitional phrase is followed by a comma in the examples above.

Punctuation Note Many words can be used either as conjunctive adverbs or as interrupters. If the words are used as interrupters, use commas to set the words off from the rest of the sentence.

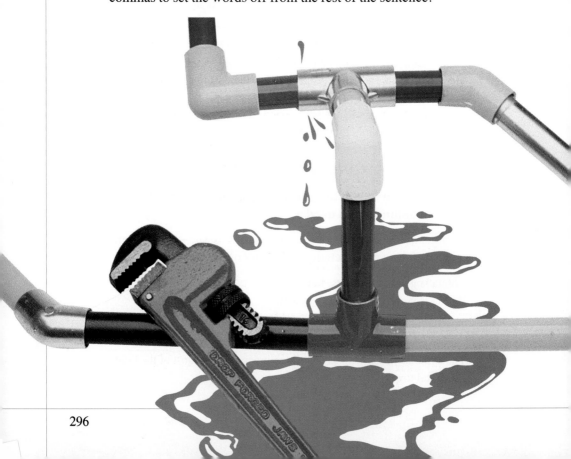

The weather was hot and humid; however, all of the participants
managed to finish the race. (conjunctive adverb)
On the day of the race, however, the weather was hot and humid.
(interrupter)

Exercise

Application in Literature Semicolons have been omitted from the
following passages. Rewrite the passages, correctly inserting semicolons where they are needed. Notice how semicolons add clarity to
the ideas.

1. In two respects it was an exceptionally safe car: first, it didn't go very
   fast second, it had three foot pedals. E. B. White
2. For her pallbearers only her friends were chosen: her Latin teacher, W.
   L. Holtz her high school principal, Rice Brown her doctor, Frank
   Foncannon her friend, W. H. Finney her pal at the *Gazette* office, Walter
   Hughes and her brother Bill. William Allen White
3. She had a painful sense of having missed something, or lost something
   she felt that somehow the years had cheated her. Willa Cather
4. We are not ignorant like the Forest People—our women spin wool on the
   wheel our priests wear a white robe. We do not eat grubs from the tree
   we have not forgotten the old writings, although they are hard to
   understand. Stephen Vincent Benét
5. Mama had not been consulted therefore, she made no comment.
   Jade Snow Wong
6. Uncle Hiram was somewhat smaller than Chig's father his short-cropped
   kinky hair was half gray, half black. William Melvin Kelley
7. Sylvia's heart gave a wild beat she knew that strange white bird, and had
   once stolen softly near where it stood in some bright green swamp grass,
   away over at the other side of the woods. Sarah Orne Jewett
8. It is a maxim of state that power and liberty are like heat and moisture:
   where they are well mixed, everything prospers where they are single,
   they are destructive. Abigail Smith Adams
9. The kitchen was warm now a fire was roaring in the stove with a
   closed-up rushing sound. Gina Berriault
10. But there we were, without a mate and it was necessary, of course, to
    advance one of the men. Robert Louis Stevenson
11. Nine times out of ten, in the arts as in life, there is actually no truth to be
    discovered there is only error to be exposed. Henry Louis Mencken
12. Here a weasel fails to see a plump white ptarmigan in the snow there
    a dragonfly snares a fast-moving mosquito in its basket of legs
    somewhere an eager fox pup grabs a toad. David Robinson

Part 2
The Colon

The colon is used to direct the reader's attention forward to what comes next in the sentence. Often a colon introduces an explanation or example.

Use a colon to introduce a list of items.

A colon often follows a word or phrase such as *these, the following,* or *as follows.* A colon is not used when a series of complements or modifiers immediately follows a verb.

> Jim is a member of the following groups: the Drama Club, the Debate Team, the International Club, and the Sophomore Swimming Team. (list)
> We visited these countries on our trip: Switzerland, France, Spain, Italy, and Austria. (list)
> The candidate's attributes are honesty, intelligence, and courage. (series of complements)
> The chart shows the primary colors, which are red, yellow, and blue. (series of modifiers)

Do not use a colon in the middle of a prepositional phrase; and, as a general rule, do not use a colon immediately after a verb.

Incorrect   Mike is interested in: chemistry, photography, and ice hockey.
Correct   These are Mike's interests: chemistry, photography, and ice hockey.

Incorrect   You should bring: paper plates, cups, and napkins.
Correct   You should bring the following items: paper plates, cups, and napkins.

Use a colon to introduce a quotation that lacks explanatory words such as *he said* or *she asked.*

> Christine wheeled around angrily: "You're going to regret this decision one day!"

Use a colon to introduce a very long or very formal quotation.

> In his Inaugural Address in 1961, President John Kennedy said: "Ask not what your country can do for you—ask what you can do for your country."

Use a colon between two independent clauses when the second explains the first.

> Then I knew we were in trouble: none of our boys could match the
> dive we had just seen.
> From then on we understood Ms. Gilroy: she was demanding, but she
> was fair.

Punctuation Note Capitalize the first word of a formal statement following a colon. If the statement following the colon is informal, however, you may begin the first word with a lowercase letter.

Other Uses of the Colon

Use a colon (1) after the formal salutation of a letter, (2) between hour and minute figures of clock time, (3) in Biblical references to indicate chapter and verse, (4) between the title and subtitle of a book, (5) between numbers referring to volume and pages of books and magazines, and (6) after labels that signal important ideas.

> Dear Sir or Madam: *The Raven: The Life of Sam Houston*
> 8:20 P.M.   *National Geographic* 171: 348–385
> Psalm 23:7   Warning: This substance is harmful if
> John 3:16   swallowed.

Exercises

A Copy the following sentences, adding the necessary semicolons and colons.

1. We ought to beat Lexington, trample Bowling Green, and slaughter Libertyville but we may lose to Russell Springs.
2. Beginning next January we shall have the following in stock treadmills, exercise bikes, rowing machines, and body-building equipment.
3. Did you read *Aging A Guide to Feeling Young Forever*?
4. Ellen has a new camera it was made in Korea.
5. On Sunday Reverend Thomas quoted from Matthew 10 12–15 in his 1100 A.M. sermon.
6. Dear Sir or Madam

   I would like to order these items from your catalog one pair of moccasins, no. 12431 one Western-style shirt, no. 23947 and one silver belt buckle, no. 67441.

   Please send the items to the following address 3810 Golden Terrace, Apt. 394, Los Angeles, CA 90052.

7. Pablo Picasso was the most prolific painter in history in fact, he produced more paintings in his career of seventy-eight years than any other artist.
8. This medicine carries a label that reads "Warning Keep this and all medications out of the reach of children."
9. Walt and Jeanne have different sports preferences Walt prefers tennis Jeanne prefers soccer.
10. The weather forecast called for low temperatures and strong winds moreover, there was a possibility of snow.

B Rewrite the following sentences, adding semicolons or colons where necessary. In some sentences, semicolons should replace commas. If the sentence requires no changes, write *Correct*.

1. Jesse Granville wrote short stories and poetry, played the trumpet, and sang in a quartet, he also did volunteer work after school as a tutor and as a hospital aide.
2. Author Tom Wolfe said of his craft "When I started writing in college, I wanted to think that genius was ninety-five percent inside your head. . . . I now believe that the proportions are more like sixty-five percent material and thirty-five percent whatever you've got inside of you."
3. The pitcher has three sure-fire pitches his fastball, his slider, and his curveball.
4. The dance was scheduled to begin at 800 P.M. the band, however, did not arrive until 842 P.M.
5. The *Readers' Guide to Periodical Literature* indicated that I could find the article on computer programs in *Newsweek* 18541. (Volume 185, page 41)
6. Barry Harper's baseball souvenir collection includes items such as the following a million baseball cards, nine hundred players' uniforms, three thousand autographed baseballs, seventy-five World Series programs, and more.
7. Did Mrs. Robertson know that the name of the first controlled and power-driven airplane, which was flown by Orville Wright, was the *Flyer I*?
8. Attention The 530 train to Ipswich and Rockport will leave from track 3.
9. My parents made themselves very clear my sister was not to watch any TV over the weekend.
10. The travelers had renewed their passports, booked their hotels, and confirmed their plane reservations, nevertheless, they were afraid they had overlooked something.

Left: Manute Bol, the tallest player in the NBA. Right: Tyrone Bogues, the shortest player in the NBA.

C *Proofreading* Rewrite the following paragraphs, correcting errors in punctuation, capitalization, and spelling.

Few profesional basketball players created the excitment that Tyrone Bogues did in his first month of play with the National basketball Association (NBA) in 1987. Basketball fans are fascinated by Bogues he is a mere 5-foot-3-inches tall. What Bogues lacks in height, however he makes up for with these charteristics speed, skill, and determanation. The shortest legitimite player in nba history. Bogues is not a publisity stunt. In fact, he was a first-round draft choice of the Washington Bullets.

In a preseason match-up against the Los Angeles lakers, Bogues entered the game after the first quarter. the Bullets were trailing 31–22. Racking up twelve points and four assists, he helped shoot the bullets ahead by eight at the half. The Laker's Magic Johnson sums up Bogues' special talent "You have to be aware of him at all times he's like a Fly that gets in your face when your trying to sleep. Every time you think you've slapped him away, he comes buzzing right back

Part 3
The Dash

Dashes are used to indicate an abrupt change of thought or a pause in a sentence. Dashes show a looser connection to the main idea than commas do. The words, clauses, or phrases set off by dashes merely add extra information to an already complete thought.

Use a dash to show an abrupt break in thought.

> The winner of today's baseball game—assuming we aren't rained out—will play in the regional semifinals.
> The appetizers—supposedly the restaurant's specialty—left us disappointed.

Use a dash to set off a long explanatory statement that interrupts the main thought of the sentence.

> They frantically searched everywhere—under the seats, in the aisle, in the lobby—before Dan finally found the car keys in his jacket pocket.
> The meeting between the two men—they had clashed violently and repeatedly over a period of years—was unexpectedly calm and friendly.

Note that in the first example, punctuation occurs within the interrupting statement. Here the dash serves as a guide to the reader, signaling the addition of extra, nonessential information.

Use a dash to set off a summarizing statement from the rest of the sentence.

> Insufficient heating, leaky roofs, cluttered stairways, and unsanitary corridors—for all these violations of the housing code, the landlord was brought into court.
> Photographs of rock-and-roll stars, concert posters, souvenir T-shirts—these covered the walls of her room.

Be careful not to overuse dashes. When used in the correct circumstances, dashes can add interest, variety, and emphasis to your writing. However, too many dashes may confuse the reader and make your writing seem choppy and less precise.

Note In typewritten work, press the hyphen key twice to form a dash.

When writing dialogue, use a dash to show an abrupt break in thought.

In dialogue, the break in thought is often caused by uncertainty or hesitancy, as in the first example below.

> "Photosynthesis is an action——I mean, it's what happens——well, it's sunlight doing something to chlorophyll."
> "The movie opens with a spectacular shot of the desert——oh, you've already seen it."
> "When I talked to her yesterday she said that——oh, I really shouldn't repeat it."

You will note from the last two examples above that the dash adds a casual, conversational tone to dialogue. People often change their thoughts in mid-sentence while speaking.

Exercise

Application in Literature Dashes have been omitted from the quotations below. Rewrite the passages, and return them to their original form by inserting dashes where they should occur. Notice how the authors have used dashes to separate ideas and add meaning and style to their work.

1. She detached his hand his hold was quite feeble and could not compete with her tennis biceps and leapt off the curb and up the streetcar steps, hearing with relief the doors grind shut behind her. Margaret Atwood
2. A man with murder in his heart will murder, or be murdered it comes to the same thing and so I knew I had to leave. James Baldwin
3. Impy left by the back way. Before the scrape of her hard, bare feet had died away on the back porch, a wild shriek I was sure it was hers filled the hollow house. O. Henry
4. The third day it was Wednesday of the first week Charles bounced a see-saw onto the head of a little girl and made her bleed, and the teacher made him stay inside all during recess. Shirley Jackson
5. The following spring the heavier of the two almost half the tree broke off in a spring gale. Richard Mabey
6. I would sit down to this breakfast at a round table in the dining room with my young parents or my beloved Miss Rachel. My father called Tata, the Polish for papa was my most favorite person in the world.
   Esther Hautzig
7. Sometimes you are able to "step out," but this effort in fact the pure exhilaration of easy movement soon exhausts you. Sharon Curtin

8. The freshness of the morning air, the smell of poplars, lilacs and roses, the bed, a chair, the dress which rustled last night, a tiny pair of slippers, a ticking watch on the table all these came to him clearly with every detail. Anton Chekhov

Part 4
The Hyphen

Use a hyphen in compound numbers from twenty-one to ninety nine.

    thirty-six steps   twenty-eight countries

Use a hyphen in all spelled-out fractions.

    a four-fifths majority   one-sixth of the pie

Use a hyphen in certain compound words.

    sister-in-law   T-shirt   right-of-way

Use a hyphen between words that make up a compound adjective used before a noun.

> We found a well-informed source.

When a compound adjective follows a linking verb, it is usually not hyphenated.

> The report seemed well organized.
> The source was well founded.

Some proper nouns and proper adjectives with prefixes and suffixes require a hyphen.

> Mexican-style   pre-Roosevelt   pro-Yankees

Use a hyphen if part of a word must be carried over from one line to the next.

> Gabriela Dimitrova, a Bulgarian weightlifter, defected to the
> United States after competing in the Women's World Weight-
> lifting Championship in Daytona Beach, Florida.

The following rules should be observed when hyphenating words:

1. Words are separated by hyphens only between syllables.
2. Only words having two or more syllables can be hyphenated.
3. Each line should have at least two letters of the hyphenated word.

Exercise

Rewrite the sentences below, adding dashes and hyphens where needed.

1. Squids, snails, and shellfish all these species are classified as mollusks.
2. Ms. Boynton's whimsical work cartoons of animals for greeting cards and calendars rapidly made her a commercial success.
3. Melissa and Jonathan used a six yard tape measure the longest they could find in the hardware store.
4. Turn left at the next Look out for that truck!
5. Angie bought a good looking bike yesterday at Jim's no, I think it was at Al's Spoke and Cycle Shop.
6. The tallest self supporting tower is the CN Tower in Toronto.
7. Labor saving devices such as vacuum cleaners, washing machines, and toasters became widely used in the 1920's.
8. By 1920, fifteen million Model T's had been sold at can you believe it less than $300 each.

Part 5
Parentheses

Parentheses enclose material that is only loosely connected to the sentence. Such material interrupts the continuity of the sentence and is nonessential.

Use parentheses to set off supplementary or explanatory material that is loosely related to the sentence.

> I can still clearly recall my high-school graduation twenty years ago (sometimes it seems like only yesterday).

Note the use of parentheses in the following examples:

> Though Loch Ness had been a tourist haven for the rich in Victorian times (the Queen herself journeyed up the loch in a paddle steamer in 1873), it was the road that really opened the area to large numbers of visitors.
>
> Their father was the twelfth child of a wealthy Englishman (one of whose houses, Claverton Manor, is now the American Museum).
>
> Inside was a first-aid kit (including boxes of antivenin), a can of beans (invariably rusty), malaria pills, and pliers.

When the supplementary material is more closely related to the sentence, use commas or dashes. Compare the use of punctuation in the following examples:

Comma	The best point of Kate's speech, which she saved for the end, was that every group needs leadership.
Dash	The beef was braised——that is, it was browned and then simmered in a covered container.
Parentheses	Leonardo da Vinci (he was a brilliant scientist and one of the world's greatest artists) wrote: "Those sciences are vain and full of errors which are not born of experiment, the mother of all certainty."

Use parentheses to enclose figures or letters in a list that is part of a sentence.

> A tree is different from a shrub in that it has (1) greater height and (2) a single trunk.
>
> Is your favorite time of day (a) morning, (b) afternoon, or (c) evening?

Use parentheses to informally identify a source of information you use in your writing or to give credit to an author whose ideas or words you are using.

"When the stock market went over the edge of Niagara in October and November, 1929, and the decline in business became alarming, the country turned to the President for action" (Allen 282).

Punctuation with Parentheses

Use punctuation marks inside the parentheses when they belong to the parenthetical material. However, when punctuation marks belong to the main part of the sentence, place them outside of the parentheses.

Leo's speech was on disarmament; Barb's, on acting as a career (her favorite subject); Jim's, on slum clearance.

I never guessed (would you have?) that the maid did it.

Sheldon spoke of his victory over Central's debaters (*his* victory!) as if he had been a one-man team.

The tallest player on the men's basketball team is Seamus (pronounced shay´məs!).

Checkpoint Parts 1–5

Rewrite the following sentences, adding semicolons, colons, dashes, and hyphens where needed.

1. Our school has exchange students from these countries Brazil, Kenya, Sweden, and Chile.
2. My class that meets at 930 oh, I hope I won't be late will discuss student rights.
3. The coach tried everything pep talks, privileges, rallies, toughness to try to improve the team's morale.
4. The water ballet routine was precisely choreographed furthermore, it was performed flawlessly.
5. Selina prepared for the audition she memorized her lines and practiced her dance.
6. The following are departure times for trains to Union Station 830 A.M., 1200 noon, and 430 P.M. every weekday.
7. We ate lunch at a little out of the way country restaurant that featured twenty one different appetizers.
8. In his book *On Writing Well,* William Zinsser says this "Clutter is the disease of American writing."
9. Jennifer came to a decision she would attend college after all.
10. Dr. Martin Luther King, Jr., was a great leader accordingly, his birthday has been made a national holiday.
11. We have a factory in Salem, Oregon an office in Buffalo, New York and a mill at Andover, Massachusetts.
12. The telephone rang it was Ron saying he'd be late.
13. She did not want to go it was dark and windy to the graveyard at midnight on Halloween.
14. The Ten Commandments are found in Exodus 20 7–17.
15. Alana is the sister in law of a well known actor.
16. Lou Schlanger's class at South Bronx High School I assume these students have impossible schedules begins at 710 A.M.
17. We are disappointed in the advertisement it is too small.
18. My brother in law has an astounding appetite last Thanksgiving he ate the following for dinner two large turkey legs, three twice baked potatoes, and two thirds of a pumpkin pie!
19. Walter Mitty if he's a hero then we all are lives an exciting life in his make believe world.
20. That turn of the century mansion has a well bred look.

Linking
Mechanics *&* Writing

Write a dialogue between two characters. One character is a nonstop talker who rambles on and on about trivial ideas, frequently interrupting himself or herself to insert unrelated details. The second character is a polite, quiet person who speaks precisely and correctly, but who keeps being interrupted by the first speaker. Use commas, semicolons, dashes, and parentheses to make the dialogue clear. (Parentheses may be used to describe the actions or reactions of the characters while the dialogue is going on.)

Prewriting and Drafting   To write an effective dialogue, you need to create characters with unique identities—that is, characters with specific interests, needs, and personality traits. Before you begin drafting your dialogue, brainstorm about what your characters will be like. Then make a list of character traits for each person.

After you have established the identities of your characters, jot down notes about how their relationship can be described. Then think about what their conversation will be about. Decide whether you want to treat the dialogue seriously or humorously. Remember, even a brief dialogue should tell a complete story; it should have a beginning, middle, and end.

Revising and Proofreading   After you have drafted your dialogue, ask someone to join you in a dramatic reading, with each of you speaking the lines of one character. Use the following questions to help you identify areas for revision:

1. Is the dialogue lifelike?
2. Does the unique personality of each character come across?
3. Is it easy to understand what the characters are talking about?
4. Does your dialogue "tell a story"?
5. Are there places where material needs to be cut or added?
6. Have you punctuated correctly to make the dialogue clear?

Additional Writing Topic   Dashes and parentheses are often used in informal writing, such as personal letters, because they allow the writer to express ideas and information in a conversational tone. Think of the most exciting event you have ever experienced or participated in. Then write a personal letter in which you describe that event to a good friend. Use correct punctuation, including dashes and parentheses.

Chapter 11
Application and Review

A Using Punctuation Correctly Rewrite the following sentences, adding semicolons, colons, dashes, and hyphens as needed.

1. For her extra credit report on the tragic *Titanic,* Alyssa used *The World Book Encyclopedia,* Volume 19, pages 235 236.
2. Dear Mr. Berger

     My used car business will take me to an out of town conference therefore, I would like you to forward my mail to the following address The Armstrong Plaza Hotel, 136 Fiftieth Street North, Richmond, VA 23232. The telephone number is 804-555-5300. Thank you very much.

     Sincerely yours,
Charles Ames

3. Mud slides, rock slides, premature dynamite explosions, and the deaths of 5,400 workers these were some of the problems that plagued the construction of the six mile Panama Canal.
4. It's about well, it's something like I would say it's a good eighteen miles from here.
5. The newly formed rock and roll band was scheduled to appear at a pregame party however, their bus broke down, and they spent twenty four hours in Tulsa waiting for parts to be delivered.
6. The blockbuster movie *E.T.* holds the record for the highest box office sales it grossed a mind boggling 322 million dollars.
7. Attention These computer controlled doors lock promptly at 500 P.M.
8. In reference to the Constitutional Convention, George Washington wrote this to a friend "We exhibit at present the novel and astonishing spectacle of a whole people deliberating calmly on what form of government will be the most conducive to their happiness."
9. The robber turned to the clerk "Give me all your money!"
10. At 120 years of age, Shigechiyo Izumi he has always lived on the same island in Japan has the unique distinction of having the oldest documented age of any human being.

B Punctuating Sentences Correctly Rewrite the following sentences, adding semicolons, colons, dashes, and hyphens as needed.

1. What happens in the end no, I won't give it away would surprise even the most devoted reader of mystery stories.

2. The Declaration of Independence ends with these inspiring words "We mutually pledge to each other our lives, our fortunes, and our sacred honor."
3. This must be Dolores's room lavender and green are two of her favorite colors.
4. The following plays are classified as tragedies *Oedipus the King, Macbeth, Julius Caesar, King Lear, Hamlet, Timon of Athens, Romeo and Juliet,* and *Death of a Salesman.*
5. After two weeks of intensive campaigning, twenty four well qualified students were elected to the Student Council.
6. You will find the quote in *Thomas Jefferson The Man and His Times,* Volume III 106.
7. Cats love peeking into corners, crawling under beds, perching atop bookshelves, and getting into bureau drawers but they don't like being put in confined spaces.
8. Geraldo said at least I think this is what he said that everyone would be welcome at the party.
9. With her latest performance, Jocelyn bettered her own long standing record in the play offs.
10. The Puritans, who settled in New England in the 1600's, discouraged merrymaking and festivities for example, they had laws against celebrating Christmas.

c *Proofreading* Rewrite the following passage, correcting errors in capitalization and spelling as well as errors in the use of semicolons, colons, dashes, and hyphens. Add any missing punctuation.

We eat more hamburgers char-broiled and pan-fried than any other nation in the world. Our all American hamburgers, however, began their sizzle on another continent. During the Middle Ages, Tartar Nomads in russia often ate raw meat. To tendarize the meat, they used the folowing recipe place a slab of meat under a saddel; ride on it all day, scrape and shred the meat, and mix it with salt, pepper, and onion juice. The modern version of this delicacy, no longer tenderized under a saddle, is called "steak tartar" German Soldiers from the town of Hamburg picked up the idea at Baltic seaports they brought it home with them. Sometime later, Hamburg cooks had another inspiration, they started broiling the meet. It took, however an american cook experts disagree on who this genius was to introduce hamburger patties to buns. This introduction was a tremendous success. The rest, as they say, is history.

12

Apostrophes and Quotation Marks

"Injustice anywhere is a threat to justice everywhere."

Martin Luther King

*T*hrough his powerful speeches, Reverend Martin Luther King, Jr., inspired many people to work for civil rights. Today writers and speakers still use the words of Reverend King to motivate individuals to support this cause. However, they always credit King for these words and enclose them in quotation marks.

In this chapter you will learn to use quotation marks to set off direct quotations and to use apostrophes to show ownership.

Part 1

Apostrophes

Apostrophes have several important functions. They are used to indicate possession, to show omitted letters, and to form the plurals of certain items such as numbers.

Using Apostrophes to Indicate Possession

Use apostrophes to form the possessives of singular and plural nouns.

To use apostrophes correctly, you must know whether nouns are singular or plural. To form the possessive of a singular noun, add an apostrophe and an *s* even if the noun ends in *s*.

> teacher's   city's   lass's   Chris's

Punctuation Note Exceptions to this rule about the possessive of singular nouns are *Jesus, Moses,* and names from mythology that end in *s*: *Jesus', Moses', Zeus', Odysseus'*.

To form the possessive of a plural noun that ends in *s* or *es*, add only an apostrophe. The possessive of a plural noun that does not end in *s* is formed by adding an apostrophe and an *s*. For information on forming the plurals of nouns, see pages 340–342.

> teachers'   cities'   men's   children's

To form the possessive of a compound noun, add an apostrophe only to the last part of the noun.

A **compound noun** is a noun composed of more than one word. Some compound nouns are written with hyphens between the parts.

> notary public + 's = notary public's office
> sisters-in-law + 's = sisters-in-law's coats

The possessive forms of nouns such as the *Queen of England* and the *President of the United States* are formed by adding an apostrophe and *s* to the last word only: *the Queen of England's throne*. Your writing will usually be less awkward if you reword and use an *of*-phrase instead.

> the throne of the Queen of England
> the home of the President of the United States

"Sorry, but I'm going to have to issue you a summons for reckless grammar and driving without an apostrophe."

Drawing by Maslin; © 1987 The New Yorker Magazine, Inc.

In cases of joint ownership, only the name of the last person mentioned is given the possessive form. Add an apostrophe or an apostrophe and *s*, depending on the spelling of the name.

> Tom and Wes's school
> the actors and dancers' costumes

This rule also governs the formation of the possessives of the names of firms and organizations.

> Cross and Hamilton Company's sales force
> Johnson & Johnson's corporate headquarters

If the names of two or more persons are used to show separate ownership, each name is given the possessive form.

> Madison's and Monroe's administrations
> Don's and Jim's grades

Again, to avoid an awkward sentence, a phrase using the word *of* may be substituted for the possessive form.

> the administrations of Madison and Monroe
> the grades of Don and Jim

To form the possessive of an indefinite pronoun, add an apostrophe and *s*.

> everyone's   somebody's
> one's   either's

Add an apostrophe and *s* to the last word to form the possessives of compound pronouns like those shown below.

someone else's turn   no one else's answer

Do not use an apostrophe with a personal pronoun to show possession.

The raincoat on the couch is hers. Yours is in the closet.
Is that magazine ours? Its cover is missing.

When nouns expressing time and amount are used as adjectives, they are given the possessive form.

a month's time   four days' wait   two centuries' tradition

Using Apostrophes to Show Omissions

Use apostrophes in contractions.

In contractions words are joined and letters are left out. An apostrophe replaces the missing letter or letters.

you'll = you will or you shall   don't = do not
what's = what is   Hank's = Hank is

Dialogue may use contractions that reflect regional dialects. Apostrophes are used to indicate the missing letters in such contractions.

"How d'you do, Ma'am!" he shouted. "'Tis a fine mornin'."

Use an apostrophe to show the omission of figures.

the class of '89   the blizzard of '78

Using Apostrophes for Certain Plurals

Use apostrophes to form the plurals of letters, numbers, signs, and words referred to as words.

How many *r*'s are there in *embarrass*?
Her speech has too many *therefore*'s in it.
F. Scott Fitzgerald focuses on the 1920's in *The Great Gatsby*.
To type *$*'s instead of *4*'s, depress the shift key.

Usage Note The plurals of letters, numbers, signs, and words used as words are always italicized in print. In manuscript and typewritten work they are underlined.

Exercises

A Find the words that have errors in apostrophe usage. Write each word correctly on your paper. If a sentence contains no errors, write *Correct*.

1. Somebody's jacket is hanging from the flagpole.
2. The reporter ignored the editor-in-chiefs warning and revealed one of his sources.
3. Alex's and Andrea's Health Club features exercise machines', aerobic's classes, and swimming lessons'.
4. Youll need two dollar's worth of quarters to play that new pinball machine.
5. Were Poe's and Hawthorne's short stories written during the early 1800's?
6. My father-in-laws panel truck is being repaired at Al and Ron's Auto Shop.
7. Odysseus' son searched in vain for his missing father.
8. Who's fault is the Chernobyl disaster? We discovered that its really many peoples fault.
9. When you have two *l*'s together in the Spanish language, how are they pronounced?
10. Selena wont drive me to Park and Hemsleys new store.
11. Roosevelts and Rockefeller's backgrounds were similar.
12. The Secretary of the Treasurys salary is $86,200.
13. Place *s next to the names of the books that are theirs'.
14. I especially liked Sissy Spacek's and Tommy Lee Jones' performances in *Coal Miners Daughter*.
15. Shes got two weeks worth of work to finish in one week.

B Follow the directions for Exercise A.

1. Several golfer's scores were below par.
2. Perrys last name has four es in it.
3. Bross and Bradys' Gourmet Shop sells pickled eel, goat cheese, and sun-dried tomatoes.
4. Its not likely that Saturn is inhabited, but lets investigate.
5. My teacher's first suggestion was to eliminate the *um'* s in my speech.
6. Cray Research Incorporateds computer, the CRAY-1, is the worlds most powerful computer.
7. Youll have to pay at least one months rent as a security deposit on the apartment.
8. That drive-ins sound system isnt working.

9. Weve used my brother-in-laws cabin in northern Vermont every summer.
10. Everythings under control; Ginas teaching the three-year-olds their *ABC*'s.
11. The client's cars are ready for them.
12. I'll write a children's story for the magazine's next issue.
13. Have you ever eaten at Anthonys and Cleopatras Diner in Cairo, Illinois?
14. Arent you reading Hemingways novels in your new course, American Literature of the 20s and 30s?
15. Michael Jackson set the record in 84 for winning the most Grammy Awards in one years time.

c *Proofreading* Rewrite the following paragraph correctly. You will find errors in spelling, capitalization, and punctuation. Pay special attention to the use of apostrophes.

One of ice hockeys greatest players is Bobby Orr, the National Hockey Leagues all-time top-scoring Defenseman. Orrs incredible record include's six one-hundred-point season's, and more individual honor's and award's than any other player in the NHLs history. Despite Orr's fame, a reporter once remarked, after dinning with orr in one of Bostons downtown restaurants, "Hes so easygoing. I would forget that I was with one of sports greatest superstars."

Orrs thirteen-year career included six operations on his left knee. Finally, even a Surgeons skill couldnt coax the heros knee to respond. Forced to retire early, Bobby Orr became the Hockey Hall of Fames youngest member in September of 79. Their, the famous number 4s sweater remains as a tribute to its' outstanding owner.

D *Write Now* You are the writer of the "Did You Know . . . ?" column for your school paper. For this month's column, you have these news items to write about: (1) a new project by members of the science club; (2) inside information from an anonymous source; (3) the thoughts of your star football player on the upcoming game; (4) a survey conducted by the history classes; (5) a mistake by your editor in chief. Write your column, using possessive forms of some nouns and pronouns.

Part 2
Quotation Marks

Quotation marks are used to set off direct quotations, titles, and words used in special ways.

Direct and Indirect Quotations

Use quotation marks to begin and end a direct quotation.

Ricardo said, "The violinists are ready to perform."

Do not use quotation marks to set off an indirect quotation.

Ricardo said that the violinists are ready to perform.

Punctuation of Direct Quotations

The speaker's words are set off from the rest of the sentence with quotation marks, and the first word of the quotation is capitalized.

"Let's meet at my house next time," Raoul said.
Raoul said, "Let's meet at my house next time."

When the end of the quotation is also the end of the sentence, the period falls inside the quotation marks. Also note the placement of commas in the examples above.

If the quotation is a question or exclamation, the question mark or exclamation point falls inside the quotation marks.

"May I make the poster?" Lola asked.
"I deny everything!" the suspect cried.

Note that no commas are necessary in the examples above.

If the entire sentence is a question or an exclamation, the question mark or exclamation point falls outside the quotation marks.

Did I hear you say, "You're welcome to take these concert tickets"?

It's totally absurd for anyone to consider these thieves "responsible citizens"!

If there is a colon or a semicolon at the close of a quotation, it falls outside the quotation marks.

The committee said that the following states contained "pockets of poverty": Kentucky, West Virginia, and Pennsylvania.

Read the ballad "Sir Patrick Spens"; then study its relation to Coleridge's poem "Dejection: An Ode" and write an essay comparing the two.

Both parts of a divided quotation are enclosed in quotation marks. The first word of the second part is not capitalized unless it begins a new sentence.

"Part of my plan," the Governor said, "is to reduce property taxes this year."

"You must remember this," the guidance counselor said. "Ten hours of casual work will probably be less effective than five hours of real concentration."

In dialogue, a new paragraph and a new set of quotation marks are used to show a change in speakers.

"My working habits have no pattern," the author said. "Some writers set themselves very strict schedules. I prefer to remain more flexible."

"But you've written five books in five years," the interviewer replied. "You must work very hard every day."

"On the contrary, some days I spend the entire morning putting in a comma and the afternoon taking it out."

Single quotation marks are used to enclose a quotation within a quotation.

Herb said, "Then she actually said to me, 'I hope I didn't keep you waiting.'"

"The announcer just said, 'More snow throughout the state tonight,'" Len reported.

"Who wrote the song 'What I Did for Love'?" asked Jan.

A quotation may sometimes be several paragraphs in length. In long quotations, begin each paragraph with quotation marks. Place quotation marks at the end of the last paragraph only.

Usage Note A long quotation can be set off from the rest of the text by indenting and double spacing. In this case, no quotation marks are needed.

When a quoted fragment is inserted in a sentence, the first word of the fragment is not capitalized unless it begins a sentence or is a proper noun. No comma is needed to set the phrase apart from the rest of the sentence.

> Marc Antony claims that he has "come to bury Caesar, not to praise him." However, his speech has the opposite effect.

Exercises

A Rewrite the following sentences, adding the necessary punctuation marks and capital letters.

1. Zachary asked may I rewrite this composition
2. Your Honor the defendant pleaded I beg you for another chance
3. The city is not equipped to deal with a heavy snowfall the guide explained
4. Did Governor Thompson say that the state of Illinois will allot more funds for education asked Jenny
5. Don replied that he had no one to blame but himself
6. In Shakespeare's *Julius Caesar*, Cassius is described as having a lean and hungry look
7. Did you know asked Juan that the three most common names for American dogs are Rover, Spot, and Max
8. Who said look out asked the irate guard
9. Referring to her father's encouragement, Andrea Jaeger said he told me Andrea, I think you have natural talent you can be a good player, maybe even a champion
10. Who was the only American President who never married asked José
11. Did Perry's message say we have met the enemy and they are ours
12. The test was incredibly hard said Sam but it was fair
13. Sink that freethrow screamed the cheerleaders
14. In the Sand Creek Massacre the speaker added several hundred Cheyenne Indians were killed
15. Martha said that the advertisers on the Super Bowl broadcast paid $550,000 per half minute

B Application in Literature The following passage has been changed to include several errors in the use of punctuation, capitalization, and paragraphing. Rewrite the passage, returning it to its original state by correcting the errors.

(1) He was very thin and dressed in rags. (2) What I remember are his eyes. (3) He had huge, dark eyes. (4) He did not speak. (5) He just stood there, looking up at me. (6) Who are you I asked in Chinese? (7) I am no one. (8) He said. (9) But what is your name I asked? (10) I have no name he said. (11) Where are your parents? (12) I have no parents. (13) But where did you come from I asked, staring at him? (14) I came from nowhere he said. (15) And you are going nowhere? (16) Nowhere he said. (17) Then why come to me? (18) He shook his head, not able to answer. (19) Come in I said finally, you must be hungry.

Pearl S. Buck

c *Write Now* You are in the middle of a telephone conversation with your best friend. Suddenly your conversation is interrupted by loud static and a high-pitched tone. Then a voice says, in English, "Go ahead, Detroit. This is Moscow." Write down the rest of your conversation with a Russian teen-ager, being sure to follow the rules for proper English punctuation, capitalization, and paragraphing.

Setting Off Titles

Use quotation marks to set off chapter titles and other parts of books and the titles of short stories, essays, poems, articles, television episodes, and short musical compositions.

Chapter Title	"Chapter 9: The Progressive Spirit"
Short Story	"The Black Cat"
Essay	"The Joys of Science"
Poem	"Mending Wall"
Magazine Article	"Good Food for Healthy Bodies"
Television Episode	"Lucy and Desi in London"
Song	"This Land Is Your Land"

The title of a book, magazine, newspaper, TV series, play, painting, or long musical composition is italicized in print. In writing, indicate italics by underlining.

Words Used in Special Ways

Use quotation marks to set off words used in special ways and to set off slang.

Writers can show that they are using a word as someone else has used it by enclosing it in quotation marks. Slang words and phrases are also enclosed in quotation marks.

> The government official claimed he was "protecting" his country's
> interests when he lied during his testimony.
> The slang of the '80's includes such words as "nerd," "awesome,"
> "wicked," and "tubular."

A word referred to as a word is italicized in print. In writing, the word is underlined. When a word and its definition appear in a sentence, the word is italicized (or underlined) and the definition is put in quotation marks.

> Until then I'd never heard the word *boondoggle*.
> In music the word *pianissimo* means "very soft."

Punctuation Note When a comma or period immediately follows the quoted word or phrase, the punctuation mark is placed inside the quotation marks. If the quoted word or phrase comes at the end of a question or exclamation, the punctuation mark is placed outside the quotation marks: Is this what you mean by "cool"?

Exercises

A Write the following sentences, adding quotation marks and under-lining where necessary.

1. What does the word serendipity mean? asked Sandy.
2. Todd calls money bread, and Meg calls it green stuff.
3. I choreographed my dance routine to the song Hip to Be Square.
4. What does Montresor mean in the story The Cask of Amontillado when he says: For half of a century no mortal has disturbed them?
5. Why is the word nevermore repeated frequently in Edgar Allan Poe's poem The Raven?
6. One of Holden Caulfield's favorite words is phony.
7. I became ill while I was reading the chapter called Bacteria Are Your Friends.
8. One of my favorite Steinbeck short stories is The Snake.
9. When I'm Sixty-Four was a popular song from the Beatles' album *Sergeant Pepper's Lonely Hearts Club Band*.
10. The word facetious contains all five vowels arranged in alphabetical order.
11. Janie is writing an episode called The Wrath of Spock for the new *Star Trek* series.
12. Epilogue means a concluding part added to a literary work.
13. Your problem of too much spending money is one I'd like to have!
14. Triskaidekaphobia means the mortal fear of 13.
15. Kristin reported on an article in *Self* magazine called Do Women Really Assert Themselves?

B Follow the directions for Exercise A.

1. Last night's episode of *Murder, She Wrote* was called It Runs in the Family.
2. The verb eulogize means to praise highly.
3. The astronauts aboard *Apollo IX* sang Happy Birthday to You during their 1969 space voyage.
4. What is meant by the phrase manifest destiny?
5. Mom ironically referred to the tuna casserole as a gourmet treat.
6. Rachel led a thought-provoking discussion of the story The Open Boat.
7. My favorite train song is City of New Orleans.
8. Footprints is my favorite poem in our text, *Reading Literature*.
9. We read E.B. White's essay called Once More to the Lake.
10. The governor did not see many benefits in what the mayor called his public transportation solution.

Checkpoint *Parts 1 and 2*

A Rewrite the following sentences adding necessary punctuation. Be sure to use apostrophes and quotation marks correctly.

1. After reading a chapter from *The Martian Chronicles* called The Green Morning, Renee decided shed enjoy being a space traveler.
2. My kid brother is exactly like the main character in O. Henrys story The Ransom of Red Chief.
3. The TV term for an added sound track of people laughing is canned laughter.
4. Ms. Armanda, does the word subsequent mean next Sonia asked.
5. Carla asked Did Mr. Oldfield say Class is dismissed ?
6. The 84 Olympics were held in Los Angeles.
7. Joyces and Amandas term papers were the best in Mr. Chens class.
8. I guess youll be wantin some kindlin for the stove tmorrow.
9. Is the song When You Wish upon a Star from the movie *Pinocchio*?
10. Have you read Poes poem The Bells the psychiatrist asked.
11. Don and Eds Hot Dog Heaven has five 4s in its phone number.
12. Your mother-in-laws gloves were left in someone elses car.
13. Its an earthquake screamed Jody.
14. Our cruise on the *Royale* included the Caribbeans prettiest islands.

B Application in Literature Apostrophes and quotation marks have been omitted from the following passage. Rewrite the passage correctly.

(1) Why, Bert Howland, she said, how long have you been sitting here?

(2) All my life, he said. (3) Just waiting here for you . . .

(4) Flatterer, she said . . .

(5) Wearing your hair a different way or something, arent you? he asked.

(6) Do you usually notice things like that? she asked.

(7) No, he said. (8) I guess its just the way youre holding your head up. (9) Like you thought I ought to notice something.

From "The Beau Catcher" by Frederick Laing

Linking
Mechanics & Writing

Soap operas are one of the most popular types of television show. In them, families, and sometimes entire communities, share secrets, problems, and schemes.

Write the dialogue for one scene from the fictional soap opera *All My Problems*. In this scene, a conversation is taking place in a restaurant between the handsome doctor Cliff Noble and and the scheming socialite Erica Lyer. Erica is trying to undermine Cliff's confidence about an upcoming heart transplant operation that he is performing on his sweetheart Jenny. Erica wants the operation to be a failure so that she can have Cliff for herself.

In your dialogue use the various forms of quotations covered on pages 318–322. Make certain that you punctuate, capitalize, and paragraph your dialogue correctly.

Prewriting and Drafting Jot down a list of possible problems that Cliff might encounter during a heart transplant operation—physical, emotional, and technical. Erica might remind Cliff of these potential problems while appearing to sympathize with him. Cliff's responses should range from confident refutations at the beginning of the conversation to worried statements at the end. Your dialogue might begin with a line such as:

"Goodness, Cliff, you're looking terrible!" Erica observed. "You must be worried about the heart transplant."

Revising and Proofreading After you have written the dialogue, proofread your work for the use of correct capitalization and punctuation in quotations. Have you begun a new paragraph each time the speaker changes?

Additional Writing Topic You are the leader of a rock group that has been rapidly gaining popularity. Your group is coming out with an album, and you have been asked to write the history of the group for the back cover. In your story, give some background about each person, including what his or her interests and favorite things are. Give a brief description of several songs on the album. Also describe the group's accomplishments and future plans. Since album notes are an example of informal writing, you may also use contractions to give your notes a conversational tone.

From Hand to Mouth

L anguage is not always fair. When it comes to matters of right and left, for example, the lefties have been subjected to discrimination. A "right-hand man" is an important person, but a "left-handed compliment" is not really a compliment at all.

Right-handed people have traditionally outnumbered left-handers, so words having to do with the right side have had the upper hand. The supremacy of the right can be traced to the origins of several words. *Dexterous,* meaning "skillful," comes from the Latin *dexter,* meaning "right" or "right hand." Therefore, someone who is ambidexterous has two right hands, since the Latin *ambi* means "both." *Adroit,* another word meaning "skillful," comes from the French *a droit,* meaning "to the right."

On the other hand, literally, is *sinister.* This word for something evil, corrupt, or dangerous comes from the Latin for "left." *Gauche,* meaning "awkward" or "clumsy," comes from the French for "left." *Gawky,* another word meaning "clumsy," comes from a dialect phrase meaning "left-handed." Even the word *left* itself doesn't get any respect. It comes from the Anglo Saxon *lef,* which means "weak," since the left hand is weaker than the right hand for the majority of people.

Left-handed people are right to complain that language has not always treated them right.

Untitled pencil drawing,
Joseph Lileck, 1985.

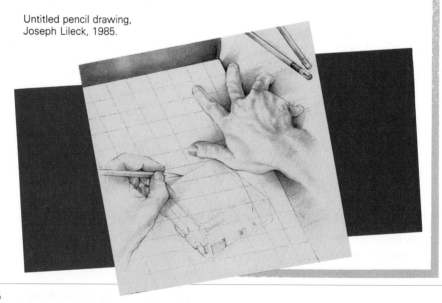

Chapter 12
Application and Review

A Using Apostrophes and Quotation Marks Rewrite the following sentences, correcting any errors in the use of apostrophes and quotation marks. Add correct punctuation and capital letters where they are needed.

1. The word refer is a palindrome, a word that is spelled the same forwards and backwards
2. Whoopee! the announcer shouted the Rangers have won
3. Sabrina asked did you read the poem Fifteen
4. You're teeths enamel said the dentist cant be replaced.
5. Is a Supreme Court Justices appointment for life Amy asked
6. Why do TV emcees say well be back after this word from our' sponsor
7. Who wrote the short story The Open Window Vivienne asked
8. Benson and Walker Companys employees have been asked to read an article in *Business Quarterly* magazine entitled How to Increase Your' Productivity
9. The students computers arent convenient remarked Mr. Day
10. The 8s and the #s on my keyboard are sticking said Joe.

B Application in Literature Apostrophes and quotation marks have been omitted from the following passage. Rewrite the passage correctly.

(1) A dark silhouette stepped into her path and demanded, Who are you? where are you going? (2) Eleni held up her flare and saw more dark figures, ranged all the way up the hill. (3) Eleni Gatzoyiannis, wife of Christos, from the neighborhood of the Perivole, she said, pointing across the ravine. (4) Im trying to find my children. (5) The figure came closer, and she could see the crown insignia on his two-pointed hat. (6) You cant go any farther, he said. (7) The guerrilla lines are all across the upper half of the village. (8) From here to there is a firing range. (9) But my children are over there! Eleni exclaimed. (10) Well have the whole village by morning, said the soldier. (11) Wait till then.

From *Eleni* by Nicholas Gage

13
Spelling

L ook at the fanciful way letters have been used in these designs.
Although you can create alphabetic pictographs such as these to represent an entire word, you cannot be quite as creative when you combine regular letters to spell words.

In this chapter you will learn the rules you must follow to spell correctly, as well as exceptions to those rules. You will also learn several ways to improve your spelling so you can communicate clearly.

Improving Your Spelling

Correct spelling is important in all types of writing. In personal messages, letters, essays, and school tests, good spelling counts. Misspelled words on a job application may even cause you to lose the job. To improve your spelling, study and apply the following rules and methods.

1. **Identify and conquer your specific spelling problems.** Know the errors you repeatedly make. Study your past writing assignments; list all misspelled words. Master those words.

2. **Pronounce words carefully.** We misspell words when we pronounce them incorrectly. If you write *liberry* for *library*, you are probably mispronouncing the word.

3. **Use memory aids, called mnemonics, for words that give you trouble.** Stationery has *er* as in *letter;* there is "a rat" in *separate; Wednesday* contains *wed*.

4. **Always proofread your writing.** Many misspellings are simply the result of careless mistakes. Proofread your writing to catch these errors.

5. **Look up new and difficult words in a dictionary.**

6. **Learn the spelling rules contained in this chapter.**

The methods listed in the following chart will help you master the spelling of particularly difficult words.

Mastering the Spelling of a Word

1. **Look at the word and say it to yourself.** Make sure you pronounce it correctly.
2. **Close your eyes and visualize the word.** Look at it again; notice any prefixes, suffixes, or double letters.
3. **Write the word from memory.** Then check your spelling.
4. **Repeat the process.** Repeat it once if you spelled the word correctly. If you made an error, repeat the process until you have spelled the word correctly three times.

Part 2
Using Spelling Rules

The English language is rich in words from many different languages. As a result, English spelling is varied and complex. The following rules can help you eliminate spelling errors.

The Addition of Prefixes

When a prefix is added to a word, the spelling of the word remains the same. When a prefix creates a double letter, keep both letters.

pre- + arrange = prearrange   co- + operate = cooperate
re- + discover = rediscover   com- + mend = commend
anti- + trust = antitrust   il- + logical = illogical

The Suffixes -ly and -ness

When the suffix *-ly* is added to a word ending in *l,* keep both *l*'s. When *-ness* is added to a word ending in *n,* keep both *n*'s.

general + -ly = generally   keen + -ness = keenness
truthful + -ly = truthfully   sudden + -ness = suddenness
wool + -ly = woolly   lean + -ness = leanness

Exercise

Write the following words, adding prefixes and suffixes.

1. im- + moderate
2. thin + -ness
3. friend + -ly
4. pre- + arrange
5. dis- + satisfy
6. uneven + -ness
7. un- + natural
8. mis- + understand
9. co- + ordinate
10. re- + examine
11. loyal + -ly
12. co- + exist
13. in- + operable
14. dry + -ness
15. careful + -ly

Suffixes with Silent e

When a suffix beginning with a vowel or *y* is added to a word ending in a silent *e,* the *e* is usually dropped.

make + -ing = making   fascinate + -ion = fascination
wheeze + -y = wheezy   facilitate + -ing = facilitating
knife + -ing = knifing   rose + -y = rosy

When a suffix beginning with a consonant is added to a word ending with a silent *e*, the *e* is usually retained.

home + -less = homeless	divine + -ly = divinely
subtle + -ness = subtleness	lone + -ly = lonely
require + -ment = requirement	fate + -ful = fateful
engage + -ment = engagement	care + -ful = careful

Exceptions include *truly, argument, ninth, wholly,* and *awful.*

When a suffix beginning with *a* or *o* is added to a word with a final silent *e*, the final *e* is usually retained if it is preceded by a soft *c* or a soft *g*.

bridge + -able = bridgeable	courage + -ous = courageous
peace + -able = peaceable	advantage + -ous = advantageous
notice + -able = noticeable	outrage + -ous = outrageous
manage + -able = manageable	gorge + -ous = gorgeous

When a suffix beginning with a vowel is added to words ending in *ee* or *oe*, the final silent *e* is retained.

agree + -ing = agreeing	toe + -ing = toeing
hoe + -ing = hoeing	decree + -ing = decreeing
free + -ing = freeing	see + -ing = seeing

Suffixes with Final y

When a suffix is added to a word ending in *y*, and the *y* is preceded by a consonant, the *y* is changed to *i* except with the suffix *-ing*.

silly + -ness = silliness	marry + -age = marriage
company + -es = companies	twenty + -eth = twentieth
happy + -est = happiest	dally + -ing = dallying
carry + -ed = carried	empty + -ing = emptying
merry + -ly = merrily	marry + -ing = marrying

Exceptions include *dryness, shyness,* and *slyness.*

When a suffix is added to a word ending in *y* preceded by a vowel, the *y* usually does not change.

pray + -ing = praying	destroy + -er = destroyer
enjoy + -ing = enjoying	coy + -ness = coyness
gray + -ly = grayly	decay + -ing = decaying

Exceptions include *daily* and *gaily.*

Donald O'Connor, Debbie Reynolds,
and Gene Kelly in the 1952 film *Singin' in the Rain.*

Exercise

Rewrite each of the following sentences, adding prefixes and suffixes as shown.

1. Gene Kelly's (un- + forget + -able) (dance + -ing) in the film *Singin' in the Rain* has become (legend + -ary).
2. The gondola was (glide + -ing) (lazy + -ly) down the canal.
3. Strike negotiators made a (courage + -ous) effort to achieve a (peace + -able) settlement.
4. The English language contains the (large + -est) number of (use + -able) words of any language in the world.
5. Our old car was (slide + -ing) slowly down the (ice + -y) hill.
6. (Creative + -ness) develops (natural + -ly) with (encourage + -ment).
7. The idea of (canoe + -ing) on the (nine + -th) longest river in North America is (un- + believe + -ably) tempting.
8. Despite our (argue + -ments), the jury was (un- + compromise + -ing) in its verdict.
9. A recluse is (lone + -ly), but a hermit is (lone + -ly + -er).
10. The (assemble + -y) of convicts began (negotiate + -ing).
11. My (radiology + -ist) is (continue + -ing) the (intense + -ive) X-ray treatment.
12. That airline's (arrive + -als) are (usual + -ly) prompt treatment.
13. The (early + -est) Mayan (write + -ing) is not (easy + -ly) read.
14. A (grace + -ful) ballerina develops (supple + -ness) by (true + -ly) endless hours of practice.
15. We climbed (clumsy + -ly) up the (danger + -ous) walls of the old (fortify + -cation).

Doubling the Final Consonant

In one-syllable words that end with a single consonant preceded by a single vowel, double the final consonant before adding a suffix beginning with a vowel.

grab + -ing = grabbing   drug + -ist = druggist
dig + -er = digger   slim + -est = slimmest

Do not double the final consonant in one-syllable words ending in one consonant preceded by *two* vowels.

treat + -ing = treating   feel + -ing = feeling
loot + -ed = looted   clean + -ing = cleaning

In two-syllable words, double the consonant only if both of the following conditions exist:

1. The word ends with a single consonant preceded by a single vowel.
2. The word is accented on the second syllable.

re · gret' + -ed = regretted   per · mit' + -ing = permitting
de · ter' + -ence = deterrence   al · lot' + -ing = allotting
oc · cur' + -ing = occurring   re · fer' + -er = referrer

If the newly formed word is accented on a different syllable, the final consonant is not doubled.

re · fer' + -ence = ref' · er · ence
prof' · it + -eer = prof · i · teer'

In some cases a word is correct with a single or double consonant: *canceled* or *cancelled, equiped* or *equipped, traveled* or *travelled.* Check your dictionary for the preferred spelling.

Exercise

Write the following word pairs, adding the suffixes as shown. Underline any words in which you had to double the final consonant.

1. control + -ed
   quarrel + -ed
2. impel + -ing
   travel + -ing
3. loot + -ed
   regret + -ed
4. admit + -ance
   disturb + -ance
5. murmur + -ing
   defer + -ing
6. heap + -ed
   tap + -ed
7. run + -ing
   hasten + -ing
8. differ + -ence
   concur + -ence
9. limit + -ed
   commit + -ed
10. panel + -ing
    propel + -ing
11. lead + -ing
    rip + -ing
12. repel + -ent
    resist + -ant

Words with ie and ei

When the sound is long *e* (ē), the word is spelled *ie*, except after *c*.

retrieve	pier	receive
belief	shield	ceiling
piece	brief	conceit

When the sound is long *a* (ā), the word is spelled *ei*.

sleigh	neighbor
beige	freight

Exceptions include *either, friend, leisure, neither, seize, sieve, species, weird, forfeit, financier,* and *Fahrenheit.*

Words with the "Seed" Sound

There are three suffixes in English pronounced "seed." They are spelled *-cede, -ceed,* and *-sede.* Learn the twelve words below and avoid misspelling "seed" words.

-cede accede, antecede, cede, concede, intercede, precede, recede, secede
-ceed exceed, proceed, succeed
-sede supersede

Exercise

Rewrite these sentences with correctly spelled words. Where letters are missing, use *ie, ei,* or one of the "seed" endings to complete the word. Note that some words may be in the past tense.

1. We rec __ ved many for __ gn telex messages.
2. Keith pro __ ed up the mountain after a br __ f stop.
3. No one pre __ d Washington as Ch __ f Executive of this country.
4. In anc __ nt Egypt pr __ sts wrote hieroglyphics.
5. The heir apparent will suc __ to the throne.
6. Colonial rule in America was super __ d by the Constitution and a bel __ f that all people have inalienable rights.
7. Drivers who exc __ the speed limit endanger the lives of others.
8. The judge ac __ d to the prisoner's request for a repr __ ve.
9. My fr __ nd and n __ ghbor sh __ lded my property from s __ zure by the financ __ r.
10. We learn about the ante __ nts of that spec __ s from w __ rd fossils.

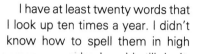

Spell Bound

When I look up something in the dictionary, it's never where I look for it.

The dictionary has been a particular disappointment to me as a basic reference work, and the fact that it's usually more my fault than the dictionary's doesn't make it any easier on me.

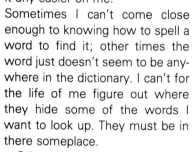

Sometimes I can't come close enough to knowing how to spell a word to find it; other times the word just doesn't seem to be anywhere in the dictionary. I can't for the life of me figure out where they hide some of the words I want to look up. They must be in there someplace.

Other times I want more information about a word than the dictionary is prepared to give me. I don't want to know how to spell a word or what it means. I want to know how to use it. I want to know how to make it possessive and whether I double the final consonant when I add -ing to it. And as often as I've written it, I always forget what you do to make a word that ends in s possessive. "The Detroit *News'* editor"? "The Detroit *Newses* editor"? I suppose the Detroit *News's* editors know, but I never remember and the dictionary is no help.

I have at least twenty words that I look up ten times a year. I didn't know how to spell them in high school, and I still don't.

Is it "further" or "farther" if I'm talking about distance? I always go to the dictionary for further details. I have several dictionaries, and I avoid the one farthest from me. Furthest from me? I am even nervous about some words I should have mastered in grade school. I know when to use "compliment" instead of "complement," when to use "stationery" and not "stationary," and "principle" not "principal;" but I always pause just an instant to make sure.

You'd think someone who has made a living all his life writing words on paper would know how to spell everything. I'm not a bad enough speller to be interesting, but there are still some words I look up in the dictionary because I'm too embarrassed to ask anyone how they're spelled. I've probably looked up "embarrassed" nine times within the last few years, and I often check to make sure there aren't two s's in "occasion." "Ocassion" strikes me as a more natural way to spell the word.

Andrew A. Rooney

Commonly Misspelled Words

abbreviate	bargain	contemptible	emphasize
absence	becoming	convenience	enthusiastic
accidentally	beginning	corps	environment
accommodate	believe	correspondence	equipped
accompanying	benefited	courageous	especially
achievement	bicycle	courteous	etiquette
acknowledge	biscuit	criticism	exaggerate
acquaintance	bookkeeper	criticize	excellent
across	bulletin	curiosity	exceptional
address	bureau	cylinder	exhaust
all right	business	dealt	exhilarate
altogether	cafeteria	decision	existence
always	calendar	definitely	expense
amateur	campaign	dependent	experience
analyze	candidate	descent	familiar
annihilate	cellophane	description	fascinating
anonymous	cemetery	desirable	fatigue
answer	certain	despair	February
apologize	changeable	desperate	feminine
appearance	characteristic	dictionary	financial
appreciate	colonel	different	foreign
appropriate	colossal	dining	forfeit
arctic	column	diphtheria	fourth
argument	commission	disagree	fragile
arising	committed	disappear	generally
arrangement	committee	disappoint	genius
ascend	comparative	discipline	government
assassinate	compel	dissatisfied	grammar
associate	competitive	economical	guarantee
attendance	complexion	efficient	guard
audience	compulsory	eighth	gymnasium
auxiliary	conscience	eligible	handkerchief
awkward	conscientious	eliminate	height
bachelor	conscious	embarrass	hindrance
balance	consensus	eminent	horizon

humorous	mischievous	practice	specifically
imaginary	missile	preference	specimen
immediately	misspell	prejudice	strategy
incidentally	mortgage	preparation	strictly
inconvenience	municipal	privilege	subtle
incredible	necessary	probably	success
indefinitely	nickel	professor	sufficient
indispensable	ninety	pronunciation	surprise
inevitable	noticeable	propeller	syllable
infinite	nuclear	prophecy	sympathy
influence	nuisance	psychology	symptom
inoculation	obstacle	pursue	tariff
intelligence	occasionally	quantity	temperament
interesting	occur	questionnaire	temperature
irrelevant	occurrence	realize	thorough
irresistible	opinion	recognize	throughout
knowledge	opportunity	recommend	together
laboratory	optimistic	reference	tomorrow
legitimate	original	referred	traffic
leisure	outrageous	rehearse	tragedy
lieutenant	pamphlet	reign	transferred
lightning	parallel	repetition	truly
literacy	parliament	representative	Tuesday
literature	particularly	restaurant	tyranny
loneliness	pastime	rhythm	twelfth
luxurious	permanent	ridiculous	unanimous
maintenance	permissible	sandwich	undoubtedly
maneuver	perseverance	schedule	unnecessary
marriage	perspiration	scissors	vacuum
mathematics	persuade	secretary	vengeance
matinee	picnicking	separate	vicinity
medicine	pleasant	sergeant	village
medieval	pneumonia	similar	villain
microphone	politics	sincerely	weird
miniature	possess	sophomore	wholly
minimum	possibility	souvenir	writing

Checkpoint *Parts 1 and 2*

A Find the misspelled words below and write them correctly. If the word is not misspelled, write *Correct*.

1. procede
2. conceed
3. dissagree
4. necessaryly
5. greeness
6. sucseed
7. awfuly
8. transslate
9. thinness
10. receed
11. supercede
12. missunderstand
13. relocate
14. wholy
15. ireverent
16. uneveness
17. seseed
18. eventualy
19. browness
20. exseed

B Rewrite any misspelled words in the following sentences.

1. Mr. Horton spent his liesure time weedding his garden.
2. Ty Cobb, the greatest batter in the history of baseball, recieved many awards for his achievments.
3. The village preist performs several wedings each year.
4. After stock prices fell, the financeir confered with his bookeeper.
5. Poe wrote many unerving tales about madmen and fiends.
6. Before diner I was seized by a strong urge for something very extravagant—caviar.
7. The ballad made referrence to a fierce knight weilding a sheild.
8. His feild is foreign diplomacy.
9. It's realy an ordinary-looking house.
10. Three beautys huried across the stage to recieve thier awards.
11. Despite hours of work, Bob was disatisfied with the results.
12. Greiving is a necessary process when a tragic loss occurs.
13. Sceintists beleive that the last dinosaur died about 65 million years ago.
14. Cheating on taxes is not only ilegal but also imoral.
15. The uneveness of the lettering ruins the whole sign.
16. Five girls succeded in their final examineations.
17. We often face requirments that exsede our knowledge.
18. Individual states may not seceed from the Union.
19. A prefix presedes the root word.
20. New laws on taxs supercede existing codes.

c *Proofreading* Proofread the following paragraph and correct errors in spelling, capitalization, and punctuation. Use the rules in this chapter, the list on pages 336–337, and a dictionary.

During world war i (1914–1918), a young leiutenant in the British royal army medical corps watched helplessly as young men died, many of them from minor wounds and infections after the war, Alexander Fleming returned to st. mary's hospital medical school, London University, to teach and continue his search for a substance that could elliminate disease-bearing microbs and save human lifes. One day in 1928, fleming examined a labaratory dish in which he had been growing *staphylococcus* bacteria. He notised that the culture had been accidentaly contaminated by a green mold, and the bacteria surrounding the mold had been killed. He found that the mold inhibitted the growth of bacteria even when it was diluted 800 times. Fleming, preparred by years of conceintious study and work, deduced that ordinary mold which he later identified as *penicillium notatum,* might work to treat bacterial infections in people

Flemings discovery—and the subsequent development of diffrent kinds of penicillins—had a great impact on medicine and the treatment of a number of deadly illnesses. Today, pencillin is used to cure such diseases as pneumonia, scarlet fever, throat infections, and spinal meningitis. For his sucess and persiverance, Fleming was knighted in 1944, he recieved the nobel prize in medicine in 1945

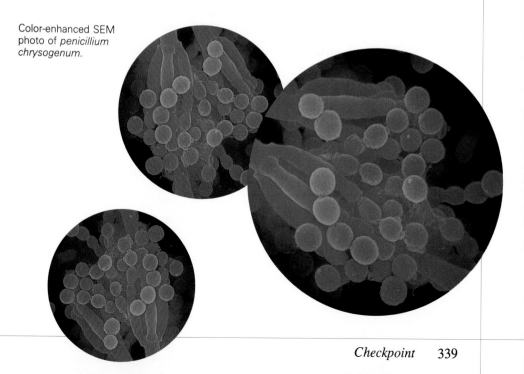

Color-enhanced SEM photo of *penicillium chrysogenum.*

Part 3

Plurals of Nouns

Noun plurals are spelled according to several rules. Study these rules for forming plurals. Also, check the dictionary whenever you are in doubt about the correct spelling of a word.

Regular Formation

Add -s to form the plural of most nouns.

building + -s = buildings   tree + -s = trees
flute + -s = flutes   oboe + -s = oboes

Nouns Ending in s, sh, ch, x, or z

Add -es to form the plural of nouns ending in s, sh, ch, x, or z.

rash + -es = rashes   waltz + -es = waltzes
bus + -es = buses   crutch + -es = crutches

Nouns Ending in y

When a noun ends in y preceded by a consonant, the plural is formed by changing the y to i and adding -es.

duty + -es = duties   party + -es = parties

When a noun ends in y preceded by a vowel, the plural is formed by adding -s.

tray + -s = trays   pulley + -s = pulleys
envoy + -s = envoys   boy + -s = boys

Nouns Ending in o

When a noun ends in o preceded by a vowel, the plural is formed by adding -s.

studio + -s = studios   ratio + -s = ratios
rodeo + -s = rodeos   duo + -s = duos

When a noun ends in o preceded by a consonant, the plural is usually formed by adding -s.

piano + -s = pianos   silo + -s = silos

Some nouns ending in *o* preceded by a consonant form the plural by adding *-es*.

tomato + -es = tomatoes	potato + -es = potatoes
echo + -es = echoes	hero + -es = heroes
cargo + -es = cargoes	veto + -es = vetoes

A few nouns in this class form the plural with either *-s* or *-es*.

mottos *or* mottoes	zeros *or* zeroes
mosquitos *or* mosquitoes	tornados *or* tornadoes

Consult the dictionary whenever you are not sure how to spell a word's plural form.

Nouns Ending in f, ff, or fe

The plural of most nouns ending in *f*, *ff*, or *fe* is formed by adding *-s*.

roof + -s = roofs	staff + -s = staffs
belief + -s = beliefs	safe + -s = safes
carafe + -s = carafes	giraffe + -s = giraffes

The plural of some nouns ending in *f* or *fe* is formed by changing the *f* or *fe* to *v* or *ve* and adding *-s* or *-es*.

calf + -es = calves	loaf + -es = loaves
life + -s = lives	self + -es = selves
half + -es = halves	wharf + -es = wharves
shelf + -es = shelves	leaf + -es = leaves
knife + -s = knives	elf + -es = elves

Nouns with Irregular Plurals

The plural of some nouns is formed by a change of spelling.

tooth—teeth	goose—geese
man—men	mouse—mice
woman—women	ox—oxen
child—children	basis—bases
datum—data	die—dice
crisis—crises	hypothesis—hypotheses

The plural and singular forms are the same for a few nouns.

sheep	corps	Japanese
deer	moose	Swiss

A few nouns have no truly singular form; they always appear in the plural form.

pants   mumps   economics   politics   scissors

Names

The plural of a name is formed by adding -s or -es.

Albert Steele—the Steeles   Jack Amos—the Amoses
Judy Lyons—the Lyonses   Bob Sable—the Sables

Compound Nouns

When a compound noun is written without a hyphen, the plural is formed by adding -s or -es to the end of the word.

armful + -s = armfuls   teaspoonful + -s = teaspoonfuls
rosebush + -es = rosebushes   skateboard + -s = skateboards

When a compound noun is made up of a noun plus a modifier, the plural is formed by adding -s or -es to the noun.

mothers-in-law (*In-law* is a modifier.)
attorneys general (*General* modifies *attorneys*.)
passers-by (*By* modifies *passers*.)
bills of sale (*Of sale* modifies *bills*.)
secretaries of state (*Of state* modifies *secretaries*.)
two-thirds (*Two* modifies the noun *thirds*.)

When a compound noun is made up of a verb plus an adverb, the plural is formed by adding -s or -es to the last word.

drive-in + -s = drive-ins   shut-out + -s = shut-outs
takeover + -s = takeovers   wind-up + -s = wind-ups

Exercises

A Write the plural of each noun below.

1. holiday	8. potato	15. Danish
2. glass	9. hypothesis	16. mouse
3. radio	10. tablespoonful	17. takeover
4. dash	11. drive-in	18. corps
5. laboratory	12. right of way	19. notary public
6. lady	13. sister-in-law	20. leaf
7. valley	14. chief of police	

B Find the errors in the formation of plural nouns in the following sentences. Rewrite the misspelled words correctly.

1. Several hanger-ons were waiting for the parties to end.
2. Don't use more than three cupsful of flour.
3. The French serve many delicious dishes covered with sauce's.
4. My sister's favorite storys are *Snow White and the Seven Dwarves* and *The Elfs and the Shoemaker.*
5. The Martin's and the Foxes have had ancestores in Canada for centurys.
6. The attorney generals for those two states are shoos-in for the next election.
7. Three-fourths of the deers in the forest preserve were driven away by the corps's of soldieres and noisy equipments.
8. There are several hypothesis to explain the existence of the twin moons of Mars.
9. Our canoes glided smoothly down the watersway of Wisconsin.
10. The dogs were good decoyes; they led the wolfs into our trap.

c *White Now* Imagine that you are one of eleven children in a family. Every Wednesday you accompany your parents to the supermarket to help with the weekly grocery shopping. Think about providing meals for eleven children and two adults. Describe the shopping trip and the quantities of food your family has to buy. You will undoubtedly use plural forms in writing about this shopping trip. Try to use as many irregular plurals as you can to demonstrate your mastery of them.

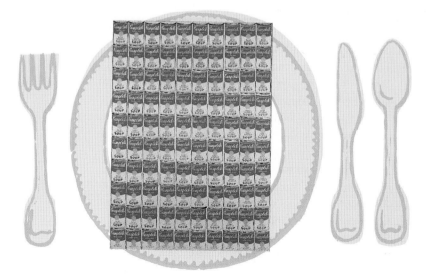

100 Cans, Andy Warhol, 1962.

Checkpoint Part 3

A Write the plural form of each noun below.

1. garage	11. zero	21. cue
2. switch	12. battery	22. brush
3. coat of arms	13. Alice	23. hex
4. donkey	14. nightmare	24. belief
5. lass	15. president-elect	25. harmonica
6. echo	16. axis	26. Romeo
7. lily	17. moose	27. kidney
8. Perez	18. gentleman	28. Lloyd
9. trousers	19. samurai	29. jackknife
10. tributary	20. breadfruit	30. honeycomb

B Rewrite the following sentences, correcting all errors in the formation of plurals. If a sentence has no errors, write *Correct*.

1. In autumn, Martin's brother-in-laws pick persimmones and blackberrys for canning.
2. Mr. Eckert says that there are three Smith's in his class's.
3. The Western democracys managed to solve both crisises peacefully.
4. Mitzner's Music sells radioes, stereoes, and pianoes.
5. Despite numerous injurys, the German and American teames still won several trophys.
6. Former Secretary of States often become professores.
7. Some dentists distribute toothbrushs to their patientes.
8. Four million American householdes have video disces or cassettes.
9. It took thirty-one days (310 hours) for Klaus Friedrich to set up 320,236 dominoes; they toppled in less than thirteen minutes.
10. The recipe's required two teaspoonsful of salt.
11. South America is the home of tomatos and potatos.
12. Fodder for the calfs and sowes is stored in the siloes.
13. Soloes by the sopranos were well received.
14. There are several Bostones, Osloes, and Athenses in the world.
15. Some college seniors write thesises before they receive diplomaes.
16. Bulrushs, sedge's, and grass's all thrive in wet places.
17. The hunter's used knifes to kill the deeres.
18. Prints of hoofs led scouts to the herdes.
19. Loafes of bread and sheafs of wheat are symbols of harvest.
20. Oboes, harpes, and violaes are featured in this symphony.

Linking
Mechanics & Writing

Imagine you are the curator of a museum. While examining a store-room, you notice a door frame behind some shelves. You remove the shelves, open the door, and step inside a musty room that is filled with incredible objects. Describe the contents of the room in a report. List the items you found; use as many different plural nouns as you can.

Prewriting and Drafting Use your imagination to invent descriptions of the unusual objects. Gather details by questioning or by using an encyclopedia. Write a first draft. In your final report include an introductory paragraph, a list, and a concluding paragraph. Remember to use plural nouns.

Revising and Proofreading Use these questions when proofreading.

1. Is there enough detail for any reader to visualize each object?
2. Are all proper nouns or adjectives capitalized?
3. Are all compound nouns or adjectives appropriately hyphenated?
4. Are correct noun plurals used, and are all words correctly spelled?

Additional Writing Topic Some very old recipes give quantities in nonstandard measurements. For example, a recipe may say, "Add as much butter as fills two walnut shells," or "Blend in three handfuls of flour." Write a recipe for a dish that you know how to make. When you list a quantity, use unconventional measures as in the examples.

Out in Left Field

"It's Greek to me." "Beat it!" "Not so hot." "Right on." Surprisingly, all of these slang expressions originated with Shakespeare. Slang comes from many less literary sources as well, including sports, jazz and rock music, crime, technology, and foreign languages. Since 1960, more than 22,000 examples have been collected in the periodically updated *Dictionary of American Slang*. This dictionary defines its turf as words and expressions that are used and understood by the majority of the American public but that are not accepted as good, formal usage.

Probably no other area has contributed as much slang to the English language as baseball. Even people who have never rooted for their home team know and use such expressions as "You're way off base" and "I liked him right off the bat."

Some slang expressions have originated with specific groups, who use the slang to exclude outsiders from their conversations. Several common slang terms have come from the criminal community. Examples include *kidnap,* a combination of "kid" (a small goat) and "napper" (thief); *cop,* from "*c*onstable *o*n *p*atrol"; and *hijack,* from the highway robber's demand to a stagecoach driver: "Hands up high, Jack!"

Most slang quickly becomes outdated, although some can remain in the language for centuries without being accepted into standard English. When slang words do become part of the language, it's often hard to remember that their origins may be "out in left field."

Chapter 13

Application and Review

Finding and Correcting Spelling Errors Identify spelling errors in the sentences below. Rewrite the complete sentences and be careful to spell each word correctly.

1. The Gettysburg Adress was only one of President Abraham Lincoln's fameous speeches.
2. It's your fault that niether of us passed the test.
3. The nieghborhood group sent a representative to the city comission.
4. The riegn of Queen Victoria preceeded that of Edward VII.
5. The worryed farmer stayed up all night with the two sick calfs.
6. It's my opinion that no musician has sucseeded like Paul McCartney in his acheivements as a composer and recording artist.
7. Sales of holiday albumes and singles have each toped the one-hundred million mark.
8. Rakeing leafs, I beleive, is Maria's chore.
9. Writting carefuly, Jeff copied the outline from the book.
10. Mother usualy dissapproves of sugared snacks.
11. The caravan stopped at several oasises on its journey through the desert.
12. On Everest unecessary equippment becomes dangerous excess bagage for the mountaineers.
13. The Japanese eat varyous specieses of fish.
14. Roger exceled at drawing inferrences in a logical way.
15. Tyrone is enjoing his twentyeth birthday.
16. Kim relatted that he had had the same wierd dream three nights in a row.
17. The looksout percieved a stationary ship through the binnoculars.
18. Leo's performance was one of his best piano soloes.
19. As a winer of both trophys, Bernice was delighted.
20. The flood waters are rising, so procede with caution.
21. My best freind is encourageing me to put in an applycation for a part-time job.
22. The audience was truely elatted when the rock star heroes made an appearance.
23. Each of my sister-in-laws has gained acceptance at three of the best universitys in the country.
24. Those televisiones hooks-up are loose.
25. The editor in chiefs of several big-city dayly papers were interviewed on TV last night.

Cumulative Review

Chapters 9–13

A Using Capitalization and Punctuation Correctly Rewrite the following paragraphs, correcting errors in capitalization and punctuation.

(1) According to some writers, the history of exploration can be divided into three major stages. (2) The first stage the Exploration of the Old World probably began with ancient egyptian and babylonian traders around 2500 BC. (3) These traders traveled South to the Indian ocean and West to the Mediterranean sea. (4) About 300 b.c., the ancient Greek astronomer Pytheas explored the North Atlantic ocean, perhaps traveling as far North as Norway. (5) Around this time the conquests of Alexander the great, extended the known world as far east as India. (6) Many centuries later, Marco Polo, an Italian adventurer, further expanded World horizons when he traveled throughout China. (7) By the late middle ages, large parts of north africa, nearly all of Europe, and a substantial part of Asia had been included in the known world.

(8) The second stage, the Exploration of the New World, started around A.d. 1450 with the search, for a sea route to China. (9) Among the most famous of these explorers were the following Christopher Columbus the Italian navigator who sailed west across the Atlantic in 1492, Vasco da Gama the Portuguese sailor who became the first European to reach India by sea and Ferdinand Magellan, the Portuguese Navigator who commanded the first world-circling voyage. (10) Thanks, largely to the efforts of intrepid explorers such as these, most regions of the world have been accurately mapped.

(11) Nonetheless exploration is still very much alive. (12) In October of 1957, the Soviet Union launched *Sputnik I* the first artificial satellite and this event launched the third stage the Exploration of Space. (13) In May of 1961, President John f. Kennedy announced, that the United States would land a manned spacecraft on the moon within a decade. (14) The culmination of Americas early space exploration came on July 20 1969. (15) On this date, Neil Armstrong became the first human being ever to set foot on the moon. (16) Since that historic walk on the moon numerous explorers have bravely ventured into the immense darkness of space.

B Correcting Errors in Quotations and Spelling Rewrite the following paragraphs, correcting all mistakes in the use of quotation marks, capitalization, punctuation, and spelling.

(1) A poor woman once asked a rich man to lend her a big silver spoon so that she could entertain a special guest. (2) "I'll let you borrow my spoon, the rich man replied But only if you return it tomorrow." (3) Then he added, "make sure you return it before the sun goes down". (4) After recieving the spoon, the woman left.

(5) She returned the next day, after having hurryed to arrive before sunset. (6) She carryed with her the big spoon and a little spoon as well. (7) As soon as the rich man spoted the second spoon, he asked the woman "what had happened." (8) "The big spoon had a baby." she answerd.

(9) "Your story is hardly beleivable, he said." (10) "However, since the mother spoon is mine," the child spoon also belongs to me." (11) Then he greedily accepted both spoons from the poor woman.

(12) A few days later, the woman came back and said. (13) "May I borrow your silver candlesticks tonight"? (14) The rich man agreed to her request, secretly hopeing that the woman would return with many little candlesticks. (15) However, the poor woman returned the next day empty-handed. (16) She said that the "candlesticks had both fallen off the table during dinner and died. (17) She also said "she regreted their loss."

(18) The rich man, angerred by this story, wanted to sieze her; instead, he took her before the three wisest people in that small town. (19) The three sages immediatly discussed the problem and arrived at a unanimous decision. (20) "If you accept the profits when a spoon has a baby, then you must take the loss when a candlestick dies.

C Adding Suffixes and Forming Plurals Number your paper from 1 to 20. Write the words listed below.

1. hobo + -s	11. persevere + -ance
2. deter + -ence	12. merry + -ly
3. teaspoonful + -s	13. transfer + -ed
4. structure + -al	14. love + -able
5. constitute + -ion	15. belief + -s
6. imply + -ed	16. father-in-law + -s
7. imagine + -ary	17. argue + -ment
8. courage + -ous	18. incidental + -ly
9. eight + -teen	19. latch + -s
10. change + -able	20. occur + -ence

Sentence Diagraming

Diagraming can help you understand how parts of a sentence relate to each other. In addition, diagraming sharpens your critical skills by requiring you to analyze sentences and classify the parts.

A sentence diagram shows how the parts of a sentence fit together. The base for a sentence diagram is shown below:

In the diagrams that follow, you will see how other lines are added to this base.

Subjects and Verbs

Place the simple subject on the horizontal main line to the left of the vertical line. Place the simple predicate, or verb, to the right.

We sang.

We	sang

Thomas had auditioned.

Thomas	had auditioned

In diagraming, capitalize only those words that are capitalized in the sentence. Do not use punctuation except for abbreviations. Place single-word modifiers on slanted lines below the words they modify.

Sentences Beginning with There or Here

To diagram a sentence beginning with *there,* first decide whether *there* tells *where* or is an introductory word. If *there* tells *where,* place it on a slanted line below the verb.

There is the document.

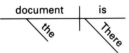

If *there* is an introductory word, place it on a horizontal line above the subject.

There have been many natural disasters.

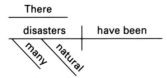

Unlike *there*, the word *here* always tells *where*. In a sentence diagram, therefore, place *here* on a slanted line below the verb.

Here comes the mayor.

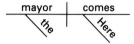

In both sentences above, the subject comes *after* the verb. Notice, however, that in the diagram the subject is placed *before* the verb to the left of the vertical line.

Interrogative Sentences

In an interrogative sentence, the subject often comes after the verb or after part of the verb phrase. In diagraming, remember to place the subject before the verb to the left of the vertical line:

Have you finished?   Can you contribute?

| you | Have finished |

| you | Can contribute |

Imperative Sentences

In an imperative sentence, the subject is usually not stated. Since commands are given to the person spoken to, the subject is understood to be *you*. To diagram an imperative sentence, place the understood subject *you* to the left of the vertical line. Then enclose *you* in parentheses. Place the verb to the right of the vertical line.

Go!

| (you) | Go |

Direct Objects

In a diagram, place the direct object on the main line after the verb. Separate the direct object from the verb with a vertical line that does not extend below the main line.

The company offered discounts.

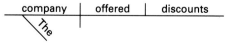

Indirect Objects

To diagram an indirect object, draw a slanted line below the verb. From the bottom of the slanted line, draw a line parallel to the main line. Place the indirect object on the parallel line.

The hairdresser paid me a compliment.

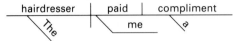

Subject Complements

In a diagram, place a predicate nominative or a predicate adjective on the main line after the verb. Separate the subject complement from the verb with a slanted line that extends in the direction of the subject.

Mary is president. (*President* is a predicate nominative.)

George seems well. (*Well* is a predicate adjective.)

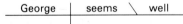

Sentences with Compound Parts

Compound Subjects To diagram a compound subject, place the parts on parallel horizontal lines as shown below. Then connect the parallel lines with a broken line. On the broken line, write the conjunction that connects the parts of the compound subject. Attach the compound subject to the main line with solid diagonal lines.

Crocodiles, snakes, lizards, and turtles are reptiles.

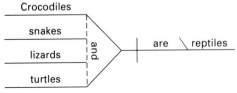

Compound Verbs To diagram a compound verb, place the parts on parallel horizontal lines. Write the conjunction on the broken line. Attach the compound verb to the main line as shown below.

Miller wrote and directed this production.

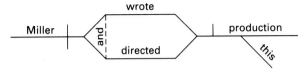

If each word in a compound verb has an object or a subject complement, place the complement on the parallel line after the verb.

The rebels won the skirmish and appeared confident.

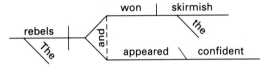

Compound Direct Objects and Indirect Objects To diagram a compound direct object or indirect object, place the parts on parallel horizontal lines. Write the conjunction on the broken line. Attach the compound object to the main line as shown below.

Houdini performed magic tricks and fantastic stunts. (*compound direct object*)

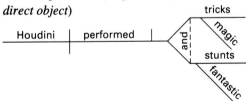

Compound Subject Complements To diagram a compound predicate nominative or predicate adjective, place the parts on parallel horizontal lines. Connect the parts with a broken line and write the conjunction on that line. Attach the compound predicate nominative or predicate adjective to the main line as shown below.

The winners are Jean and Sharon. (*compound predicate nominative*)

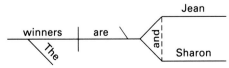

Adjectives

To diagram an adjective, place it on a slanted line below the word it modifies. Keep in mind that *a, an,* and *the* are adjectives and that more than one adjective can modify the same word.

Our new high school has a fitness trail.

When two or more adjectives are connected by a conjunction, place the adjectives on slanted lines below the words they modify. Connect the slanted lines with a broken line. Then write the conjunction on the broken line.

A playful but friendly porpoise saved the sailor's life.

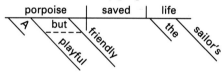

Adverbs

To diagram an adverb that modifies a verb, place the adverb on a slanted line under the verb. Keep in mind that words like *not* and *never* are adverbs.

The students did not assemble quickly.

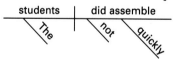

To diagram an adverb that modifies an adjective or an adverb, place the adverb on a line connected to the modified adjective or adverb as shown below.

Too many cars rust very quickly.

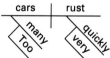

Prepositional Phrases

To diagram a prepositional phrase, draw a slanted line below the word that the phrase modifies. From the slanted line, draw a line parallel to the main line. Place the preposition on the slanted line and the object of the preposition on the parallel line. Words that modify the object of the preposition are placed on slanted lines below the object.

Eric painted a portrait of the President.

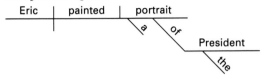

If a preposition has a compound object, place the objects on parallel lines as shown below.

Some stagecoach drivers were known for their determination and their bravery.

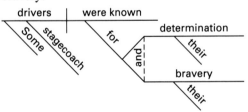

Gerunds and Gerund Phrases

To diagram a gerund, place it on a line drawn as a step (⌐_). Put the step on a forked line (⋏) that stands on the main line. The placement of the forked line shows how the gerund or gerund phrase is used—as a subject, a direct object, a predicate nominative, or the object of a preposition. If the gerund phrase includes modifiers, place these on slanted lines as shown in the example below.

We disliked taking the aptitude test. (*gerund phrase used as direct object*)

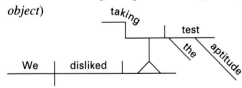

To diagram a gerund or a gerund phrase that is the object of a preposition, place the preposition on a slanted line that extends from the modified word. Then place the step and the forked line below the main line as shown below.

After swimming, we relaxed. (*gerund phrase as object of a preposition*)

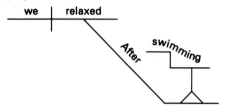

Participles and Participial Phrases

To diagram a participle, place the participle on an angled line below the word it modifies. Place any modifiers on slanted lines below the participle they modify.

Purring softly, the kitten lay down.

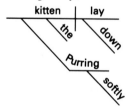

To diagram a participial phrase that includes a direct object and modifiers, place the object on a straight line extending from the base of the angled line. Place any modifiers on slanted lines below the words they modify.

Sailing his boat brilliantly, Jeff won the race. (*participial phrase including a direct object and modifiers*)

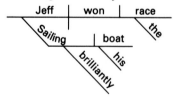

Infinitives and Infinitive Phrases

To diagram an infinitive used as a noun, place the infinitive on an angled line. Write the word *to* on the slanted part of the angled line and write the verb on the horizontal part of the angled line. Put the angled line on a forked line that stands on the main line. The placement of the forked line shows how the infinitive or infinitive phrase is used in the sentence. Place any modifiers on slanted lines below the words they modify.

We want to have a beach party soon. (*infinitive used as direct object*)

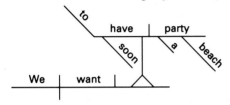

To diagram an infinitive used as a modifier, place the angled line on a horizontal line below the modified word. Attach the horizontal line to the main line as shown below.

This mountain is difficult to climb. (*infinitive used as adverb*)

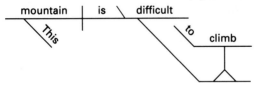

Appositives and Appositive Phrases

To diagram an appositive, place the appositive in parentheses after the word it identifies or explains. Place any modifiers on slanted lines below the appositive.

The ostrich, a native bird of Africa, can run swiftly.

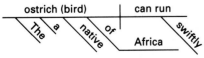

Adjective Clauses

Place the clause on its own horizontal line below the main line, diagraming the clause as if it were a sentence. Use a broken line to connect the relative pronoun in the adjective clause to the word in the independent clause that the adjective clause modifies.

The route that they took went through Washington.

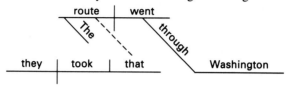

Adverb Clauses

Place the clause on its own horizontal line below the main line, diagraming the clause as if it were a sentence. Use a broken line to connect the adverb clause to the word it modifies in the independent clause. Write the subordinating conjunction on the broken line.

When the car stopped, we lurched forward.

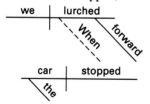

Noun Clauses

To diagram a noun clause, place it on a separate line that is attached to the main line with a forked line. The placement of the forked line shows how the noun clause is used in the sentence.

Diagram the word that introduces the noun clause according to its use. If the introductory word simply introduces the clause, place it on a line above the clause as shown in the second example.

What Juri saw was an illusion. (*noun clause used as subject*)

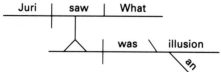

I know that they are going. (*noun clause used as object of the verb*)

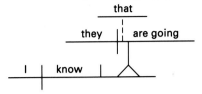

We have a job for whoever is qualified. (*noun clause used as object of a preposition*)

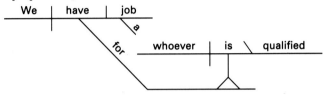

Compound Sentences

To diagram a compound sentence, place the independent clauses on parallel horizontal lines. Use a broken line with a step to connect the verb in one clause to the verb in the other clause. Write the conjunction on the step. If the clauses are joined by a semicolon, leave the step blank.

The game was close, but we finally won.

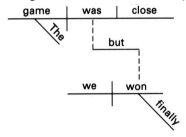

Complex Sentences

To diagram a complex sentence, first decide whether the subordinate clause is an adjective clause, an adverb clause, or a noun clause. Then use the information presented on pages 358–359 to diagram the sentence.

Compound-Complex Sentences

To diagram a compound-complex sentence with an adjective or an adverb clause, diagram the independent clauses first. Then attach the subordinate clause or clauses to the words they modify. Leave enough room to attach a subordinate clause where it belongs.

> Franklin Pierce, our fourteenth president, accidentally collided with an old lady while he was riding on horseback, and a policeman arrested him.

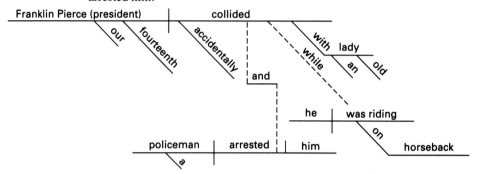

To diagram a compound-complex sentence with a noun clause, decide how the noun clause is used in the independent clause. Then diagram the noun clause in the position that shows how it is used.

> Who started the mutiny was never decided, but the British government blamed Mr. Christian. (The noun clause *who started the mutiny* is the subject of the verb in the first independent clause.)

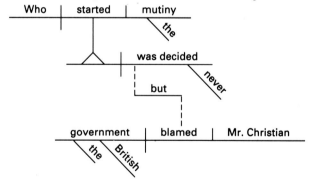

Index

diagraming, 358–59
Nouns, 7–9
  abstract, 7
  as adjectives, 25
  as adverbs, 28
  collective, 8, 217
  collective, agreement of verb with,
    184
  common, 7, 249
  compound, 8, 313, 342
  concrete, 7
  defined, 7
  gerund phrases as, 85
  gerunds as, 84–85
  infinitive phrases as, 79
  infinitives as, 78
  as objective complements, 61
  plurals of, 340–42
  possessives of, 313–15
  predicate, 62
  proper, 7, 24, 305
  singular, with plural forms, agreement
    with, 185
  singular/plural, agreement of verb
    with, 173–74
  verbs distinguished from, 20
Number, of pronouns, 10
  pronoun–antecedent agreement in,
    215–17
  subject–verb agreement in, 173–74
Numbers
  apostrophes with, 315
  commas with, 287
  hyphens in, 304

parentheses with, 306
periods with, 272

O

Objective case, pronouns, 199, 202–203
Objective complements, 61
Objects
  of prepositions, 34
  of verbs, 19–20
  see also Direct objects; Indirect objects
Objects of prepositions, 71
  confused with indirect objects, 60
  diagraming, 355
  pronouns as, 203
On the Lightside, 32, 73, 229, 335
Outlines
  capitalization in, 263
  periods in, 272

P

Parentheses, 306–307
Parenthetical expressions
  commas with, 279
  semicolons with, 296
Participial phrases, 81–82, 119
  diagraming, 356
  essential, 82
  nonessential, 82, 285
Participles, 81–82
  dangling, 82
  defined, 81
  diagraming, 356
  fragments and, 118
  misplaced, 82

conjugation, 145–46
defined, 16
diagraming, 350
emphatic forms, 151
future perfect tense, 146, 148
future tense, 146, 147
helping, 17
historical present tense, 147
in idioms, 28
imperative mood, 162
improper shifts in tense and form, 153
indicative mood, 162
intransitive, 19–20, 160
irregular, 134–35, 138, 140, 142
linking, 16–17, 20, 24, 62, 226–27
main, 17
mood of, 162
nouns distinguished from, 20
objects of, 19–20
passive voice, 159–60
past perfect tense, 146, 148
past tense, 146, 147
perfect tenses, 146, 148
present perfect tense, 146, 148
present tense, 146

present tenses, 147
principal parts of, 133–35, 138, 140, 142, 146
progressive forms, 150–51
regular, 133–34
simple tenses, 146, 147
subjunctive mood, 162
tenses, 145–49
transitive, 19–20, 160
voice, 159–60
Voice, of verbs, 159–60

W

Weasel words, 243
who, whom, 207–208
Word order, 34, 53, 55–57, 72
    commas and, 278
    subject–verb agreement and, 175
Write Now, 15, 21, 27, 30, 54, 58, 75, 84, 98, 101, 122, 140, 156, 161, 179, 182, 205, 228, 234, 256, 265, 277, 281, 284, 318, 321, 343
Writing. *See* Linking Grammar & Writing; Linking Mechanics & Writing; Write Now

Sources of Quoted Materials

32: Dave Barry: For excerpts from *What Is and Ain't Grammatical;* copyright © 1982 Dave Barry. **73:** Franklin Watts, Inc.: For excerpts from "The Perils of Syntax," from *How to Win a Pullet Surprise* by Jack Smith, copyright © 1982 Jack Smith. **229:** Harper & Row, Publishers, Inc.: For excerpts from *The Garden of Eloquence* by Willard R. Espy, copyright © 1980 Willard R. Espy. **229:** Clarkson N. Potter, Inc.: For excerpts from *Another Almanac of Words at Play* by Willard R. Espy, copyright © 1983 Willard R. Espy. **294:** Harcourt Brace Jovanovich, Inc.: For the first stanza of "All Ignorance Toboggans into Know," from *Complete Poems 1913–1962* by E. E. Cummings, copyright 1944 E.E. Cummings; renewed 1972 Nancy T. Andrews. **335:** Atheneum Publishers, an imprint of Macmillan Publishing Co.: For excerpts from "Dictionaries," from *And More by Andy Rooney* copyright 1982 Essay Productions, Inc.

The authors and editors have made every effort to trace the ownership of all copyrighted selections from this book and make full acknowledgment for their use.

Photographs

Assignment photography: Ralph Burke: **46, 73, 95, 120, 121, 156, 168, 169,** *all* **182, 193, 265, 275, 277, 296,** *all* **304;** Gregg Eisman: **114,** *all* **148;** Richard Hellyer: **123, 172, 321;** Gregg Gillis: *all* **236, 238, 248. 6:** Laimute Druskis, Taurus Photos; **9:** © 1987 The Detroit Institute of Arts, City of Detroit Purchase; **13:** © 1986 Universal Press Syndicate, Inc.; **15:** *r* Edward Bock, Frozen Images; *l* Ann Duncan, Tom Stack and Assoc.; **19:** L. West, FPG; **21:** Tim Thompson; **25:** Togashi; **26:** FPG; **30:** *in* Keith Berr; **35:** *r* Len Kaufman; *l* The Bettmann Archive; **40:** © 1987 Newspaper Enterprise Assoc., Inc.; **43:** *r* J. Carnemolla, West Light; **50:** *l* Marilyn Gartman; **50:** *r,* The Bettmann Archive; **55:** © 1981 United Features Syndicate, Inc.; **58:** Marche, FPG; **63:** Dennie Cody, FPG; **65:** *c,* NASA;/NASA; *r* NASA, Grant Heilman; **70:** L. T. Rhodes, Click/Chicago; **75:** © 1986 Universal Press Syndicate, Inc.; **80:** The Tate Gallery A.D.A.G.P.; **84:** Greg Nikas, Picture Cube; **86:** David Austen, Click/Chicago; **90:** *l,* Fran Barakas; *r* Brent Jones; **95:** *l,r* John Reader; *c* John Reader; **103:** Jean Gaumy, Magnum Photos; **105:** Roger Miller, Image Bank; **108:** Curtis Willocks, Document Brooklyn; **111:** *all,* John Running; **116:** George Robbins, The Stock Solution; **118:** Uniphoto; **125:** Photri, Gartman Agency; **132:** Don Clegg; **135:** © 1986 Universal Press Syndicate, Inc.; **136:** Culver Pictures; **140:** Lorie Novak; **143:** Benson & Hedges Illustrators' Gold Awards 1984, Courtesy Sharp Practice; **145:** Ralph Nelson, Universal City Studios, Inc.; **150:** Uccello, Photo Researchers; **151:** Richard Brown Baker Collection, Yale University Art Gallery; **155:** Courtesy MacMillan-London; **161:** Andrew Lautman, Ford's Theatre; **164:** Michael Melford, Wheeler Pictures; **175:** Diana Rasche; **178:** Joe McNally, Wheeler Pictures; **187:** Bill Tucker; **188:** Peter Marlow, Magnum Photos; **191:** Sam Griffith, Click/Chicago; **193:** Amon Carter Museum, Fort Worth; **198:** *all* Andreas Dannenberg, Wheeler Pictures; **200:** Lorie Novak; **203:** David Madison; **208:** © 1978 United Feature Syndicate, Inc.; **210:** Culver Pictures; **213:** Larry Kolvoord; **218:** Uniphoto; **221:** *l* Henley and Savage, *r* John Newbauer; **224:** Jacques Dirand, Courtesy House & Garden. © 1984 by The Conde Nast Publications, Inc.; **230:** Photri; **243:** Yuri Dojc, Image Bank; **248:** Greg Gillis; **250:** © 1984 Universal Press Syndicate, Inc.; **252:** Sygma; **256:** Richard Burda, Taurus Photos; **263:** Courtesy Interview Magazine; **267:** Susan Van Etten; **270:** Photri, Marilyn Gartman; **273:** © 1985 Universal Press Syndicate, Inc.; **280:** Charles Palek, Animals, Animals; **284:** Joseph Szaszfai, Yale University Art Gallery; **287:** Phyllis Galembo; **290:** The Bettmann Archive; **294:** Phil Schofield, West Stock; **301:** Focus on Sports; **307:** *l* The Bettmann Archive; *b* Historical Pictures Service, Chicago; **312:** Ernst Haas, Magnum Photos; **314:** Drawing by Maslin. © 1987 The New Yorker Magazine, Inc.; **317:** Gerard Vandystadt, Agence Vandystadt, Photo Researchers; **326:** Courtesy Joseph Lileck; **332:** Movie Still Archives; **335:** Courtesy Andrew Rooney; **339:** Manfred Kage, Peter Arnold; **343:** Albright-Knox Art Gallery, Buffalo, NY. Gift of Seymour H. Knox, 1963; **345:** F. G. Samia; **346:** *r,* Bernard Brault Photography.

Illustrations

Lynne Fischer (hand coloring of photographs): **290, 328;** Precision Graphics: **256, 344–345;** Laura Tarrish: *c* **153**